Mosh the Polls

Mosh the Polls

Youth Voters, Popular Culture, and Democratic Engagement

EDITED BY
TONY KELSO AND BRIAN COGAN

LEXINGTON BOOKS

A division of
ROWMAN & LITTLEFIELD PUBLISHERS, INC.
Lanham • Boulder • New York • Toronto • Plymouth, UK

LEXINGTON BOOKS

A division of Rowman & Littlefield Publishers, Inc.
A wholly owned subsidary of The Rowman & Littlefield Publishing Group, Inc.
4501 Forbes Boulevard, Suite 200
Lanham, MD 20706

Estover Road
Plymouth PL6 7PY
United Kingdom

British Library Cataloguing in Publication Information Available

Library of Congress Cataloging-in-Publication Data

Mosh the polls : youth voters, popular culture, and democratic engagement / edited by
Tony Kelso and Brian Cogan.
    p. cm.
Includes bibliographical references and index.
ISBN-13: 978-0-7391-2230-3 (hardcover : alk. paper)
ISBN-13: 978-0-7391-2231-0 (pbk. : alk. paper)
ISBN-13: 978-0-7391-3046-9 (electronic : alk. paper)
ISBN-10: 0-7391-2230-4 (hardcover : alk. paper)
[etc.]
    1. Youth—United States—Political activity. 2. Popular culture—United States. 3.
Political campaigns—United States. 4. Presidents—United States—Election. I.
Kelson, Tony. II. Cogan, Brian, 1967-
HQ799.2.P6M66 2008
324.084'20973—dc22   2008037201

Printed in the United States of America

♾™ The paper used in this publication meets the minimum requirements of American
National Standard for Information Sciences—Permanence of Paper for Printed Library
Materials, ANSI/NISO Z39.48–1992.

For Tony's son, Emil, and Brian's daughter to be, Zoe, who will someday navigate the terrain of popular culture—one whose shape we cannot possibly foresee—on their way to the voting booths.

Contents

Foreword

Over the last two presidential election cycles we have seen an increase in political participation by young voters, the age group least likely to be engaged in our political system. We have also seen an increase in popular culture's engagement in politics, with the development of programs such as *The Daily Show* and *The Colbert Report*, and the now mandatory appearance of candidates on the late night talk show circuit trading jokes with Jay Leno and David Letterman. There has been an explosion in computer based social networking. And the number of people using the Internet as a major source of information about politics continues to grow.

Social scientists are just beginning to turn our attention to these developments and their impact on our politics. But most studies focus on just one of these trends. We examine the impact of the Internet on our politics. We look at the growing influence of entertainment and popular culture on society. We explore young citizens and debate whether increased voter turnout reflects permanent changes in our democracy or short-term, election-specific factors.

The collection of essays in this volume puts these trends and changes together, for they do seem related. How does popular culture engage young voters in politics? Does new technology provide a way to reach citizens who are unlikely to read newspapers or watch the evening news, the most common ways for older citizens to connect with political events?

If our democracy is to prosper, citizens need to be engaged. Concern that younger, less engaged citizens are replacing older citizens has been a common theme of observers of our political scene. This collection helps us understand how our newest cohort of voters behaves, and how popular culture and new technologies may be bringing them into, not separating them from, our politics. It is too soon to know if the optimism implied in most, though not all, of these studies, is warranted. But they present a good place to start that discussion, providing an overview of these issues and case studies that examine the specific ways in which this engagement might—or might not—come to fruition.

Arthur Sanders
Drake University

Acknowledgments

We would like to thank our editor at Lexington Books, Joseph C. Parry, for his guidance and for his confidence in this collection of essays. We are also grateful to all of our contributors, who not only challenged us with new insights, but produced work that made the editing process relatively painless, even enjoyable.

Tony wishes to express his gratitude to his wife, Tricia Capistrano, as well. Her dedication to giving me the space and time I needed to complete this book was invaluable—I can only hope I display the same warmth and patience when it is her turn to enter into solitude and focus on her writing projects. And although, at four-years-old, our son Emil was too young to fully understand what his papa was always up to on the computer, he still somehow sensed it was important to find a separate place to play in our small Manhattan apartment whenever I was clacking on the keyboard. By always believing in me, my mother, Patrice Heath, also had a hand in the text. Moreover, for a group of chapters about politics and popular culture, image counts too—so a big shout out must go to my longtime friend, Ken Young, for his contribution to the book's cover design. I would also like to convey my appreciation to my co-editor Brian Cogan for his ability to both work hard and play hard. I am glad that our association developed into a full-blown friendship through our joint effort on this project. Finally, I am thankful to the many friends and fellow scholars who have influenced my thinking about media, popular culture, and politics over the years. An exhaustive list of these sources of inspiration would be impossible to provide, but Todd Gitlin, Josh Klein, Ted Magder, and William McCarthy deserve special mention. Todd's and Ted's mentorship and my many enlightening conversations with Josh and William helped make my perspectives on the topics in this book considerably richer and more nuanced than they would be if we had not fortuitously crossed paths.

Brian would like to thank his wife Lisa for her patience, support, and occasional bemused comments, such as, "You said yes to *another* new project?" I also wish to thank my parents and brothers and their families—although they were not exactly sure why I was so busy, they assumed that writing was somehow keeping me off the streets. In addition, a thank you goes to my co-editor Tony Kelso for his dedication, patience, wonderfully dry sense of humor, and superb taste in hats. In terms of the theoretical development that went into this book, I owe a debt of gratitude to Terence Moran and Jonathan Zimmerman for asking questions that have continued to puzzle me for years about politics—I hope that some of the answers are articulated in this work.

Lastly, both Brian and Tony would like to thank all of you who purchased this book. Your investment means you are interested in topics that we of course believe are especially salient. It is our wish that the arguments and debates this book sets in motion continue long after you have finished reading it.

Introduction

At the Intersection of Politics and Popular Culture: Over Two Hundred Years of Great Entertainment

Tony Kelso and Brian Cogan

On a typical weeknight in the United States, to catch up on the political happenings of the day, hundreds of thousands of young fans shun the traditional evening network news broadcasts (as well as FOX, MSNBC and other cable news stations) and, instead, later grab their remotes to turn to the faux news program, *The Daily Show*. Immediately afterwards, they might stay tuned to *The Colbert Report* for another dosage of hilarious, fake news that, to them, comes across more honestly than the "serious" version they could watch on CNN. Or they might flip to Jay Leno or David Letterman to see comedic monologues peppered with political commentary. Or some of them might indeed switch to CNN because they perceive its political coverage, with its music, its graphics, its shouting pundits, and the blow-dried hair of its anchors, as entertainment in itself. Various studies have shown that younger viewers are far less likely to watch traditional television sources of news than their counterparts were in previous generations.[1]

But the fusion of politics and entertainment is not simply a television phenomenon. Increasingly, politics has merged with diverse elements of popular culture. During the 2004 U.S. presidential election, for example, rapper Sean "P. Diddy" Combs was "keeping it real" by touring the country and encouraging young eligible voters to "vote or die" (a presumably grim choice, if we are to believe the pundits and their disgust at

1

young voter apathy), a campaign that also featured accompanying T-shirts, hats, buttons, and other merchandise, and spilled into many forms of media. Meanwhile, even as his controversial movie *Fahrenheit 9/11* played nationally in movie theaters, Michael Moore, too, traveled around the nation, speaking on college campuses to filled auditoriums during his "slacker tour," which itself was later parodied by Trey Parker and Matt Stone, the producers of the popular television program *South Park.*

Whether it's television, radio, concerts, live appearances by comedians, commercial Internet websites, or even the political party conventions themselves, the mixing of politics and popular culture is frequently on display and, it appears, there is an increasing nexus between the two, to the extent that it is often hard to distinguish parody from legitimate political engagement. The purpose of *Mosh the Polls: Youth Voters, Popular Culture, and Democratic Engagement* is to undertake an analysis from a variety of scholarly and knowledgeable—but not obscure—standpoints of the new and innovative ways in which both the political process and the entertainment industry appeal to the youth voter—roughly those voters between the ages of eighteen and twenty-nine—and how these endeavors are *received* by the intended audience; along the way, the book will shed light on the state of the modern American political system and its relationship to entertainment and popular culture. The book especially explores the junction between politics and popular culture within the context of young voters and democratic engagement. Does connecting politics with various forms of entertainment, for example, tend to further promote cynicism and alienation? Or, conversely, could meeting young people on their own terms actually help them reconnect to the political process? Whatever the case, it is clear that the manner in which many politicians and political parties choose to draw in, or in some cases, disenfranchise, young voters, is through popular culture, which is why, we believe, this book is plainly relevant.

The Trivialization of Politics versus Engaging Entertainment

Over the years, the blending of politics and popular culture has generated considerable debate as to its significance for American democracy. Perhaps one of the most vehement critics of this seemingly dichotomous tendency was Neil Postman, who argued that television, by its very "nature," has probably been the chief force behind the "dumbing down" of political discourse and the trivialization of politics in general. Evaluating political campaigning in nineteenth-century America, he maintained that because print, with its analytical "bias," was the dominant communication medium of the time, everyday citizens were prone to enter into sustained mental deliberation over the issues of the day and who merited political office. As evidence, he portrayed a hypothetical account of the 1858 Lincoln-Douglas senatorial debates; although each event lasted for several hours, the attendees supposedly devoted their unbroken and rapt attention to every eloquent word delivered by the orators. Today, Postman pointed out, television represents the culture's dominant communication technology (the author wrote before the Internet had become a part of daily life for many Americans—whether television's "reign" comes to an end remains to be seen but it is still, without question, one of the key sources that most Americans use to find out information and entertain themselves), and, because of its visual bias, inevitably fosters an entertaining approach to *everything* it depicts—including political events and other "major" news of the day. Accordingly, it evokes not an analytical but a visceral response. Extended argumentation and rational debate are replaced by sound bites and comedy show appearances by politicians. This, in a sense, trivializes key current issues and pushes entertainment to the forefront of American consciousness. In an era biased toward the visual and the exaltation of amusement, Postman and other like-minded critics would say, it is no wonder that politics, one of the most important subjects for any American to be knowledgeable about, becomes intertwined with popular culture.[2]

Countering this rather bleak account are scholars who contend that entertaining popular culture does not necessarily taint the political process—indeed, it can even promote substantial political engagement. Liesbet van Zoonen, for example, strongly advances this point of view. The Lincoln-Douglas debates, she notes, were not a "pure" analytical, print-inspired series of contemplative episodes. In fact, the atmosphere surrounding the debates was carnivalesque, replete with hawkers, vendors, games, and other amusements. It is no leap to assume that many of the people interested in the debates weaved back and forth between the "high-minded" discourse and the "low-brow" activities on the ground. Rather than bemoan the ostensible loss of elevated citizen political participation, van Zoonen indicates that politics has never occupied a space completely separated from entertainment and suggests there is no reason why politics should not be enjoyable, even fun. Popular culture, in its capacity to resonate with most of the population, can actually rejuvenate citizenship, stir greater political commitment, and increase political knowledge and awareness.[3] While applying their observations to youth voters, the authors of the essays in *Mosh the Polls* take up various positions along the spectrum represented by Postman and van Zoonen, which should inspire dynamic critical debate and allow the reader to reach his or her own conclusions.

Defining Popular Culture

Because the term *popular culture* is central to the framework of this book, a working definition and delineation of its usage in the pages ahead is in order. Like van Zoonen, *Mosh the Polls* borrows John Street's designation, which posits, "Popular culture is a form of entertainment that is mass produced or is made available to large numbers of people."[4] As van Zoonen points out, however, entertainment and popular culture are not precise synonyms. From one perspective, entertainment can refer to specific industries (i.e., "Hollywood"), genres (situation comedies, for example), or products (music, for instance). But some scholars take a different approach by looking at entertainment as an *effect* rather than a type of output produced by the media industries. Viewed through this lens, a person revealing gossip about a neighbor to a friend might evoke an entertainment effect; but one would be hard pressed to include this interpersonal exchange within the realm of popular culture. Yet more significantly for the purposes of this book, media products such as "hard" news and other educational fare are generally not associated with popular culture—but some people might indeed gain a degree of pleasure from these vehicles too.

One problem with the focus on effects, according to van Zoonen, is that it can render the concept of popular culture—if linked to entertainment—as essentially meaningless since anything could qualify. Furthermore, when applied to politics in particular, it is clear that only a small number of citizens actually find entertainment value in it; otherwise, why would politicians and their consultants go so far out of their way in their attempts to make politics somehow seem more compelling? Thus, like van Zoonen and others, this book will generally employ popular culture and entertainment interchangeably but with the understanding that entertainment refers to the specific media genres and products (media "texts") commonly assigned to this category, rather than the amusement it might incite (effects) in certain audience members. Accordingly, television entertainment, advertising, music, movies, Internet sites whose sole purpose is not informational, "soft" news, and live concerts all represent examples of popular culture that furnish modes of entertainment for sizeable audiences. On the other hand, hard news, for the most part, lies outside the boundaries of popular culture. Yet even here, as many scholars assert, the field of journalism has increasingly obscured the border between "serious" and "light" news in many of its offerings.[5] Consequently, the news can sometimes slip in and out of the sphere of popular culture as well.

At the same time, in line with the cultural studies tradition, the book will not simply position these creations of the media industries as static texts that impose messages on an often unknowing populace, but as tools through which people can generate their own interpretations that serve their interests.[6] In other words, popular culture involves a transaction between the producers and consumers (a distinction that is progressively blurring due to the rise of "new media" and the digital convergence of all forms of media) of media products—only together is meaning cultivated. Popular culture is also a loaded phrase because it presupposes that it can be separated from "high" culture and that there are different levels of cultural comprehension. The essays in this book shun from taking an elitist approach to popular culture, instead regarding it as worthy of contemplation. Ultimately, though, *Mosh the Polls* is interested in the issue of young people and their engagement with democracy. It is this concern that informs the examination of the intersection of politics and popular culture throughout the chapters.

The Focus on Youth Voters

For many observers, it is young people's apparent *lack* of engagement with the political process that they find so disturbing, which is another reason why the core topics of this book merit strong attention. Pundits on both sides of the political spectrum have, for the past several decades, branded young voters as apathetic, lazy, and unmotivated. There is some evidence to back up their claim. Leading up to the 2004 Presidential election, statisticians were quick to repeat the familiar refrain. In the 2000 presidential election, for instance, the percentage of eighteen- to twenty-four-year-old citizens who voted was 28 percent less than the percentage of citizens twenty-five-years-old and above who cast their ballots.[7] Jack M. McLeod wrote: "Voter turnout, as one among many

criteria of participation, averaged 37 percent in the ages eighteen to
twenty-four category in the past three presidential elections; this was 21
percent lower than among all citizens."[8] Yet the 2004 presidential election actually demonstrated that young voters had turned out in numbers
not seen in years. What is more, polling numbers are not the only crite-
rion by which political engagement can be measured. So why is the label
of apathy so likely to stick to younger voters? This may have as much to
do with an overall perceptual bias of the commentators as it does with
the activities younger voters are participating in on a daily basis. As we
have seen, video games, certain Internet activity, and television are considered by many to be pure entertainment and not worthy of substantial
discussion as it relates to politics. Whether there is some truth to these
stereotypes or not, it is clear that to political researchers, critics, practi-
tioners, and citizens of other stripes, the pattern among people new to the
political process has been specifically troubling. Consequently, one of
the main motivations behind the creation of this book is the feeling
shared by the authors that gaining a better grasp of youth voters in relationship to a changing media environment deserves critical reflection and
that popular culture should be taken seriously. Are eighteen- to twenty-
nine-year-olds really too young to care? Or is their concern merely hidden from view because it does not boldly manifest itself at the polls but
reveals itself through less-direct means instead?

Furthermore, popular culture, a classification of phenomena that appeals to nearly everyone, nonetheless, is especially associated with the
young.[9] Not surprisingly, then, politicians and interest groups have increasingly recognized the potential of popular culture for reaching this
fickle demographic. Eighteen- to twenty-nine-year-olds progressively
turning to forms of entertainment to gain political information and an
understanding of social issues, as well as the intense campaign emphasis
on young voters during election seasons, are relatively recent developments. For this reason as well, *Mosh the Polls* attempts to fill a gap that
other texts on politics and popular culture do not fully address. While
other books, such as Liesbet van Zoonen's *Entertaining the Citizen* and
Jeffrey P. Jones's *Entertaining Politics*, admirably examine this convergence, with the former treating it at large and the latter applying it specifically to humorous political talk shows, they tend to regard it in connection with the general audience, rather than the youth audience per
se.[10] This marks a point of departure for the collection of essays in the
pages ahead. Each author probes a particular issue with the motivation of
better comprehending the relationship between popular culture and

young people within the context of politics and democratic engage-ment—especially during national election campaigns. The book analyzes topics as diverse as *The Daily Show*, Rock the Vote, Michael Moore, Hollywood movies, and Sean Comb's Vote or Die initiative; illustrates the ways in which popular culture and politics overlap for young adults in today's mediated environment; and evaluates the potential conse-quences of these articulations. As a means of giving the book a consis-tent structure, each essay incorporates findings from the 2004 U.S. presi-dential election, a political event that has generated considerable discussion. The relevance of popular culture for the youth voter acquir-ing political capital was in full view during the heated election battle be-tween Senator John Kerry and incumbent George W. Bush for the top office in the United States. While, as we show below, this is not a new phenomenon, the 2004 presidential election was a watershed moment for the intersection of popular culture and politics for the young voter. Yet because the propensity to mix politics and show business will likely only continue, each essay to follow will also extend its treatment by consider-ing the implications of its findings for future elections and other political events, thus offering a perspective that should remain fresh. Before out-lining the book, however, it would be wise to put the fusing of politics and popular culture into historical context. By realizing that this blending has been transpiring for generations, the reader can then better enter the debate without adopting an overly alarmist position toward it.

Back in the Day: Politics and Popular Culture in Perspective

As Liesbet van Zoonen reveals, the linking of politics and entertainment is nothing new. If truth be told, by the turn of the twentieth century, this convergence was already becoming established in the United States. It was previously mentioned that the Lincoln-Douglas debates were staged within a festival-like setting. Starting before then and building through-out the century, during any presidential campaign season, in towns and cities across the country, swarms of citizens would line walkways and cheer as they viewed the spectacle of bands, dignitaries, flags, colorful banners, badges, and smiling faces streaming by.[11] Modern advertising, which emerged and began to assume its pervasive presence in the cul-tural landscape during the second half of the nineteenth century, had its political forms as well. Campaign advertising, including broadsides and posters designed to appeal to the emotions and imagination, was a staple publicity tactic by the dawn of the new century. The presumption of many politicians campaigning in the nineteenth century was that to reach voters, one had to engage them on their level, which brings to mind the issue of how the potential audience is regarded by politicians, public figures, and entertainers today, a topic that chapters of this book will also take up.

It could actually be argued that at least loose connections between politics and popular culture extend still further back—even to the early days of the country's formation. Contemptuous attacks in the press against candidates for office were common. Could not parallels be drawn between these stern rebukes designed to evoke a type of perverse enjoyment and *The O'Reilly Factor*'s host mounting another tirade against politicians who are "soft" on the "War on Terror"? Surely the partisan newspapers and partisan handbills sensationally depicting Adams as a no-good monarchist were meant to incite delight among Jefferson supporters, while the lurid accounts of Jefferson as nothing but a vile atheist and unfit to lead were intended to instill a sense of pleasure for backers of Adams. The struggles during the writing of the constitution were also particularly bitter, with clearly identified partisan papers all but calling those on the other side of the debate potential traitors, a charge that surely has added resonance in the modern political environment. Attacks in the form of editorial cartoons, pamphlets, and popular songs were seen as especially effective ways of mobilizing public opinion. During Grover Cleveland's second presidential race, for example, followers of his opponent charged that Cleveland had fathered an illegitimate child and serenaded campaign appearances with shouts of, "Ma, ma, where's my pa? Gone to the White House, haw, haw, haw!"[12]

In fact, as Schudson, McChesney, and others spell out, not until well into the twentieth century did the U.S. press fully develop the method of *objectivity* as a means of promoting standards of professionalism and defending itself against both sources attempting to distort events for political gain, and criticism that it was merely reflecting the views of its business-friendly owners. Previously, partisanship was the rule; citizens on both ends of the political spectrum commonly sought out papers that simply reinforced their views—these papers were often clearly named after the political party that each one endorsed.[13] A number of scholars, such as Jay Rosen, convincingly reason that news production and reception are moving in the same direction today.[14] Although the notion of objectivity is still spouted as an almost sacred tenant of responsible journalism, many newspapers, television news programs, talk radio shows, and news bloggers, even if they do not readily admit it, present a decidedly partisan stance—and countless readers, viewers, and listeners are only too eager to engage with those news media that are crafted to dramatically drum up sentiment in support of worldviews they already hold. Even if they are delivering "important" (albeit often dubious) information, vehicles such as *Hannety and Combs*, *The Don Imus Show*, or The Daily Kos are intended to amuse their audience members, triggering increased heart palpitations and a tingle in the spines along the way. These media products, in a sense, validate the outlook and partisan opinions of the listener or viewer and imply that subjects such as the war on terror are not matters of debate, but settled matters that one is either "for" or "against," which would seem to lead to consequences that need examination. Conservative advocate Ann Coulter has even gone so far as to suggest in her latest book and in television interviews about the text that reporters for the *New York Times* be shot for treason for reporting stories contrary to the government's point of view.[15]

Of course, today's political books are just the latest manifestations within a long tradition. Even before the nineteenth century was three decades old, the book industry had already entered into the political campaign fray. During the 1828 presidential election season, when Andrew Jackson, who was affectionately labeled by his followers as "Old Hickory" to symbolize a brave act of battle he had once executed in support of his troops, participated in what could be regarded as a precursor to the "image campaign," citizens could learn of his purported strong character through a biography published four years earlier.[16]

Sloganeering, a device commonly employed to reduce an idea to its bare-bones essence in a way that stirs up certain emotions among large numbers of people, notably stood out twelve years later. Throughout the campaign of 1840, William Harrison was enshrined in the alliterative phrase, "Tippecanoe and Tyler Too." The expression was intended to remind citizens of Harrison's role in a battle against the Shawnee Indians at Tippecanoe in 1811, an event of questionable merit that resulted in the massacre of Indians yet weakened their strength. The reference, cleaned up for the purpose of mythologizing the candidate, was even encoded in song. Supplemented with parades and symbols that signified Harrison was a man of the people (though he was solidly a member of the well-to-do), such as the display of log cabins, the distribution of hard cider, and the donning of coonskin caps, the cheer of "Hurrah for Tippecanoe" could be heard loud and clear at campaign gatherings.[17] In effect, the campaign demonstrated that reality could be reorganized and that mere facts about economic status did not matter so much as the proper image. Similar activities continue to this day, with wealthy politicians "rolling up their shirt sleeves" and snacking on pork rinds to exhibit their connection with "average citizens."

Yet perhaps the most preeminent form of popular culture throughout much of the nineteenth century was staged theater—and this dramatic vehicle was not immune from the sway of politics. Although it appears that office-seekers did not commonly turn to the stage to further their campaigns, nonetheless, the theater did produce work that promoted certain causes and offered political commentary on the concerns of the day. As John W. Frick illustrates, for instance, the temperance movement relied heavily on drama to support its mission.[18] Temperance melodramas, according to Reynolds and Rosenthal, could "touch the feelings with electric quickness."[19] And they could attempt to rouse people to action. For example, in the 1880s, a production described as a "pro-prohibition musical for children," *A Temperance Picnic with the Old Woman Who Lived in a Shoe*, "advocated the vote as the remedy for intemperance and stressed the importance of exerting political pressure on legislators."[20] Nor was a pox on drinking the only cause for which theater could serve as a tool of propaganda. For the popular audience, Hays and Nikolopoulou state, melodrama "served as a crucial space in which the cultural, political, and economic exigencies of the century were played out and transformed into public discourses about issues."[21] Even P. T. Barnum, the notorious showman and master of hype, would use his bully pulpit as a master of ceremonies in traveling spectacles, pushing for temperance and asking his large audiences to consider his political agenda.

Another dramatic genre, blackface minstrelsy, which was hugely popular during the Antebellum period and foreshadowed the burlesque and vaudeville shows to come, especially carried political implications—and not only in relationship to race. Social satire was endemic to the performances. Moreover, as Alexander Saxton argues, "from the mid-1840s through the 1860s, overt partisanship linked it to the Democratic party." Symbolically fusing the urban worker with the planter in the South, minstrelsy was "an attack on the moral and economic premises of whiggery," politically well-disposed toward European immigration and territorial expansion, while hostile to the temperance movement.[22] Sometimes, it even overly promoted a political candidate. Described by Saxton, minstrelsy, for example, mounted a campaign in 1864 for George McClellan in his election fight against the Republican Abraham Lincoln. The words of one sketch plainly indicated where the show's war sympathies lied:

> We're willing, Father Abram, ten hundred thousand more
> Should help our Uncle Samuel to prosecute the war;
> But then we want a chieftain true, one who can lead the van,
> George B. McClellan you all know he is the very man.[23]

Or in another case:

> Abram Linkum said to me
> Send de sojers down!
> He's gwine to make the niggers free
> Send de sojers down![24]

In *Julius the Snoozer*, an 1875 burlesque of Shakespeare's *Julius Caesar*, the characters mocked the perceived corruption of New York's William Marcy "Boss" Tweed, as evidenced in the following exchange:

> Cassius: Our dirty streets want cleaning; to this you've no objection?
> Julius: We'll have them cleaned just before our next election.[25]

Political cartoons were also a significantly influential popular-culture force. The political cartoons of Thomas Nast (the man who drew the most iconic version of Santa Claus), for instance, commented on and influenced the American debates on both the political fortunes of Boss Tweed, as well as the immigrant and nativist disputes of the time period. Nast's cartoons of Irish and Catholic immigrants as buffoonish, gorilla-like figures probably helped stir nativist resentment as much as any political factor in the city of New York during the latter half of the nineteenth century.

Still, in terms of direct campaign tactics, eventually the prominence of parades and brass bands was supplanted by the rise of the nation's first broadcast medium. Radio offered an expanding array of opportunities for reaching the populace at the level of popular culture. In 1923, Calvin Coolidge delivered the first State of the Union address ever transmitted through the airwaves. Before then, just a proportionately small number of people had ever had access to the words of a President as the utterances were actually unfolding—they could only hear them within earshot at a live event. Hard as it is to imagine for twenty-first-century audiences awash in diverse forms of media, to be able to listen to the country's leader in an everyday setting caused quite a stir. People enthusiastically gathered around radio sets in homes and offices; stores selling radios even projected the speech to passers by. And whether or not a State of the Union address qualifies as popular culture per se, as Kathleen Hall Jamieson explains, "By 1928 political proselytizing guised as entertainment had overflowed from the parades onto the airwaves."[26] The trend continued. For instance, in 1944, celebrities, including Lucille Ball and Irving Berlin, endorsed their favorite presidential candidate during the radio broadcast, the "Roosevelt Special." Four years later, a series of comedic shows targeting women in the home was produced for the Democrats and their choice for President, Harry Truman. The programs featured songs, pointed jokes, and contests aimed at involving the listener.[27]

Today, critics of the intersection of politics and popular culture might lament the birth of political radio broadcasts, identifying it as a turning point in the supposed decline of the nation's political discourse. Yet interestingly, none other than Franklin Delano Roosevelt, the President who, through his "Fireside Chats," best demonstrated the efficacy of radio in establishing a bond with the public, contended that the medium actually heightened the level of campaign communication because it removed citizens from the "surroundings of brass bands and red lights" and thus, he stated at the time, "mere oratory and mere emotion are having less to do with the determination of public questions . . . final opinions are arrived at in the quiet of the home."[28] Moreover, according to an author of the *New York Times* in 1928, unlike the days of the partisan press when constituents would gravitate toward their favorite biased newspapers, radio allowed them to hear a range of speeches and, consequently, attain a more neutral state of mind.[29]

At about the same time, the interplay of politics and popular culture found another new expression through newsreels. These short films were screened by movie patrons before the featured selections. Mostly a forerunner to the contemporary television news show (in fact, the introduction of television quickly led to the newsreel's extinction), the newsreel was also exploited by political candidates for self-promotion, somewhat prefiguring political television advertising. For example, Hollywood was called into service to help defeat Upton Sinclair, a socialist running for governor of California in 1934. Actors were hired to play the roles of everyday citizens who conveyed anxiety regarding the prospect of a newly elected Sinclair.[30] The following year, Huey Long, a U.S. Senator from Louisiana, unwittingly undermined his own campaign by participating in a newsreel produced by the "March of Time." Little did he realize that the makers of the short film were partial to Long's competitor; presaging television attack commercials—or even segments on news spoof shows such as *The Daily Show*—the newsreel was edited in such a manner as to make him appear ridiculous.[31] Other films, including the silent movies intended to generate support for the "Great War," featured Douglas Fairbanks, Mary Pickford, and Charlie Chaplin. Indeed, George Creel, head of the United States Committee on Public Information (eventually known as, simply, the Creel Commission), drew on a broad array of media sources to launch what was then perhaps the most comprehensive propaganda campaign ever implemented, designed to encourage U.S. citizens to back the country's entrance into World War I; turning to Hollywood, Creel included film among his diverse assortment of tactics.[32] Later, other government attempts at propaganda through film, such as the *Why We Fight* series, were of limited success yet still demonstrated that popular opinion could be influenced though the relatively new medium of moving pictures.

Television, which quickly took residence in millions of Americans' homes by the end of the 1950s, of course, provided the capacity for politics and popular culture to interlink like never before and, arguably, stands as the central culprit to which critics point when they grumble about the purported decline of the nation's political discourse. By the close of the following decade, people had the pleasure—or the irritation, depending on their perspective—of witnessing the presidential "candidacy" of the comedian Pat Paulson on *The Smothers Brothers Comedy Hour* (although his routine, which continued for years through other venues, was grounded in humor spiced with social commentary, he actually appeared on primary ballots in New Hampshire in later years—even finishing second to Bill Clinton in 1992) and the stiff performance of Richard Nixon (who had successfully used television to revive his flagging political fortunes during his notorious "Checkers" speech a decade earlier) on the zany comedy sketch show, *Laugh In*, which featured the soon-to-be President delivering one of the lines the program turned into a cliché, "sock it to me." In the 1970s, *Saturday Night Live* burst onto the scene and became a symbol of tongue-in-cheek, political satire. Many of its comedic skits—particularly its regularly slated mock news segment—revolved around issues of the day or poking fun at government officials. One of the recurrent routines that catapulted the comedian Chevy Chase into the limelight was his impersonation of a bumbling President Gerald Ford. Chase utterly ridiculed the President, who was probably unfairly stigmatized for his supposedly frequent mishaps, by falling over furniture and carrying out other clumsy activity.

More recent notorious instances of politics and popular culture overtly coming together through television include the dark-sunglasses-adorning and saxophone-blaring Bill Clinton during his 1992 surprise appearance on The *Arsenio Hall Show* (or even his admission on MTV of what his preference of underwear was); Bob Dole's expression of lust toward a scantily clad, gyrating Brittney Speers in a Pepsi commercial produced after Dole's loss to Clinton in the 1996 campaign; and John Edward's announcement of his presidential candidacy on *The Daily Show* in 2003.

Scores of films over the years, of course, have also brought together entertainment and politics, either serving the function of disseminating propaganda or delivering scathing critiques of current events. For instance, in the classic movie, *Mr. Smith Goes to Washington*, released in 1939, James Stewart plays the role of a naïve Senator who confronts political corruption; the scene in which he spearheads a filibuster goes down as a particularly memorable Hollywood moment. The next year, Steinbeck's *The Grapes of Wrath*, a biting commentary on the profound troubles sparked by the industrial revolution and capitalism run amuck, was turned into a motion picture that still receives considerable attention today. In the 1950s, releases included *The Last Hurrah* (1958), featuring Spencer Tracy as the Irish-American mayor, Frank Skeffington, who strives—yet ultimately fails—to obtain one last term in office. One of the standout films of the 1960s is *Dr. Strangelove* (1964), a startling satire of the policies of politicians ominously engaged in defending the nation in the incipient nuclear age. Nixon's Watergate scandal supplied the impetus for *All the President's Men* (1976), which was based on Bob Woodward's and Carl Bernstein's non-fictional account of the cover-up. By the 1980s, the nation was ostensibly ready to process the Vietnam War, as evidenced by the appearance of *Apocalypse Now* and *The Deer Hunter* in 1979, and *The Killing Fields* (1984), *Full Metal Jacket* (1987), and *Born on the Fourth of July* (1989) within the decade. More recent cases in point, from the 1990s and beyond, include *Bob Roberts* (1992), *Primary Colors* (1998), *Wag the Dog* (1998), *Bulworth* (1998), and documentaries (the form making a comeback of late) such as *Control Room* (2003) and, yes, *Fahrenheit 9/11* (2004).

Reams of other examples could be readily identified from the realm of popular culture at large. Moreover, this brief historical overview has barely even touched on political themes in popular music, which occurred long before the highly recognized political protest songs of the 1960s. And still more connections between politics and popular culture could be explored, including political advertising, "horse-race" news coverage of elections, and political conventions themselves as forms of entertainment; former performance celebrities who later became politicians (i.e., President Ronald Reagan, U.S. Representative Sonny Bono, California Governor Arnold Schwarzenegger, Minnesota Governor Jessie Ventura, Clint Eastwood as mayor of Carmel, Jerry Springer as mayor of Cincinnati, et al.)—or, indeed, politicians who became celebrities in their own right; and certain political "media events" (e.g., FDR's "Fireside Chats," the Kennedy-Nixon debates) that, at least to some extent, assumed popular-culture status by becoming a part of the nation's folklore. But without unnecessarily turning this introduction into an exhaustive historical treatise, we hope the point here is clear: the fusion of American politics and entertainment or popular culture is not something of only recent vintage or simply a product of the television age; instead, it can be traced from the very founding of the nation (and surely still earlier, both in the New World and elsewhere). Yet, we would suggest, some developments *are* different today, including the degree to which politics and popular culture intersect, the much greater selection of popular-culture tools that can be used for campaigning (which, since the rise of the full-time media consultant in the 1960s, have been enthusiastically exploited), and the emphasis on potential *youth* voters in particular. Whether this is cause for celebration or regret is a topic on which the essays in *Mosh the Polls* intend to evoke discussion and debate.

Preview of the Book

Mosh the Polls is uniquely situated to be used by both scholars for research, and teachers and students for classes in politics, government, media studies, cultural studies, popular culture, and other related courses. While the book is rigorous in its approach and scholarship, it is designed so that it can be read by academics and undergraduate and graduate students alike, as well as by the everyday reader interested in how politics and popular culture are increasingly intersecting.

Given that the sphere of politics and the entertainment industry are entwined now more than ever, numerous concerns come to mind regarding the way in which Americans (particularly young Americans) use media (both traditional news media and entertainment based coverage) not only as a source of information but as a way of engaging in the political process as well. Are a greater number of young Americans, in an age of declining ratings for network news, ever more turning to entertainment programming such as *The Daily Show* for their political news? Does viewing documentaries and witnessing personal appearances by Michael Moore and the activists of Rock the Vote demonstrate true political agency? Or are these ways in which real engagement in the nation's version of democracy are counterfeited? This media environment deserves a critical look, one that scrutinizes not just the political process, but also the means in which modern young voters make sense of and engage, or do not engage, in political events. *Mosh the Polls* seeks to take up this mission. The text features a multidisciplinary group of young scholars who specialize in analyzing youth culture and political engagement. It also presents its investigations from a variety of spectrums, including historical and textual analyses, and both qualitative and quantitative work. As a collection of essays reflecting a range of viewpoints, the book offers a critical assessment of both the potentially negative and positive consequences for the youth voter negotiating a symbolic milieu in which the line between politics and entertainment is decidedly blurred.

Mosh the Polls is structured in a way that, by playing off of the idea of politics as part of the realm of entertainment, subtly reinforces some of the text's central motifs and gives the collection of essays coherence. Part I, entitled "Setting the Stage," provides key general themes that set the groundwork for subsequent chapters. Robert Klotz discusses in Chapter 1 how young adults experience mediated political campaigns differently than other adults—especially because of their association with popular culture. In particular, young adults not only turn to the Internet more often than other adults, but also participate in different types of political activity while online. Laura Tropp also focuses on the Internet in Chapter 2, looking at various sites that have been used to mobilize youth voters—including Rock the Vote and Declare Yourself—and questioning their efficacy. Ultimately, she concludes, with their product ads and other forms of hype, these vehicles seem to replicate the messages of popular culture through a new medium and further contribute to the commoditization of the political process, thus rendering democratic engagement problematic.

Part II, entitled "The Performance," examines specific texts and explores their circulation among their intended audiences. The authors also consider how these "performances" offer both direct and indirect opportunities for political engagement. In Chapter 3, Aaron Teeter and Brandy Chappell, who both worked for Rock the Vote during the 2004 presidential election, supply an "insider's" account of the organization's efforts to mobilize youth voters, as well as analyze both its strengths and short-comings. In Chapter 4, Brian Cogan centers his study on *The Daily Show* and other comedy shows that feature political satire and appeal to young audiences. Along the way, he poses the question, Are these TV programs facilitating political engagement or merely functioning as additional resources for amusement? Michael Grabowski, in Chapter 5, turns his attention to Michael Moore's "Slacker Tour." Using medium theory, the author probes Moore's rhetoric and some of the heated responses to his live performances. Here again, Grabowski challenges the reader to consider whether a form of popular culture—in this case, stand-up routines staged at college campuses—can work to motivate political engagement or, instead, is likelier to diffuse the energy that students could channel toward more direct political participation.

In Chapter 6, Marco Calavita goes in a different direction from the other essays in the book. He conducts a textual analysis of a number of recent Hollywood movies and television shows that have targeted young people and whose narratives emphasize torture. Observing the ways in which these products of popular culture mirror current U.S. foreign policy, Calavita contemplates whether they indirectly encourage youth audiences to accept the dubious actions of their government. Ultimately this matters because, as Calavita argues, among other things, the ideological influence of these media texts could make a difference on behavior at the polls. Tony Kelso completes Part II with an investigation of the initiatives designed to reach young African Americans active in hip-hop culture. Blending textual and audience reception methodologies, the author contends that efforts targeting African-American youth can have an impact on voter participation. Still, he adds, hip-hop culture's capacity to play a central role in instigating political change is probably limited.

The title of Part III is "Evaluating the Show." Here, the authors present general reflections on some of the issues raised by the previous chapters and the implications of these findings for participatory democracy, especially as it relates to young adults. The tone of the essays in this section ranges from cautiously optimistic to highly skeptical. Xiaoxia Cao, in Chapter 8, eschews a dismissive tone as she examines so-called soft news, a kind of journalism that is commonly linked to popular culture, and its relationship to young voters. Instead, she reveals that this type of coverage can actually serve as a legitimate source of information and contribute to the democratic process. Shawn McIntosh presents a mainly contrary point of view in Chapter 9. He explores the rise of interactive media and questions whether they are facilitating a movement toward "strong democracy" or are, instead, primarily operating in a manner that further transforms the citizen into a consumer. In the final chapter, Marc Leverette brings the book to a provocative close. Incorporating a discussion of the work of Trey Parker and Matt Stone, the creators of *South Park*, the writer suggests that, given the current media and political climate, *un*involvement might stand as the most "powerful" response young citizens can generate.

In sum, within an increasingly politicized climate in which reputable journalists are often afraid to broach serious subjects, *Mosh the Polls* asks the reader to consider the legitimacy of our current political discourse and the extent to which the American mediated public sphere functions as a place where significant political issues can be engaged and debated. When self-professed comedians such as Jon Stewart and Michael Moore are regarded by many as having more political capital and depth than mainstream reporters, it is clear that something radical has taken place in American political discourse, American civic life, and the way in which mass media are used as a tool of engagement by youth voters. Some readers might draw rather dour conclusions, fearing that American politics, which inevitably yields concrete outcomes for real human beings, is suffering considerable harm through its association with seemingly light-hearted entertainment. Others, no doubt, will view this evolving political climate with hopefulness, apprehending the possibility that a greater percentage of the population could be motivated to become involved in matters of substance. Were politics ever free from "crass" communication influences and other "contaminants" that render distorted representations of political policies, candidate positions, and the state of the nation's affairs? Could it even be true that the potential for young people to subvert and deconstruct deceitful messages has never been greater, given the abundant media resources, such as the alternative news sites and blogs of the Internet, that they have at their disposal in comparison to yesterday's citizenry, which could be kept in the dark through blatantly biased newspapers and printed propaganda? If after reading the following essays, readers are energetically discussing these and other questions, then *Mosh the Polls* will have done its job.

Notes

1. See for example, Kevin G. Barnhurst, "Politics in the Fine Meshes:

Young Citizens, Power and Media," *Media Culture & Society* 20, no. 2 (April 1998): 201-18.

2. Neil Postman, *Amusing Ourselves to Death: Public Discourse in the Age of Show Business* (New York: Penguin Books, 1986).

3. Liesbet van Zoonen, *Entertaining the Citizen: When Politics and Popular Culture Converge* (Lanham, MD: Rowman & Littlefield, 2005).

4. John Street, *Politics and Popular Culture* (Cambridge: Polity Press, 1997), 7.

5. See, for example, Edward J. Epstein, *News from Nowhere: Television and the News* (Chicago: Ivan R. Dee, 2000); Robert McChesney, *The Problem of the Media: U.S. Communication Politics in the Twenty-First Century* (New York: Monthly Review Press, 2004); Neil Postman and Steve Powers, *How to Watch TV News* (New York: Penguin, 1992).

6. For example, see Chris Barker, *Cultural Studies: Theory and Practice*, second ed. (London: Sage, 2003).

7. Carrie Donovan and Mark Hugo Lopez, "Youth Voter Turnout in the States during the 2000 Presidential and 2002 Midterm Elections," *Center for Information and Research on Civic Learning and Engagement*, June 2004, http://www.civicyouth.org/PopUps/FactSheets/FS_Youth_turnout_%20states_2 002.pdf (accessed July 10, 2006).

8. Jack M. McLeod, "Media and Civic Socialization of Youth," *Journal of Adolescent Health* 27, no. 2 (August 2000): 45.

9. Denis McQuail, *McQuail's Mass Communication Theory*, fifth ed. (London: Sage, 2005).

10. van Zoonen, *Entertaining the Citizen*; Jeffrey P. Jones, *Entertaining Politics: New Political Television and Civic Culture* (Lanham, MD: Rowman & Littlefield, 2005).

11. Kathleen Hall Jamieson, *Packaging the Presidency: A History and Criticism of Presidential Campaign Advertising*, third ed. (New York: Oxford University Press, 1996).

12. Alyn Brodsky, *Grover Cleveland: A Study in Character* (New York: St. Martin's Press, 2000).

13. Michael Schudson, *Discovering the News: A Social History of American Newspapers* (New York: Basic Books, 1980); Robert McChesney, *Rich Media, Poor Democracy: Communication Politics in Dubious Times* (New York: Free Press, 2000).

14. Jay Rosen, *What Are Journalists For?*, New Ed ed. (New Haven, CT: Yale University Press, 2001).

15. Ann Coulter, *Godless: The Church of Liberalism* (New York: Crown Forum, 2006).

16. Jamieson, *Packaging the Presidency*, 6.

17. Jamieson, *Packaging the Presidency*, 8-9.

18. John W. Frick, *Theatre, Culture and Temperance Reform in Nineteenth-Century America* (Cambridge: Cambridge University Press, 2003).

19. David S. Reynolds and Debra J. Rosenthal, eds., *The Serpent in the Cup: Temperance in American Literature* (Amherst: University of Massachusetts Press, 1997), 4

20. Frick, *Theater, Culture*, 164.

21. Michael Hays and Anastasia Nikolopoulou, "Introduction," in *Melodrama: The Cultural Emergence of a Genre*, ed. Michael Hays and Anastasia Naikolopoulou (New York: St. Martin's Press, 1996), viii.

22. Alexander Saxton, "Blackface Minstrelsy," in *Inside the Minstrel Mask*, ed. Annemarie Bean, James V. Hatch, and Brooks McNamara (Hanover, NH: Wesleyan University Press, 1996), 67.

23. Saxton, "Blackface," 81.

24. Saxton, "Blackface, 81.

25. William J. Mahar, "Ethiopian Skits and Sketches: Contents and Contexts of Blackface Minstrelsy, 1840-1890," in *Inside the Minstrel Mask*, ed. Annemarie Bean, James V. Hatch, and Brooks McNamara (Hanover, NH: Wesleyan University Press, 1996), 201.

26. Jamieson, *Packaging the Presidency*, 25. The authors wish to point out that much of the material in this section of the introduction derives from this important book.

27. Jamieson, *Packaging the Presidency*, 26-27.

28. Franklin D. Roosevelt, *The Public Papers and Addresses of Franklin D. Roosevelt* (New York: Russell & Russell, 1969), 659.

29. John Calvin Brown, "Broadcasting is Called a Vital Campaign Vehicle," *New York Times*, November 4, 1928, 154.

30. Jamieson, *Packaging the Presidency*, 30.

31. Raymond Fielding, *The March of Time 1935-1951* (New York: Oxford University Press, 1978).

32. A full account of Creel's and the United States Committee on Public Information's massive propaganda campaign is captured in George Creel, *How We Advertised America* (1920; reprint, Manchester, NH: Ayer, 1972).

Part I: Setting the Stage

Chapter 1

Different Experiences of Young Adults and Other Adults in Mediated Campaigns

Robert J. Klotz

College student Alexandra Trustman was ready to ask a question of the Democratic presidential candidates during a debate preceding the 2004 primaries. The CNN producer had not liked the question that she suggested about technology policy and instead handed her a note card. Alexandra asked the presidential candidates the question on the card: "Macs or PCs?"

The aftermath of the question tells us something about mediated politics and young voters. Alexandra Trustman was ridiculed for the superficiality of her question. Writing in her campus newspaper, she explained that the Macs or PCs question had not been her idea. A CNN spokesperson apologized for the network's role in the incident: "In an attempt to ensure a lighthearted moment in this debate, a CNN producer working with Ms. Trustman clearly went too far."[1] CNN's patronizing attitude toward the young audience of its Rock the Vote debate reflects the continuing struggle of political establishment culture to reach young adults through traditional media. This struggle has increased the relative role of popular culture and the new media in the political lives of young adults.

In this chapter, I will examine how young adults and other adults experience mediated presidential campaigns with a focus on the 2004 election. Survey data will be used to identify age-based differences in reliance on political establishment culture and the traditional media versus popular culture and the new media. Having identified a strong impact of the Internet on young adults, the nature of Internet use will be examined further. Similarities and differences in the online political behavior of young adults and other adults will also be identified. Finally, the implications of the findings will be considered.

Popular Culture and Politics

While recognizing that popular culture influenced politics long before television, scholars have viewed television as a medium that has especially linked politics with popular culture. Alan Schroeder has described how television led politicians to become entertainers: "And with television in the 1950s, it added the kind of effect of having the president in your home night after night, and becoming a television character in addition to being the chief of state. . . . Presidents can use entertainment and pop culture as a means of reinforcing their bond with American voters."[2] The connection also holds true for political messages in entertainment, including the most basic conception of citizenship. In *This Is the City*, Ronald Schmidt tied the Los Angeles Police Department's support of the production of the television show *Dragnet* to promoting a particular view of citizenship: "In the 1950s, the citizens at home could strive to emulate the citizens on television as they strove to emulate [Sergeant Joe] Friday."[3] The effect of both fictional and non-fictional television is shown in the research of Delli Carpini and Williams. They found that three focus groups that watched a television newsmagazine story on toxic waste and three focus groups that watched a fictional television movie with a toxic waste story line incorporated a similar number of references to the television programs in a subsequent general discussion about the issue of pollution.[4]

The impact of television and popular culture on politics has sparked a vibrant debate among scholars about whether this is good or bad. Most recently, several scholars have articulated a positive view of the potential for entertainment with political messages to activate citizens. In *Entertaining the Citizen*, Liesbet van Zoonen identifies problems with a rigid demarcation between popular culture and politics: "[T]o set politics apart from the rest of culture is not a feasible option for the maintenance of citizenship; not only will it not survive the competition for spare time, but more importantly it will also be separated, different, and distant from everyday life."[5] In *Entertaining Politics*, Jeffrey Jones finds that the new political television of Bill Maher, Jon Stewart, and Dennis Miller promotes civic dialogue by approaching subjects with humor and without the ideological constraints of political insiders: "In short, popular culture is just as capable of shaping and supporting a culture of citizenship as it is of shaping and supporting a culture of consumption."[6]

These positive perspectives are a reply to a growing indictment of television for disengaging people from public life. Robert Putnam's *Bowling Alone* placed much of the blame for the decline in civic participation on the solitary pursuit of watching television.[7] Neil Postman argued that television had impoverished political discourse by making "entertainment itself the natural format for the representation of all experience."[8] When Postman wrote these words, today's young adults were less than ten years old.

Yet there probably has been an acceleration of the influence of popular culture on the political lives of young adults. By asking for open-ended life histories, Kevin Barnhurst has investigated how young adults come to understand a political issue. He has found increasing alienation from traditional news sources: "Young American citizens remember learning that newspapers were supposed to be an important avenue for political information, but their own encounters with the medium taught them that the products of institutional journalism are largely irrelevant to their lives."[9] Barnhurst concludes that young adults come to understand political issues from "many genres (especially entertainment media)" and personal discussion.[10]

The increasing influence of popular culture on the political perceptions of young adults may also be seen as a response to watershed political events. The most enduring news story about the first president vividly remembered by many of today's young adults centered on when President Clinton was impeached by the U.S. House of Representatives for lying to the special prosecutor about his sexual relationship with Monica Lewinsky. The underlying subject matter obviously offered little role for political expertise. It is not surprising, then, that a scholarly study has found that the perspectives offered by political outsiders on the television show *Politically Incorrect* about the Clinton scandal were more diverse and resonated better with the public than the perspectives of political insiders on *This Week with Sam Donaldson and Cokie Roberts*.[11] The establishment political culture and traditional media also failed young adults in the 2000 campaign. This failure is symbolized by the third presidential debate, when the two candidates were given an open-ended question to address issues of special concern to young adults. In their awkward answers, neither candidate was able to resist a reference to the importance of providing prescription drugs for seniors under Medicare. Al Gore let young people know that "the big drug companies are against the prescription drug proposal that I've made"; George Bush said that "Medicare is relevant for all of us, young and old alike."[12] Only 42 percent of young adults voted in the 2000 election.[13]

While the political establishment communicating through traditional media has clearly struggled to speak the language of young adults, there were hints early in the 2004 campaign that the Internet was engaging young voters. Scholars have found that the 2004 Democratic primary candidates gave a prominent role to interactive functions in their online campaigns.[14] The opportunity for interactivity may have had a special appeal for young voters. In particular, the Howard Dean campaign was able to energize young voters through Internet appeals. Reflecting on his campaign's success in mobilizing young voters, Dean's campaign manager Joe Trippi described the Internet as having characteristics that are well suited to the high energy of young adults:

> As one of the first mainstream organizations to tap into this demographic vein, we were learning that, unlike generations of dull and deadened TV watchers, these young people actually *wanted* to be engaged politically. They were out there asking questions, organizing, and just waiting for someone who could speak their language back to them, the language of the Net.[15]

Research has suggested that young adults may seek different things from the Internet than other adults. For example, using an experimental design, Lupia and Philpot exposed young adults and other adults to nine different political websites for a five-minute period. They asked participants to evaluate the quality of the information presented on the website. Subjects were also asked how the website affected their political interest—whether it made them want to learn about politics, talk about politics, and vote in the 2000 presidential election. The results showed significant differences between age groups in how websites were evaluated. The different quality rankings then had an impact on whether the website increased interest in politics.[16]

The literature's suggestion that young adults may be drawn more to popular culture and the new media suggests a pairing. An alternative pairing would be establishment political culture and traditional media. These loosely competing pairings will frame this chapter's analysis of news consumption during presidential campaigns. The goal will be to move beyond anecdote to examine if there are systematic differences between young adults and other adults in how they experience mediated presidential campaigns. It is hypothesized that young adults are more likely than other adults to experience the mediated presidential campaign through popular culture and the new media. Conversely, it is expected that other adults are more likely to experience the campaign through establishment political culture and the traditional media.

Methods

In order to examine the different experiences of young adults and other adults during presidential campaigns, this chapter will rely heavily on a survey from the Pew Internet & American Life Project taken immediately after the 2004 election. This survey provides the best and most recent available data for understanding how presidential campaigns are experienced through the media. The survey had a large sample size and asked a wide range of detailed questions about media use during the 2004 election. It was conducted during the period from November 4-22, 2004. Media use during the campaign was fresh on the minds of respondents. The Pew Internet & American Life Project is well-respected for the quality of its survey research. I am grateful to the Pew Internet & American Life Project for making its data available to scholars, although the organization is not responsible for my interpretations of its data.

The first key step in analyzing the data is to define young adults. Any definition, of course, is arbitrary and different age ranges for young adults abound. For the purposes of this chapter, young adults will be those aged eighteen to thirty in November 2004. Other adults are the rest of the adult population. This distinction has intuitive appeal, which means that, given that the top cohort of young adults were born in 1974, the entire range of young adults generally would have entered high school after Bill Clinton was elected. Because the goal is to ascertain whether young adults have distinct characteristics, the chapter does not draw further distinctions among other adults.

The findings in this chapter are based on the primary data set and a relevant subset. The primary data set includes the entire sample of respondents whose age is indicated in the Pew post-election survey. The final sample includes 378 young adults and 1,768 other adults. As with any subgroup in a survey, the smaller number of young adults means that there is a little more uncertainty about the responses of this group. For young adults, the margin of error (at the conventional 95 percent confidence interval) of the survey is approximately ±5. For other adults, it is ±2. For the question about the use of traditional media sources (reported in Table 1), there were so many potential outlets that the survey only asked people about half of the items, thereby creating two panels of about half of the total sample. The average panel size for the traditional media source question was 189 young adults and 884 other adults, with margins of error of ±7 and ±3, respectively.

The subset is the entire sample of respondents who are Internet users. This includes all people who answered "yes" to the following question: "Do you ever go online to access the Internet or World Wide Web or to send and receive e-mail?" For the subset of Internet users, there were 287 young adults and 1,016 other adults, providing margin of errors of ±6 and ±3, respectively. In both the primary data set and subset, respondents who refused to answer or didn't know about their use of a particular media source were coded as non-users. This minor coding adjustment has intuitive appeal, since people who can't recognize a media type or recall using it were unlikely to have used it, but has no real impact on the results, since lack of knowledge responses were so rare (typically no more than 1 percent).

The key question in the chapter is whether young adults are systematically different than other adults in their mediated experiences of campaigns. In a poll, it is possible that what appears to be a meaningful difference occurred by chance. Before identifying something as a difference, scholars must be fairly sure that pure mathematical chance is not responsible for the difference. The two most common standards in social science are that scholars must be at least either 95 percent or 99 percent sure that the differences would not have occurred by chance. In this chapter, I will err on the side of caution and use the at least 99 percent sure standard for significant findings. Stated in another way, the probability that the difference between age groups could have occurred by chance must be less than 1 percent ($p < .01$) before a finding will be considered statistically significant. In presenting results, I will highlight only those differences that are statistically significant.

Results

Table 1 reveals both similarities and differences between how young adults and other adults consumed traditional media in the 2004 campaign. The major differences are consistent with the hypothesis that young adults are less likely to have campaign exposure to establishment political culture and the traditional media. This can be seen in the dramatic difference between young adults and other adults in watching the nightly network news. While only 34 percent of young adults regularly watched the nightly network news, 52 percent of other adults did. A difference of similar magnitude was also found in the lower viewing of local television news by young adults. Reading a newspaper was also less common among young adults (42 percent) than other adults (57 percent). As denoted by the asterisks in Table 1, there are a number of other statistically significant differences between young adults and other adults. Young adults were less likely consumers of cable news, Sunday morning talk shows, and the PBS *News Hour* with Jim Lehrer.

The few categories in which young adults had greater media use than older adults have ties to popular culture. The media source for which young adults enjoyed the greatest advantage over other adults was *The*

Table 1: Regular Sources of Information About 2004 Campaign

Information Source	Young Adults (%)	Other Adults (%)
Local television news *	53	72
Local daily newspaper *	42	57
Nightly network news *	34	52
Cable news *	30	44
Morning television shows	16	23
National Public Radio	13	16
News magazines	13	12
Late night television	12	10
Daily Show with Jon Stewart *	12	3
Sunday morning news shows *	10	16
National daily newspaper	8	10
C-SPAN	5	6
Howard Stern *	5	2
Rush Limbaugh	4	6
Business magazines	4	5
Magazines like *Harper's*	4	4
PBS *News Hour* with Jim Lehrer *	2	7
Political magazines like *New Republic*	1	2

*p < .01

Source: 2004 Pew Internet & American Life Project Post-Election Survey Primary Data Set.
Notes: Q: "How often do you get news or information from the following sources? Regularly, sometimes, or hardly ever?" Percentages are for "regularly." Significance levels take into account all three ordinal response categories.

Daily Show with Jon Stewart on the cable channel Comedy Central. While 12 percent of young adults reported regularly watching *The Daily Show*, only 3 percent of older adults did. There was also a statistically significant gap in listening to Howard Stern.

For news magazines and about half of the information sources, there were no statistically significant differences between young adults and other adults. Although Table 1 may show small differences in these categories, the differences between the two groups are so small that there is a decent possibility that they would have occurred by chance. They are not statistically significant. Thus, in some ways young adults and other adults behaved similarly. Where differences exist, it is clear that young adults relied less on political establishment culture and more on popular culture than other adults.

Next, I turn to whether there are differences in the general type of media used by young adults and other adults. Pew asked people about their principal means of getting campaign information. Respondents were allowed to give up to two answers. As shown in Table 2, the relatively new medium of the Internet turns out to be very important for young adults. While 30 percent of young adults named the Internet as a principal means of learning about the campaign, only 14 percent of other adults did. The other side of the picture is that older adults were significantly more likely than young adults to have newspapers as a principal source. Both groups relied on television as the most important way of learning about the campaign.

Table 2: Principal Sources of 2004 Campaign News

News Source	Young Adults (%)	Other Adults (%)
Television	73	80
Internet	30	14
Newspapers	28	45
Radio	16	16
Magazines	3	4

Source: 2004 Pew Internet & American Life Project Post-Election Survey Primary Data Set.
Notes: Q: "How have you been getting most of your news about the presidential election campaign? From television, from newspapers, from radio, from magazines, or from the Internet?" Since respondents could give up to two answers, the totals exceed 100 percent.

The magnitude of the difference between young adults and other adults in reliance on the Internet for campaign information prompts further investigation. Certainly, part of the difference in Internet use in politics emerges from greater overall use of the Internet by young adults. In the survey, 76 percent of young adults and 58 percent of other adults reported going online. Once the population is limited to Internet users, is there a difference between how young adults and other adults use the Internet for politics? To answer this question, this chapter examines the subset of Internet users. The survey asked respondents about their political use of the Internet generally and during the campaign specifically. Both types of questions will be helpful in understanding Internet use.

Table 3 presents the general nature of Internet use at the time of the 2004 campaign. It shows that among Internet users, there is not a statistically significant difference between young adults and other adults in seeking online information about politics.

Table 3: Selected Internet Activities at Time of 2004 Campaign

Online Behavior	Young Adults (%)	Other Adults (%)
Look for info about politics and campaign	63	56
Look for info from government website *	49	59
Read someone else's blog *	34	25
Create content for Internet (blog, post, etc.) *	25	16
Get or send invite to meeting with online service *	22	12

*p < .01

Source: 2004 Pew Internet & American Life Project Post-Election Survey, subset of Internet users.
Notes: Q: "Please tell me if you ever do any of the following when you go online. Do you ever? Did you happen to do this yesterday, or not?" Percentages are for "yes" to ever doing. Significance levels take into account all ordinal response categories.

The absence of a significant difference or perhaps even a small advantage for young adults over other adults in seeking political information on the Internet is especially important in light of the imbalance in traditional media. Beyond general political information seeking, there are significant differences in online behavior. It is not just that young adults are more likely to be online. They behave differently than other adults when they are online. Young adults are significantly more likely than other adults to send or receive an invitation to a meeting through online services like meetup. They are also significantly more likely to read someone else's blog or create content for the Web. These dimensions suggest that young adults are more likely to encounter popular culture. Their online lives have a greater potential for voices outside of the political establishment, including their own as content producers. In contrast, other adults are significantly more likely than young adults to look for information from a federal, state, or local government website.

The results are similar when looking only at online behavior related to the 2004 campaign. The differences in Table 4 show a more popular orientation for young adults. While 9 percent of young adult Internet users participated in chats about the election, 3 percent of other adult Internet users engaged in this interactive activity. The 22 percent of young adults who voted in an online poll was significantly more than the 14 percent of other adults who did. Another important area in which online political behavior differed is in finding information on how to vote. Young adults were more than twice as likely as other adults to use the Internet to learn about the logistics of voting. On the other hand, activities with no statistically significant difference between age groups were more closely related to establishment political culture, such as finding a candidate's voting record or identifying the candidate preferences of interest groups.

Table 4: Political Use of Internet During 2004 Campaign

Online Campaign Behavior	Young Adults (%)	Other Adults (%)
Get or send e-mail with election jokes	39	36
Seek more info on candidate issue positions *	39	29
Check accuracy of candidate claims	30	28
Watch online video clips about campaign *	28	19
Get info about when and where to vote *	24	11
Register opinion in online poll on election *	22	14
Get info about candidate voting record	20	18
Find group ratings or candidate endorsements	19	18
Be in online discussion (chat) about election *	9	3
Contribute money online to candidate	3	5

*p < .01
Source: 2004 Pew Internet & American Life Project Post-Election Survey, subset of Internet users.
Notes: Q: "When you went online to get information about the elections, did you ever do any of the following?" Percentages are for "yes." This question was a follow-up question for people who had earlier indicated that they had gone online for information about the election. If they answered "no" to the overall questions, "no" is imputed for specific categories of online campaign activity.

The absence of a statistically significant difference on e-mailing jokes is also important. The results definitely do not suggest that other adults lack a sense of humor about politics. Indeed, it is clear that the use of online humor had appeal across the electorate. It crossed age and, perhaps more importantly, partisanship. Humor may be a potential bridge in a polarized election. A powerful example of this can be seen in the overwhelming popularity of the JibJab.com video, "This Land Is Your Land," in which animated versions of George Bush and John Kerry hurled insults at each other. During summer 2004, visits to the parody website far exceeded visits to the official presidential candidate websites.[17]

The combination of Internet activities during the campaign had an impact on election day. The survey asked all Internet users whether online information was important to how they voted. As shown in Table 5, young adults were significantly more likely to say that they were influenced by online information. While over half of young adults reported that the Internet was at least somewhat important to their vote, only 35 percent of other adults felt that it was. Within the population of Internet users, young adults relied more on the Internet than other adults.

Table 5: Importance of Online Information to How Internet Users Voted in 2004

Importance	Young Adults (%)	Other Adults (%)	Total (%)
Very important	19.5	11.0	12.9
Somewhat important	31.4	23.6	25.3
Not very important	19.2	18.8	18.9
Not at all important	30.0	46.6	42.9
Total	100%	100%	100%
(n)	(287)	(1,016)	(1,303)

$p < .01$; tau-c = -.142; gamma = -.284

Source: 2004 Pew Internet & American Life Project Post-Election Survey, subset of Internet users.

Notes: Q: "How important, if at all, has the Internet been in terms of providing you with information to help you decide how to vote in the November election? Very important, somewhat important, not very important, or not at all important?"

Not only do young adults believe that the Internet helped their decision making on election day, but also that the Internet improved the overall quality of the campaign. Pew asked Internet users for a summary assessment of online information: "Thinking about all of the information available online about this year's campaign, do you think the Internet has raised the overall quality of public debate about the candidates and issues, has lowered the overall quality of public debate, or that the Internet hasn't made much difference?" Fifty-seven percent of young adults believed that the Internet raised the quality of public debate; while only 4 percent believed that it had lowered the quality of the debate. Older adults were less enthusiastic, but still overwhelmingly believed that the Internet raised, not lowered, the quality of public discourse.

Conclusion

The results show that popular culture and the new media are more a part of the mediated presidential campaign experience of young adults than of other adults. Young adults are significantly less likely than older adults to receive news from conventional cable, local, and national television newscasts. The format of the traditional newspaper has struggled to engage young adults. While conventional political programming in the traditional media has had less appeal to young adults, some entertainment programming with political messages in the traditional media has found an audience with young adults. Late-night comedy often uses the news of the day as a springboard to humor. The television program that has served as a news source for the most disproportionately young audience is *The Daily Show* with Jon Stewart. Entertainment programs clearly have potential relevance for the political lives of young adults. Yet, entertainers may have mixed feelings about their role as a news source. On the December 7, 2006, episode of NBC's *Tonight Show*, Jay Leno teased some young adults in his studio audience who were visibly surprised by the news that he had used as the background for a monologue joke. "If you get your news from me, you're in a lot of trouble," Leno told them.

In addition to documenting how popular culture in the traditional media conveys political information to young adults, this chapter also illuminates the important role of the Internet in the political lives of young adults. Of course, Internet content may or may not be a part of popular culture. The data show that young adults are attracted to both entertainment and non-entertainment political content on the Internet. The Internet has become a vital source of information for many young adults who have been turning away from traditional media sources. It should not, however, be blamed for the decline of other media. Indeed, the declining appeal of traditional sources was a trend in place well before the Internet. What the Internet has done is to counterbalance declining consumption of traditional sources. The Internet clearly has characteristics that appeal to young adults and may help them relate to politics.

What characteristics of the Internet make its use for political purposes appeal to young adults? The Internet has many characteristics, not all of which may be relevant to the question. For some reason, scholars have found it helpful to think of relevant Internet characteristics as alliterative triads, such as the three characteristics that have been said to explain why the Internet may foster addictive behavior—accessibility, affordability, and anonymity.[18] In the case of Internet political use and young adults, the characteristics of immediacy, interactivity, and intractability seem to stand out.

Growing up in a 24/7 culture of cellular telephones and the Internet, young adults may be drawn to the immediacy of the Internet. When asked why they go online for political information, young adults gave convenience as the major reason. Young adults are more likely to cite convenience than other adults. The Internet is available for immediate access.

The interactive nature of the Internet clearly appeals to young people. The establishment political culture and traditional media are greatly invested in the one-way communication of political messages. The Internet allows for more interactive communication. It provides new ways of collaboration. Even within the online population, young adults are more likely to take advantage of the interactive features for politics.

The Internet is also intractable. It is not easily controlled or managed. Young adults have less investment in the established political order and long-standing ideologies. They may look for a way to rebel in the context of mediated politics. Young adults may be more enthusiastic about an online environment in which the regular order of politics is not as pronounced. They may be attracted to the more bottom-up communication structure of the Internet.

While the appeal of some Internet activities may rest on only one characteristic, other activities may reflect all three of them. The appeal of video sharing, for example, seems to capture all three characteristics. Although most of their content is not political, video-sharing websites have started to influence political campaigns. Candidates, for example, may assign workers to videotape opponents with the hope that an opponent's mistake could be captured and posted to cyberspace. It is not surprising that it was a young adult, twenty-year-old S. R. Sidarth, who videotaped George Allen insulting him as "macaca" while working for Allen's opponent Jim Webb during the 2006 U.S. Senate campaign in Virginia. In this case, a young adult was not merely the passive recipient of one-way communication; instead, he immediately responded with his videotape of the event, which was beyond the control of the videotaped person. The way in which this video quickly took on a life of its own shows how video sharing exhibits the characteristics of being immediate, interactive, and intractable.

The combination of these characteristics suggests the resonance of the mosh analogy in this book. Young adults and other adults behave differently online. In the 2004 presidential campaign, the Internet use of

young adults was more at the forefront in exploiting the special characteristics of the Internet. It was more uninhibited and interactive. Even
among Internet users, young adults were more likely than other adults to
participate in chats, vote in online polls, create their own content, read
blogs, and send or receive meeting invitations through online services.
The only specific online political activity that young adults were significantly less likely than other adults to engage in was visiting a government website, which is a more regulated outlet from an establishment
source. The Internet and popular culture clearly helped young adults to
connect with campaign 2004. Even if they were not on the stage, young
adults used the Internet as a vehicle for participation beyond being part
of the audience. This mediated experience stands as one of the possible
reasons why voter turnout by young adults increased from 42 percent in
2000 to 51 percent in 2004.[19]

Of course, the question is whether increased political activity will
continue. There are many challenges to that outcome. Young adults start
from a lower base of overall political awareness. The Pew survey asked
respondents how often they "follow what's going on in government and
public affairs." While only 39 percent of young adults reported following
politics "most of the time," 63 percent of other adults said they do. Even
without a lower base of political awareness, enthusiasm can fade. Others
may not encourage it. Joe Trippi has described how other adults may find
it difficult to relate to the uninhibited high energy of young adults:

> In Vestavia Hill, Alabama, an earnest nineteen-year-old named Gray
> Brooks listened to Howard Dean once on the radio, got on the Inter-
> net to research him, decided Dean was "a good man," and the next
> thing you knew, was in his car and on the freeway, driving to Ver-
> mont to volunteer for the campaign, to work seventeen-hour days and
> sleep on the floor. A handsome, clean cut, lifelong Boy Scout and
> Baptist, Gray couldn't help but be courtly, calling everyone ma'am
> or sir. . . . I would think of Gray often later in the campaign, when
> Republican operatives, our Democratic opponents, and some in the
> press caricatured young Dean supporters as pierced, vegan weirdos.
> Here for the first time in decades were young voters inspired to get
> involved—and believing that they could make a difference—and
> they were being painted as some kind of freak show. For wanting to
> be involved![20]

The age of the median voter and median news consumer may cause politicians and traditional media to fail to exert the effort required to reach
young adults. Indeed, CNN may trivialize young adult interest in tech-

nology as a choice between Macs or PCs.

Ultimately, however, technology has important political implications for young adults. When online, young adults behave differently than other adults. To some extent, their use of technology reflects a desire for a different kind of politics. It has certainly brought many young people closer to politics. Overwhelmingly, young adults believe that the Internet elevates the quality of public debate during a presidential campaign. No one doubts that further elevation is possible. The prospects for future elevation will depend increasingly on Internet users, regardless of whether they access the Internet on Macs or PCs.

Notes

1. Howard Kurtz, "'Light' Not Quite Right for this Forum," *Washington Post*, November 11, 2003, 4(A).

2. Jennifer Jacobson, "Verbatim: The President as Entertainer," *Chronicle of Higher Education*, May 14, 2004, 16(A).

3. Ronald J. Schmidt Jr., *This Is the City: Making Model Citizens in Los Angeles* (Minneapolis: University of Minnesota Press, 2005), 89.

4. Michael X. Delli Carpini and Bruce A. Williams, "Constructing Public Opinion: The Uses of Fictional and Nonfictional Television in Conversations about the Environment," in *The Psychology of Political Communication*, ed. Ann N. Crigler (Ann Arbor: University of Michigan Press, 1996), 149-76.

5. Liesbet van Zoonen, *Entertaining the Citizen: When Politics and Popular Culture Converge* (Lanham, MD: Rowman & Littlefield, 2005), 3.

6. Jeffrey P. Jones, *Entertaining Politics: New Political Television and Civic Culture* (Lanham, MD: Rowman & Littlefield, 2005), 32.

7. Robert D. Putnam, *Bowling Alone: The Collapse and Revival of American Community* (New York: Simon & Schuster, 2000), 216-46.

8. Neil Postman, *Amusing Ourselves to Death: Public Discourse in the Age of Show Business* (New York: Elisabeth Sifton, 1985), 87.

9. Kevin G. Barnhurst, "Politics in the Fine Meshes: Young Citizens, Power and Media," *Media, Culture & Society* 20, no. 2 (April 1998): 203.

10. Barnhurst, "Fine Meshes," 216.

11. Jones, *Entertaining Politics*, 141-48.

12. Commission on Presidential Debates, "Debate Transcript: The Third Gore-Bush Presidential Debate," http://www.debates.org/pages/trans2000c.html (accessed December 20, 2006).

13. Thomas E. Patterson, "Young Voters and the 2004 Election," http://www.vanishingvoter.org/Releases/Vanishing_Voter_Final_Report_2004_Election.pdf (accessed December 6, 2006).

14. Kaye D. Trammell et al., "Evolution of Online Campaigning: Increasing Interactivity in Candidate Web Sites and Blogs Through Text and Technical Features," *Mass Communication & Society* 9, no. 1 (Winter 2006): 21-44.

15. Joe Trippi, *The Revolution Will Not Be Televised: Democracy, the Internet, and the Overthrow of Everything* (New York: Regan Books, 2004), 88.

16. Arthur Lupia and Tasha S. Philpot, "Views from Inside the Net: How Websites Affect Young Adults' Political Interest," *Journal of Politics* 67, no. 4 (November 2005): 1122-42.

17. Al Gibes, "Giggle All the Way to the Polls with JibJab," *Las Vegas Review-Journal*, September 6, 2004, 1(D).

18. Al Cooper, "Online Sexual Activity in the New Millennium," *Contemporary Sexuality* 38, no. 3 (March 2004): i-vii.

19. Patterson, "Young Voters."

20. Trippi, *Revolution*, 87.

Chapter 2

Links, Chicks, Blogs, Banners: Using the Internet for Youth Voter Mobilization

Laura Tropp

P. Diddy, Russell Simmons, and Norman Lear all have something significant in common: they are part of a celebrity trend to create organizations to mobilize young voters. Interestingly, these campaigns rely on mass media for their mobilization efforts. This is not a completely new phenomenon. Celebrities have been involved in media voter drives in radio and television since at least the 1950s. Yet now the celebrities are not simply a small part of the voter drive but a key feature of the campaign. In 2004, two organizations, Rock the Vote and Declare Yourself, two organizations that rely on celebrity appeals, used the Internet specifically to mobilize young people for the election. Their Internet campaigns used the celebrities and visual aides to stimulate visitor response, capitalized on the ability to supply a degree of personalization for the visitor, encouraged a type of interactivity within their websites, and ultimately, commoditized their messages for their young audiences. Yet these campaigns were limited by how the Internet was conceived and dominantly used during the 2004 campaign period. The characteristics of the Internet shaped and drove these campaigns as much as their creators did. This chapter explores the media environment that drove Internet usage during the 2004 campaign and how this landscape is changing right now, in the midst of the 2008 campaign. By situating the 2004 campaign in comparison to earlier broadcast media efforts to appeal to voters, this chapter will examine the characteristics of the Internet and how they worked both with and against the goals of the organizations.[1] Along the way, it will discuss the limits of websites for mobilization efforts and offer some suggestions for how political strategists and scholars will need to reconceptualize their uses of the Internet for future mobilization efforts.

Rock the Vote is a non-profit organization, sponsored in part by the music industry, that uses various media and celebrities to encourage young people to vote. Though Rock the Vote began using the Internet in earlier campaigns, this chapter focuses on its—as well as Declare Yourself's—2004 voter mobilization drive as a case study.[2] Television producer Norman Lear created Declare Yourself in 2003 to increase voter turnout among young people for the 2004 election.[3] With a budget of nine million dollars, the organization claims to be non-partisan, despite the fact that Lear is a major donor to the Democratic Party.[4] The choice in this chapter to specifically emphasize two campaigns devoted to young people is in part inspired by a key characteristic of the Internet. The Internet surpasses previous mass media technologies in its ability to target specialized audiences, a technique that was attempted during Rock the Vote's use of MTV as its primary channel for disseminating its television public service announcements. In addition, appealing to young voters has become a popular trend as more celebrities are becoming involved in voter mobilization efforts.[5]

The Internet, Politics, and Popular Culture

Scholars in the field of study known as medium theory or media ecology argue that each medium carries with it certain characteristics that structure, bias, or limit the way that society uses the technology. Harold Innis and Marshall McLuhan, two early leaders in this field, argued respectively that the structures of technologies shape civilizations and that each medium serves to extend our senses. Innis writes, "A medium of communication has an important influence on the dissemination of knowledge over space and over time and it becomes necessary to study its characteristics in order to appraise its influence in its cultural setting."[6] McLuhan builds on this argument: "[T]he personal and social consequences of any medium—that is, of any extension of ourselves—result from the new scale that is introduced into our affairs by each extension of ourselves, or by any new technology."[7] In the past few decades, scholars have built on their arguments to explore how the latest technologies influence changes in the scope of society. Neil Postman, in his well-known book, *Amusing Ourselves to Death*, decried that a television saturated world creates a society of people who always expect entertainment in every aspect of life.[8] More recently, scholars have turned to understanding how the Internet contributes to the shape of society. Some of these scholars are taking an approach that focuses on an examination of the nature of the medium.

Some scholars are quick to point out the irony between the original purpose of the Internet and the current uses of the medium. Hafner and Lyon describe the history of the growth and development of the Internet, beginning when the Internet, formally Advanced Research Projects Agency Network (ARPANET), was intended to be "used for resource-sharing."[9] The Internet as a term is often incorrectly used to denote more specific media within the Internet, such as e-mail or the World Wide Web. The Internet encapsulates all of these different communication tools as part of its network.

Sheizaf Rafaeli proposes five defining characteristics of the Internet: emphasis on sensory appeal, disruption of linearity, no main hierarchical structure, options for synchronous communication, and interactivity.[10] Each of these characteristics distinguishes the Internet from previous media, such as radio and television. For example, synchronous communication allows for people to transmit messages at the same time, while the lack of hierarchy prevents one government or producer from dominating the medium. The user has an unprecedented level of control. Interactivity allows the user to respond directly to the producers of information. Douglas Rushkoff, though, in 1999, writes of his disappointment in the use of the Internet not benefiting from these inherent characteristics. He explores the transformation of the Internet from a potentially interactive to a broadcast medium. Many early users of the Internet relished the interactivity of e-mail, chat sessions, discussion boards, and listservs, which allowed them to collaborate with the technology. But Rushkoff laments the way in which advertisers have largely taken over the medium to use websites mainly to sell and market goods.[11] Meanwhile, some political scientists have seen the potential of this medium. Deborah G. Johnson writes, "As a result of the Internet, like-minded individuals who separately were ineffective minorities can join forces and promote their interests collectively."[12] She also notes the paradox of the Internet's potential to offer anonymity while providing reproducibility, which allows information to be collected, surveyed, and stored.[13]

This chapter draws on scholarly literature on the Internet and a media ecological approach to examine the way in which organizations have

tried to use this new technology to reach young people for voter mobilization. The following case-study of two initiatives demonstrates how the
transformation of the Internet to a predominantly broadcast medium has
influenced the means through which campaign producers approach the
issue of interactivity within their mobilization campaigns. Yet these examples also illustrate how some organizations have been able to collectively join resources to build a potentially powerful network that they
may not have been able to accomplish without the Internet. The pages
ahead will illustrate how the Internet itself guides messages; consequently, the producers are limited, in many ways, in their use of this medium.

This study also examines how the organizers of these voter drives
embrace popular culture in their use of the Internet. Communication
scholars have studied popular culture across different media. Janice
Radway explored how women read and shared romance novels, found
their own meanings within them, and used them on their own terms.[14]
John Fiske has put forward various ways of understanding how fans understand and interpret codes and meanings within their favorite television
programs.[15] But what happens when political and popular cultures
merge? In their study of politics in primetime television, Allan McBride
and Robert K. Toburen explore how politics represented on television
may lead to an emphasis on individualistic culture and a decline of political participation.[16] Lauren Cohen Bell, Joan L. Conners, and Theodore
F. Sheckels explore political rhetoric in appearances on popular culture
programs. While this rhetoric works to increase candidate connectedness
with some viewers, the authors are concerned about the larger effects:
"Comedy may inadvertently convince some pop culture consumers that
politics is absurd. At the same time, it may undermine our leaders and
our candidates for leadership."[17] The Internet also poses problems in
terms of political participation within popular culture. Alan Wexelblat
calls into question the assertion that the use of new forms of communication via the Internet will automatically transfer power from producers of
media to consumers: "Old models of authorial power operate just as well
within the literate computer-accessing population as they do anywhere
else, especially given a strong authorial presence whose words and actions reinforce that kind of model at every turn."[18] These researchers call
into question the consequences of using popular culture to reach voters.
This study both examines what impact the use of the Internet has on
voter mobilization drives and investigates how attempts to reach voters
through the use of popular culture commoditize the political participation

process and voting.

Sponsorship

One strength of these websites is that they encourage a new level of openness in terms of identifying sponsors. Each organization clearly identified its sponsors on its website. The interconnection that is a key characteristic of the Internet allows organizations to partner up. Historically, the television industry created the single sponsor system, in which a program was sponsored by one company or product.[19] This system declined, and then disappeared, in part as a result of the quiz show scandals in the 1950s, which demonstrated that sponsors had gained too much power over program content. Since that time, television has displayed more variety in identifying its sponsorships. Advertisers can sponsor one or more spots in a program, as well as vary the length of their spots.[20] Television, though, is a time-based medium. There is a definite separation between when the program ends and the commercial begins (although this separation is diminishing as product placement becomes more prominent—see endnote 21). On the Internet, however, there is less delineating between program content and sponsorship. In addition, the Internet allows more malleability to organizations to offer different levels and visibility of sponsorship.

On the websites, the ability exists for clearly labeling the connection and involvement of the sponsors. For example, Rock the Vote lists different types of sponsors under a section labeled "Partners" on its website. Inside the "Partners" section, Rock the Vote categorizes "Nonprofit," "Creative," and "Corporate" partners. Unlike television, where the viewer has little knowledge of how the sponsors contributed to the content (one assumes they simply bought commercial time), with the Internet, there is always room to explain the role of the sponsor. Similarly, Declare Yourself's website allows access to information about its sponsors by merely clicking on "About Us" and navigating links that distinguish between "Co-Chairs and Friends," "Sponsors," and "Partners." Yet how each sponsor is categorized is not explained. This illustrates that, though the Internet offers the possibility for providing more information, producers of this information may not necessarily take advantage of the opportunity.

The characteristics of the Internet also allow sponsors more flexibility in soliciting visitors. Traditionally, the only place to insert sponsorship in television has been before or after programs, or during program breaks.[21] There are no such restrictions for sponsor identification for these websites. Declare Yourself lists some of its sponsors, including Yahoo.com, friendster, and ClearChannel, on the front page.

In addition, becoming a sponsor or having an affiliation with the organization need no longer require a monetary exchange. Many of these organizations link to each other because of promotional networking opportunities. Unlike with radio and television advertisements, there are more opportunities to promote other organizations and easier ways to do so. Within the Internet, time and space is limitless. Rock the Vote, in a section called "Partners Rock," indicates that it does not restrict who sponsors it: "ANYONE, and we mean everyone can add a link or banner to Rock the Vote on a website, personal web page, blog, e-mail blast or wherever to drive people to register to vote." Declare Yourself advertises, "Do your part to help democracy work in this year's election! This DY 'Register to Vote' campaign button is your site's online link to voter registration. Please feel free to download this image and add it to your homepages (or paste it to any pages)." This illustrates the disconnection between those sponsoring the organization and the organization itself. They will allow anyone to promote a cause and bring people to a particular website.

Even as levels of sponsorship are more easily achieved, each sponsorship is also more easily visible to the visitor. Televised public service announcements (PSAs) require the viewer to wait until the end of the spot to see who the sponsor is (if he or she is still looking). In contrast, there are plenty of opportunities on the websites to promote sponsorship connections.

Within the websites, organizations can be found easily and their agendas are available for anyone to read. For example, Rock the Vote lists an organization labeled "SEIU" as one of its non-profit sponsors. Clicking on the link allows one to find out more about this organization, whose focus is on healthcare. These websites allow visitors to learn more about the organizations sponsoring (or partnering) with the main concerns, because almost every organization can be clicked on to link to its homepage.

Individualization

Websites also allow for a degree of visitors' individualization and personalization that was unavailable with previous mass media, such as radio and television. Susanne Langer explores the difference between discursive and presentational communication. Discursive communication requires that words and ideas be strung side by side and in a particular order to be fully understood by their recipient.[22] Non-discursive communication, on the other hand, does not have this requirement. As non-discursive media, websites are nonlinear; the visitor can choose what links to click on and in what order to read website material. Visitors can look up the sponsors first, ignore them and browse the merchandise for sale, or even leave a website entirely by clicking on the link to one of its sponsors. Wisely, Rock the Vote's website is arranged so that when someone clicks on a sponsor link, a new window opens up—the original webpage, then, remains on the screen. Declare Yourself has only some of its links set up in this manner, so in some cases it is possible to completely lose track of the website; clicking on the "Back" function of the browser is the only way to return. Despite some limits placed by the organization, visitors have a level of control previously unavailable to them with other media.

The websites have capitalized on this freedom of control by allowing visitors a degree of personalization. Both Declare Yourself and Rock the Vote enable visitors to type in their zip codes in order to find specific voter and polling information, including information on absentee ballots and registration forms. Also, the Internet in general allows individuals to watch and read material within a timeframe of their own choosing. Declare Yourself makes all of its spots available for downloading. Letting visitors download material encourages them to pass on their favorite downloads to their friends. Interestingly, Rock the Vote does not allow downloads from its websites. Possibly the reason for this may be that the sponsors—members of the music industry, in particular—wish to discourage young people from the practice of downloading and sharing material online.

The websites are used to tailor pitches to specific populations. Even Rock the Vote, which already targets a particular cohort of voters in its television spots, has taken advantage of its group of websites to become yet more specific. Rock the Vote devotes special sections to Rap the Vote, an organization sponsored in partnership with Russell Simmons, and Rock the Vote Latino, designed to reach a Latino audience. They even have a "Chicks Rock, Chicks Vote!" section. Just as the advent of cable television triggered the capacity for narrowcasting, the Internet extends these options still further with a potentially unlimited number of web pages for different audiences, along with reinforcing messages sent through targeted e-mail. Unlike radio and television, the Internet gives these organizations the ability to make their messages more specific, since there is no need for every person to read the same message.

While Declare Yourself offers opportunities to download information from its organization, Rock the Vote goes a step further in providing the means to receive e-mail updates from its organizations. This encourages visitors to become part of a community, although in this case, visitors have less control since these messages ultimately signify one-way communication: the organization can forward updates and information to those who sign up, but the visitors do not have the same opportunity to send messages back.

Rock the Vote, though, has created a blog in which visitors can respond to ideas and posts initiated by the Rock the Vote organization. The blog serves many functions. First, like many blogs, it is a vehicle for self-promotion. For example, a posting on April 28, 2004, discussed a successful event: "Yesterday was Free Cone Day at Ben & Jerry's. Ben & Jerry's has given out free ice cream one day a year for like the last 28 years. But this year they did it a little different; they asked us to come to the store and register voters." The end of the post encouraged readers to "Join our street team today—find the button on our front page and get rolling!" Other posts reacted to negative publicity, such as one titled, "Wack-ass article in Salon.com," and dated, April 24, 2004; the post responded to a critical article on Rock the Vote's techniques for selling voting: "The author obviously misunderstands the role of Rock the Vote and similar efforts. That's why we end up with criticism instead of praise." Yet, visitors are allowed to respond to these posts. One person wrote, "Give me a break, RTV is all about selling stuff to young people. Look at the website. Look at the sponsor—MTV and it's [sic] parent company—Viacom." Here, we see that visitors have a chance to voice their opinions and debate with others. However, there is not an opportunity for live debates, and the discussions are all initiated by Rock the Vote, the creator of the blog. Thus, there is interaction, but it is controlled by the producers of the website more than those visiting it.

Consequently, the websites have opportunities for both narrowcasting and broadcasting. In some cases, information (such as finding a polling location) is tailored to specific people; in other instances, material is aimed at the youth population at large. McBride and Toburen have explored how televised depictions of politics may lead to an emphasis on an individualized culture. In this case, the use of the Internet also can lead to an emphasis on the individual instead of the community, as people tend to view these sites alone, personalizing their visits.[23]

The websites also vary in their degree of interactivity. Declare Yourself has no place for discussion by the visitors but does give them the chance to download information on their own time. Rock the Vote has a greater amount of interactivity, yet it is still guided and shaped by those in control of the website. Neither website has created a discussion board or chat room for visitors to engage in synchronous or asynchronous debates on ideas and issues. For the most part, the "politics" of politics is still left out of the discussion.

Issues

The websites, with their lack of space and time constraints, would seem to offer the opportunity for, if not a discussion of issues, then at least the dissemination of information about issues. However, the websites examined are limited in the information they provide. Both websites combine discursive and non-discursive information. Most pages limit text to either captions under pictures or no more than a paragraph or two of explanation. Declare Yourself uses a page of text to describe its mission, although it is only two paragraphs long. In its candidates section, Declare Yourself includes pictures of candidates and short biographical information (date of birth, career, religion, family, and so on), and links to the website of each campaign. Rock the Vote displays a header and sidebar, both containing images, that remain on the top and side of pages so that when visitors link to the more informative pages, the pages are still surrounded by visual elements. The front pages of both organizations emphasize visuals and minimize text.

Though the websites have the capacity to include lengthy biographies of the candidates, they instead create short bios that do not provide much information, mimicking the thirty- or sixty-second political advertisements typically found on television. The George W. Bush biography on Declare Yourself, for example, reads:

> Birth date: July 6, 1946; Hometown: Austin, TX; Education: Bachelor's degree, Yale University, 1968; MBA, Harvard University, 1975, Military Service: Air National Guard, 1968-1973; Career: Founder/CEO of oil and gas company, 1975-1987; managing general partner, Texas Rangers baseball team, 1989-1998; Elected office: Texas governor, 1994-2000; U.S. president, elected 2000; Family: Wife,

Laura; two daughters; Religion: Methodist; Campaign website: www.
georgewbush.com; White House website: www.whitehouse.gov/
president.

Here, the name, rank, and serial number are about all that is provided for
the visitor.

Rock the Vote lists sections on the environment and education but,
like Declare Yourself, its organization avoids details about such issues.
Instead, after raising general questions about each issue, it directs visitors
to more specific organizations. For example, Rock the Vote's page on
violence reads: "**Violence:** Every day in America 2,402 children are
abused or neglected. A woman is raped every sixty seconds. In 2001
there were 12,020 victims of hate crimes in the United States. What's
being done to make our schools and streets safer? Want a less violent
society? Tolerate, educate and speak your mind." Like the Declare Yourself biographies, little information is provided.

A primary reason why these organizations do not capitalize on the
flexibility of this medium is their supposedly non-partisan motives. In
their desire to appear to be fair, they avoid supplying detailed information about particular candidates and issues. However, they do take advantage of one aspect of the Internet—the ability to connect to other websites for information, which is an element that is not available through
radio and television advertisements. Visitors can link to other organizations rather than simply end with an initial site's message. Declare Yourself provides links to political parties, and a news section links to stories
by Yahoo, its online partner. Another section links to civic engagement
organizations, where visitors can find more information devoted to specific issues. Rock the Vote has developed even more specific information
for visitors. Its most lengthy webpage is titled, "Election 101," where it
gives general information about the electoral college, national conventions, and the general election. Yet instead of providing detailed information about issues or evaluating candidates' positions on them, these sites
act as little more than a directory to other sites that supply this information. When search sites such as Google can just as easily allow audiences
to find this information, the necessity of Rock the Vote's and Declare
Yourself's sites becomes questionable. Another reason for their avoid-
ance of any partisan issues within their websites is recent election law.
Trevor Potter and Kirk L. Jowers cite an Advisory Opinion issued by the
FEC, which concludes that "nonpartisan activity on the Web—loosely
defined as providing campaign-related information and candidates'
statements in a way that treats all candidates on an equal basis—is ex-

empt from any FEC reporting requirements."[24] Thus, these organizations must present themselves as non-partisan to avoid being subjected to regulation.

The consequence of this desire (or need) to avoid the appearance of partisan interests is that these Internet sites mimic previous media, such as television and radio, which, aside from airing political advertisements leading up to elections, create mostly apolitical content. Barnes writes that the computer is currently being adapted "to a television-oriented model." She argues, "the linear and logical biases embedded in the machine could eventually become characteristics of the medium."[25] The creators of these websites do not take advantage of the opportunity to provide copious information; instead, they constrain themselves as if they were restricted by the same limitations of other electronic media. They emphasize the visual over print and consequently create messages that discourage thought and reflection. The causes of violence in society are not debated on the Rock the Vote website; instead, the issue is treated vaguely. Serious discussion and candidates' ideas and issues are replaced with graphics, pictures of celebrities, advertisements for stars and products, and pictures of the members of the organizations themselves, ultimately leading to the commoditization of their messages.

Commoditization and Self-Promotion

During the 2001 UK election, the Labour party produced a website aimed at young voters. Julian Bowers-Brown describes the website, Ruup4it.org.uk:

> [The website] contained games and competitions as well as information on the party's youth manifesto and details of celebrities who were endorsing the party. Given that a large number of the online population are under thirty, this was an admirable attempt to capture their interest. However, it was let down by a limited marketing campaign that largely centred on university campuses.[26]

The criticism of this campaign rests on the lack of publicity and the narrow focus of the campaign. However, though Declare Yourself and Rock the Vote have much larger and more integrated marketing campaigns, the commercialism embedded in them is what limits them in the way their messages are shaped and defined.

Like on televised campaigns, the use of celebrity is a component of the public service drive online. Declare Yourself displays a headline on its homepage titled, "Hollywood Celebrates Democracy," accompanied by pictures of celebrities in the background. It also has a short video to download, narrated by actors Ben Stiller and Vince Vaughn. Potential voters are encouraged to identify with these stars of popular culture. Norman Lear, the founder, is featured in an interview on NBC's *Today*. Actually, this interview took place prior to the start of Declare Yourself's campaign, and its subject is one of Lear's other projects, which focuses on celebrities reading the Declaration of Independence. One can also download country music stars singing *America the Beautiful*, another component of Lear's Independence Project. In fact, these clips may be just another opportunity for Lear to promote his other projects while serving as additional content for the website. Thus, the messages of popular culture replicate as the same content is recycled through a new medium. Celebrities are used within a larger promotional campaign to sell voting. The celebrities help to position patriotism as "cool." Visitors must make their own connection between patriotism and voting.

Rock the Vote uses celebrities in an even more aggressive fashion, as demonstrated with its televised PSAs. Moreover, like on Declare Yourself, celebrities are featured on Rock the Vote's home page. Amber Tamblyn, of the CBS television show *Joan of Arcadia*, is described as a spokesperson for Rock the Vote in the "Chicks Rock, Chicks Vote" section. The site celebrates that Natalie Maines, a member of the country band, Dixie Chicks, designed the Rock the Vote T-shirt. In fact, the Dixie Chicks, themselves, sponsor the entire "Chicks Rock, Chicks Vote" Section, with a link on the bottom to their own website. Names of rap stars and other African-American celebrities, such as Cornell West, are listed as the Advisory Board on the Rap the Vote section. Similar to their appearance on the Declare Yourself site and the televised PSAs, celebrities are used here to tout the importance of a cause.

Within the Rock the Vote website, there are so many "advertisements" for all sorts of "products" that it becomes necessary to put both of these words in quotes. The products include celebrities, beverages, and films. Advertisements either look like traditional television commercials or simply display a graphic with a link. Rock the Vote advertises, with a short commercial trailer, a new beverage from 7-Up, which is a corporate sponsor. Yet at other times, the products and advertisements are not so easy to recognize. The website advertises the HBO film *Iron Jawed Angels*: "The right to vote wasn't just given, it was fought for. Check out this new movie by HBO Films and witness how these amazing women

Rocked the Vote." One can then click on the link and be taken to HBO Films, which prominently features an advertisement for Rock the Vote.

Yet, there is no information on the nature of the relationship between Rock the Vote and HBO. Is HBO promoting its film on Rock the Vote's website simply because the film is about women's suffrage? Or is it because Time Warner's music division is already a sponsor of Rock the Vote? The website purposely blurs advertisements for all types of products, whether they are educational or not. Although the Declare Yourself website proudly lists its sponsors on many pages, it otherwise does not place outright advertisements within its pages. As discussed below, however, this does not mean that no advertisements exist.

While the organizations use the websites to advertise all types of products (Rock the Vote more so than Declare Yourself), both also engage in the practice of using the campaigns for self-promotion. In addition to press releases about the websites that are sent to various news outlets, the websites themselves serve as an integral part of the self-promotion process. In fact, it is often difficult to separate campaign messages from the promotion of the organizations. Declare Yourself, for instance, allows visitors to click on a special section containing its press releases. Thus, the website serves as a self-touting archive while it promotes its cause. Both websites show pictures of the tours and events the organizations have hosted, which promote their activities and encourage visitors to join in future events. As discussed earlier, both websites also have banners that people can download and place on their own personal websites.

Each website features a type of store. Under "Order Stuff," Declare Yourself's main offering is the other pet project of Norman Lear, the video of celebrities reading the Declaration of Independence. However, Rock the Vote has many more offerings as part of its "Rock the Vote Gear" section. This part is clearly labeled, "Rock the Vote Official Merchandise" (one wonders how much unofficial merchandise is floating around). Rock the Vote is working hard to have voting tied not only to the American political process but also to its own organization.

Declare Yourself offers a different incentive to vote. The "Sign Up Sweepstakes," sponsored in conjunction with Yahoo.com, offers potential prizes for registering to vote. One can win a lunch on the set of *The O.C.* or an iPod mini. In affiliating voting with sweepstakes, voting is commodified like any other product. Rushkoff argues, "The problem with reducing online interaction to an exchange of bits, and the interactive age to an information age, is that it allows cyberspace to be quantified and, ultimately, commodified."[27] On these websites, information has been commercialized, mimicking other websites whose main purpose is to sell. They attempt to associate the organization with as many celebrities, television programs, music, and artists as possible in order to affiliate their causes with the hipness of popular culture. In their desire to brand patriotism as a cool stance that encourages young people to vote, mobilizers risk creating the impression of voting as a fashionable but temporary fad. The concept of hip is situated within specific cultural trends that shift in and out of young people's lives, not unlike clothing, jewelry, or shoes. A generation of young people taught to see voting as cool in the last election may, in 2008, declare: "Voting was sooo 2004!"

Levels of Activism

Neither website relies completely on mediated communication to mobilize voters. Instead, they encourage visitors to move beyond the websites to become involved in mobilizing others. This is particularly important for the target group that they seek. In their work studying the "Millennials," people born after 1982, William Strauss and Neil Howe discuss this age cohort's participation in the political process: "In politics . . . the weird argot of 'rock the vote' campaigns that once amused Gen-Xers is less interesting to Millennial activists, who would rather join forces with like-minded adults and change the national outcome."[28] Rock the Vote is responding to this by inviting young people to become involved in the political process.[29] The website encourages visitors to join the "Street Team," which organizes young people to set up voter registration tables at colleges, rock concerts, and other places where young people congregate. The name "Street Team" implies a separation between mediated and interpersonal communication; it offers real physical engagement rather than a virtual one.

Rock the Vote's website section called "Action" suggests other ways to become politically involved. One series of activities listed is the "Meetups," in which days are set aside for people around the country to meet and discuss issues. Declare Yourself attempts to inspire visitors to meet with others by attending one of the college tours. The website encourages them to "'Do it with your friends' (sm) . . . register to vote that is :-)."

This interpersonal strategy is reminiscent of earlier political periods, especially the nineteenth-century age of partisan politics. George Washington Plunkitt, one of the most active leaders of Tammany Hall partisan politics in New York City, dismissed the usefulness of newspapers and other campaign literature for transmitting political information to the public. Plunkitt asserted, "To learn real human nature you have to go among the people, see them and be seen."[30] Michael Schudson describes nineteenth-century voting as "a performance of community with the local party integrated into communal functions."[31] The online organizations, then, do not treat voting as a solitary process. They encourage people to meet with others and to engage as part of a community; the Internet is only the beginning of this process.

A larger organization, The Youth Vote Coalition, connects other organizations that are committed to increasing voting among young people. Within both Rock the Vote and Declare Yourself, a visitor can easily link to Youth Vote Coalition, at which she or he can then access over one hundred additional organizations. Even though both Declare Yourself and Rock the Vote position themselves as non-partisan, they link to organizations that have more focused agendas or partisan interests, such as the Young Republican National Federation (www.yrock.com).

While these organizations attempt to connect young people to each other, they are also interdependent with previous media technologies. Declare Yourself was founded by Norman Lear, former producer of such television shows as *All in the Family, Good Times, Maude, Sanford and Son*, and films such as *Princess Bride* and *Fried Green Tomatoes*. In fact, the organization describes itself on its website as having "unique alliances with technology and media partners, educators, the entertainment, music and fashion industries." It had plans to host television specials during the summer of 2004. It also associated itself with members of the music industry and performance artists. MTV's *Real World* cast members appeared on the college tour.

Rock the Vote has shown its strong ties to other media, in particular the music industry and MTV. These relationships are promoted on its website. For example, the website advertised Rock the Vote events held during the week of the Grammys. One of Rock the Vote's sponsors was the television show, *The West Wing*. In addition, not long ago, Rock the Vote announced a nine-month partnership campaign with Motorola, combining technologies to encourage young people to vote.[32] On its website, Rock the Vote announces: "Who R U Voting 4 . . . Sign up below to receive poll questions on your phone, updates on the top issues, special messages from the hottest artists on the scene, and exclusive opportunities to get ringtones, concert tickets, CDs and other cool stuff—

only for those who Rock the Vote *Mobile*." A press release states, "For nine months, Motorola and Rock the Vote will take familiar Election year grassroots efforts, blend them with the power of wireless technology and pop culture, and enable people to opt into the process in new and compelling ways."[33]

The two websites examined here suggest how links to other organizations are essential for bringing traffic back to their sites. Thus, the characteristics of the medium help define these campaigns: the organizations must reach out to others to promote their causes, so they naturally encourage young people to do the same. Since the producers of the campaigns have connections to other media, they bring these ties to the voters. Within these websites, visitors can seek more information, contributing to both a greater sense of control and the possibility of connecting to a greater community. The Internet's inherent ability to link communities and organizations fosters new levels of community building. This can certainly help activists because organizations have the ability to share resources. However, the danger of confusing activism with promotion must be recognized. When organizations share links with one another or the young people they are seeking, is their purpose to mobilize a group to political action or simply to promote their organization? Robert McChesney argues that large media conglomerates receive the most benefit from the Internet: "The media giants can bring their audiences to their sites on the Internet. By 1998, it was argued that the only way an Internet content provider could generate users was by buying advertising in the media giants' traditional media. . . . Otherwise, an Internet website would get lost among the millions of other web locations."[34] Certainly, the power of young people to share links and create buzz for a particular website challenges McChesney's claim. Yet these organizations are not engaged in true activism. As noted above, they limit their content to neutral political fare. What they are promoting is simply voting for voting's sake, and they do it in a way in which they use their websites as advertisements for their organizations. Rushkoff criticizes this strategy of using the Internet as a broadcast model: the organizations see themselves as leaders in disseminating information; though they seek out young people to help promote their cause, they follow a top-down approach. This hierarchy limits the 2004 election mobilization efforts, even though these organizations are using a medium that supposedly defies hierarchy. This model will not work in the 2008 election, as young people have discovered ways to network online and create bottom-up movements.

Conclusions: Young People Take Charge

Scholars argue that a unique feature of the Internet is its ability to provide more control to the visitor:

> In the traditional print and electronic media, while there is competition between individual producers of information, the consumer is essentially a passive recipient of news from a limited number of sources. The Internet, however, cedes information control to the individual consumer, who can actively search out the desired information and can edit and collate the relevant news sources.[35]

Each of these websites was ostensibly set up to empower young visitors. The names of the websites and organizations themselves promoted a feeling of action. One was encouraged to "Declare Yourself" and "Rock the Vote." These phrases were reaffirmed within each website, where action verbs were plentiful. Rock the Vote tried to persuade its visitors to act: "Get Informed, Get Rock the Vote Gear, Get Registered to Vote." Declare Yourself asked young people to "Get Informed, Watch and Listen, Register." Many visitors probably felt a sense of control simply because the medium allowed them to decide what to click on and when. They could choose to find out about upcoming events or information about candidates (though they may have been disappointed with the lack of coverage). Visitors could control when they wanted to leave the websites and go to others for more information. Unlike their relationship to radio and television public service announcements, with the Internet, visitors have the opportunity to become active participants in receiving messages.

Having said that, users were not necessarily as empowered as it might first appear. While visitors had a choice as to what they could seek out, they were still confined by the information that was provided to them by the hosts. Neither organization devoted much space to exploring partisan or political issues. Therefore, those who wanted to seek additional information were forced to leave these websites for others that may not have been as easy to negotiate or may have had partisan interests that were not readily apparent. Sure, these websites might have facilitated access to more information, but they did it under the charade of offering a unique and necessary service. Ultimately, they were just amplifying and replicating messages rather than providing any new information.

The websites mimicked previous media technologies in that they emphasized visuals and de-emphasized linearity and language. The websites also associated themselves as much as possible with places and people that are part of our popular culture. Here, the content of popular culture was often taken from previous media. Thus, in this model, the Internet becomes a repository for re-visiting and recycling popular culture artists. The messages became commoditized and contemplation was discouraged, as words were replaced by sounds and images, analysis was replaced by celebrities, and debate was replaced by slogans and advertising.

Because young people are more networked than ever before, youth voter mobilization organizations must rely on websites to inform and motivate these potential voters. Yet a case-study examination of these two websites that were used in 2004 illustrates the limitations of this medium. However, the technological landscape since the 2004 political campaign, has made huge leaps in development. Rushkoff bemoans the Internet being used as a broadcast model, dominated by commercial advertising on its websites. In 1999, when he wrote his critique, this was probably the case. Yet the 2004 case study presented in this chapter illustrates that the way in which these organizations used the Internet was also quite limiting. Though there were opportunities for interaction, the main way in which these organizations communicated on-line was by "broadcasting" messages to its constituents on websites. Young people had only limited opportunities to interact and, when they did, they often had to go beyond the organization for more information rather than communicate with the organization. Thus, these initiatives also followed the model of a commercially dominated medium. Many of their messages were framed from a commercial or consumer model, positioning voting as no more important as choosing between television programs or buying an item of clothing. This chapter has illustrated how the medium itself guided these messages. Yet the medium has expanded since the 2004 campaign.

As politicians execute the 2008 presidential campaign and other future elections, newer technologies will likely influence how these mobilization efforts take place. Internet sites such as YouTube.com, on which anyone can post videos for others to see, could motivate these organizations to find ways to seed viral videos and prompt interactions among the very people they are trying to reach themselves. No longer will organizations need to stick to a primarily broadcast model in which they the organizers are the key people generating the messages and sending them out through one main website. Instead, the idea of "organization" could shift so that anyone can begin a voter mobilization campaign. Political strategists looking at the 2004 campaign as a model for 2008 and beyond should focus on adapting to the earlier constraints of the medium and consider ways in which structure and organization in delivering messages could change. There may indeed be a shift from the organization leading the message to individuals—in particular, the young people who know how to use these new technologies—creating the content. In addition, convergent technologies that offer mobile telephone service, text messaging, and video and Internet access put young people in a position to receive even more timely and responsive outreach efforts. Perhaps young people's increased access to digital cameras and editing software will contribute to yet another shift in voter mobilization, in which centralized organizations give way to peer-to-peer mobilization activities. Future research could examine how these organizations encourage, discourage, and adapt to these changes.

Notes

1. Certainly, people have used the print medium to appeal to voters in the past. However, this chapter focuses on broadcast media because it is here where money has been increasingly spent by politicians as they attempt to appeal to younger voters, who spend less time with print media than with radio, television, and newer media.

2. Rock the Vote. http://www.rockthevote.com (accessed February 18, 2003).

3. Declare Yourself. http://www.declareyourself.com (accessed February 18, 2003).

4. Jennifer Lee, "TV Producer Starts Campaign to Register Young Voters for '04," *New York Times*, November 14, 2003, 24(A).

5. P. Diddy announced on July 20, 2003, that he was creating Citizen Change, an organization to mobilize young, in particular Black and Latino, voters. Russell Simmons created the Hip-Hop Summit Action Network to appeal to this same group of young voters.

6. Harold A. Innis, *The Bias of Communication* (Toronto: University of Toronto Press, 1951), 33.

7. Marshall McLuhan, *Understanding Media: The Extensions of Man* (New York: McGraw-Hill, 1964), 23.

8. Neil Postman, *Amusing Ourselves to Death: Public Discourse in the Age of Show Business* (New York: Penguin Books, 1986).

9. Katie Hafner and Matthew Lyon, *Where Wizards Stay Up Late* (New

York: Touchstone, 1998), 189.

10. John E. Newhagen and Sheizaf Rafaeli, "Why Communication Researchers Should Study the Internet: A Dialogue," *Journal of Computer-Mediated Communication* 1, no. 4 (1996): http://www.ascusc.org/jcmc/vol1/issue4/ rafaeli.html (accessed July 16, 2003).

11. Douglas Rushkoff, *Coercion: Why We Listen to What 'They Say* (New York: Riverhead Books, 1999), 264.

12. Deborah G. Johnson, "Reflections on Campaign Politics, the Internet, and Ethics," in *The Civic Web*, ed. David M. Anderson and Michael Cornfield (Lanham, MD: Rowman & Littlefield, 2003), 13.

13. Johnson, "Reflections," 14-16.

14. Janice Radway, *Reading the Romance: Women, Patriarchy, and Popular Literature* (Chapel Hill, NC: University of North Carolina Press, 1991).

15. John Fiske, *Television Culture* (New York: Routledge, 1993).

16. Allan McBride and Robert K. Toburen, "Deep Structures: Polpop Culture on Primetime Television," *Journal of Popular Culture* 29 (Spring 1996): 181-200.

17. Lauren Cohen Bell, Joan L. Conners, and Theodore F. Sheckels, *Perspectives on Political Communication: A Case Approach* (Boston: Pearson Education, 2008), 352-70.

18. Alan Wexelblat, "An Auteur in the Age of the Internet: JMS, *Babylon 5*, and the Net," in *Hop on Pop: The Politics and Pleasures of Popular Culture*, ed. Henry Jenkins, Tara McPherson, and Jane Shattuc (Durham, NC: Duke University Press, 2002), 225.

19. Interestingly, television is now returning to different tiers of sponsorship, with programs such as *24* or *Survivor* often prominently featuring products of some sponsors within the show, and occasionally even having one company sponsor a program.

20. William Baker and George Dessart, *Down the Tube: An Inside Account of the Failure of American Television* (New York: Basic Books, 1998), 98.

21. Of course, today, the proliferation of product placements is changing this. Product placements are needed because of consumer technologies that allow viewers to skip commercials easily. However, perhaps companies that are now regularly using the Internet now demand the same level of visibility or flexibility of sponsorship placement in the older medium of television.

22. Susanne K. Langer, *Philosophy in a New Key: A Study in the Symbolism of Reason, Rite, and Art* (Cambridge, MA: Harvard University Press, 1979), 81.

23. McBride and Toburen, "Deep Structures," 181-200.

24. Trevor Potter and Kirk L. Jowers, "Election Law and the Internet," in *The Civic Web*, ed. David M. Anderson and Michael Cornfield (Lanham, MD: Rowman & Littlefield, 2003), 67.

25. Susan B. Barnes, "The Development of Graphical User Interfaces and their Influence on the Future of Human-Computer Interaction," *EME: Explorations in Media Ecology* 1, no. 2 (2002), 81-95.

26. Julian Bowers-Brown, "A Marriage Made in Cyberspace," in *Political Parties and the Internet: Net gain?* ed. Rachel Gibson, Paul Nixon, and Stephen Ward (New York: Routledge, 2003), 112-13.

27. Rushkoff, *Coercion*, 264.

28. William Strauss and Neil Howe, *Millennials and the Pop Culture: Strategies for a New Generation of Consumers in Music, Movies, Television, the Internet, and Video Games* (Great Falls, VA: Life Course Associates, 2006), 6, 72.

29. Although, community activism is not new for Rock the Vote. In addition to their television spots in the 1990s, Rock the Vote always used some type of activism that involved young people connecting with others beyond the mediated experience.

30. William L. Riordan, ed., *Plunkitt of Tammany Hall* (New York: Penguin Books, 1991), 25.

31. Michael Schudson, *The Good Citizen: A History of American Civic Life* (New York: The Free Press, 1998), 173

32. Michael Krauss, "Motorola Joins Push to Get Out Young Voters," *Chicago Sun-Times*, March 8, 2004, 56.

33. "Headline: Rock the Vote and Motorola Team to Mobilize Electorate," *PR Newswire*, March 2, 2004.

34. Robert W. McChesney, *Rich Media, Poor Democracy: Communication Politics in Dubious Times* (New York: The New Press, 1999), 171.

35. Stephen Ward, Rachel Gibson, and Paul Nixon, *Political Parties and the Internet: Net gain?* (NewYork: Routledge, 2003), 4.

Part II: The Performance

Chapter 3

Rock the Vote: An Insider's Account of the 2004 Campaign Strategy

Aaron Teeter and Brandy Chappell

For the first time in American political history, twenty million youths, ages eighteen to twenty-nine, established themselves as a decisive voting bloc capable of swinging the 2004 presidential election. A number of organizations emerged during the 2004 presidential campaign to garner support from this new group of swing voters, each often claiming to represent the political will of young Americans. Many of these organizations utilized elements of popular culture to reach their target audience. Rock the Vote (RTV), established in 1990, remains the archetype and most recognizable organization to employ the links between America's popular culture and the nation's youth.

Founded in 1990 to defend attacks against freedom of speech and artistic expression, members of the recording industry banded together to create an organization that could link political issues to America's supposedly apathetic youth.[1] In its infancy, Rock the Vote sought to stimulate interest among this voting population by registering young voters, and staging national media campaigns with facilitated dialogues between political candidates and America's youth. In its first seven years RTV developed into the premiere organization for communicating political issues to American youths, and in 1998 RTV expanded the organization's mission to "dedicating itself to protecting freedom of expression, and helping young people realize and utilize their power to affect change in the civic and political lives of their community."[2]

In 2004, RTV accomplished its campaign goals of registering one million new voters and mobilizing twenty million young Americans to vote on Election Day. However, the organization failed in its mission of youth empowerment through political participation. This begs the question: to what extent did RTV succeed in effectively shaping the 2004 general election? Furthermore, given RTV's financial difficulties, what implications will this have on the organization's role and other similar youth-oriented initiatives in future elections?

The purpose of this chapter is to provide an insider's account of RTV, offering a critical analysis of the organization's 2004 campaign by detailing the multiple inconsistencies between the organization's mission, its donor base, and its campaign strategy. This analysis will examine RTV's mission, the organization's 2004 campaign goals, and how it employed tactics of pop-culture utilizing technological advancements, strategic partnerships, and celebrity endorsements to market and sell the RTV brand. Finally, the 2004 general election's impact on the organization will be discussed.

Rock the Vote's Mission: Empowering America's Youth

> Rock the Vote is a non-profit, non-partisan organization, founded in 1990 in response to a wave of attacks on freedom of speech and artistic expression. Rock the Vote engages youth in the political process by incorporating the entertainment community and youth culture into its activities . . . Rock the Vote mobilizes young people to create positive social and political change in their lives and communities . . . and take action on the issues they care about.[3]

Historically, RTV embodied the progressive nature inherent in many young Americans and their desire for greater reforms in politics. The organization received its largest contributions from the entertainment industry and liberal donors. However, the 2004 general election, expected to have the largest amount of campaign contributions and voter turnout in U.S. history, produced numerous challenges, especially for partisan organizations. The new McCain-Feingold Campaign Finance Reform law would dynamically alter how previous campaigns fundraised. This provided a rare opportunity for Rock the Vote; the organization could bridge the partisan divide by emphasizing its mission to register and turnout young American voters. At the height of the 2004 election, RTV employed twenty-eight full-time staff members, dozens of interns, and thousands of volunteers across the nation. The staff all believed in the organization's mission, but many employees found a glaring contradiction between their jobs and their personal agendas for political change. RTV's leadership and staff faced a major challenge in determining how to fulfill the organization's progressive mission and its new 2004 campaign strategy while maintaining its non-partisanship.

Two fundamental constraints developed from this. The first obstacle, which RTV struggled with since its inception, deals explicitly with empowering young Americans. To empower America's youth inevitably requires helping them to feel a sense of confidence and authority—that their vote matters. The organization's non-partisan mission complicates this act by not expressly advocating for either a candidate or any specific issue. Furthermore, the youth empowerment platform cannot narrowly be defined by the simple phrase, "all that applies to the MTV generation, is all that is important to young people." RTV volunteers represent almost every facet of the political spectrum from neo-conservatives to socialists, and each member maintains a differing perspective on what a youth platform should encompass. Voting itself may empower some, but to truly feel confident in one's choice and retain a sense of authority in determining a candidate, that vote must result in a victory. However, RTV could not accomplish this and needed to maintain its non-partisan objectivity. To circumvent this issue the organization continually stressed its mission: to protect first amendment rights, and promote youth voter registration and political participation by providing information on youth related issues.

The second constraint RTV faced further articulates the contradictions between the organization's mission, its donor base, and its campaign strategy. To succeed in shaping the 2004 general election, RTV needed to meet not only its campaign goals of one million new voters and a turnout of twenty million young Americans on Election Day, but the organization also had to satisfy its liberal donors. The organization's financial contributors believed they were investing in young new progressive voters, which contradicted RTV's non-partisan mission. This created a difficult situation for the organization: RTV could not openly advocate a political perspective, yet it needed to appease its donors. The organization's youth empowerment mission further complicated this issue. Ultimately, the organization's success gambled on the election's final outcome, requiring the results to favor its donors' wishes and to be consistent with the organization's constituent youth voters, who were assumed to be inherently more progressive. If RTV could accomplish these objectives, the organization could claim a place among the most successful grassroots political movements in American election history. To undertake this mission, Rock the Vote needed to develop a cohesive strategy, building upon its previous strengths and new technologies, while marketing the youth empowerment message to a more diverse audience.

Marketing Empowerment: New Technology, Strategic Partnerships, and the RTV Brand

To repeat, in 2004, Rock the Vote maintained two centralized goals for the general election: register one million new voters, and mobilize twenty million young Americans on Election Day. To fulfill these mandates, the organization relied heavily upon its previous campaign successes utilizing American pop-culture through technological advancements, strategic partnerships, and celebrity endorsements. To market the youth empowerment message, RTV employed these three techniques in concert in hope of connecting the nation's youth culture to politics. The organization's target audience focused primarily on eighteen- to twenty-four-year-olds, with a secondary audience extending to thirty-years-old.

Rock the Vote and New Technology

In Rock the Vote's early days, the organization depended on volunteers to register and engage young voters at the concerts and nightclubs they frequented. By 2004 the Internet had drastically altered how young Americans congregate; the virtual world created greater accessibility, but it also compartmentalized people by their interests into smaller and more diverse groups. To reach its disparate audiences RTV focused its campaigning programs around the Internet and cell phones, the two technological tools that had most recently become hugely popular with eighteen- to twenty-four-year-olds. The most prominent programs supplemented the organization's web presence with RTV's Online Voter Registration (OVR) tool, the grassroots Community Street Team (CST) volunteers, and RTV mobile.

In 1991, Rock the Vote had endorsed the National Voter Registration

Reform Act (NVRA), better known as the Motor Voter bill. In the organization's early stages it recognized that the largest constraint to voting is registration. The U.S. Census Bureau notes that, beyond voting's obvious required registration, "historically, the likelihood that an individual will actually vote once registered remains high."[4] Registration also poses a greater challenge to young voters who lead more transient lives, frequently moving for college or new jobs. The Motor Voter bill sought to increase registration with young voters by connecting it to the driver's licensing process, thus eliminating the hardships in dealing with government registrars. In 1991, President Bush vetoed the bill, but RTV continued to lobby the U.S. Congress. In 1993, President Clinton passed the Act, making it law, and highlighted RTV's contribution during the White House signing ceremony.[5]

The Motor Voter bill marked the organization's innovative approach to voter registration and aided in the future development of the Online Voter Registration tool. The OVR tool fundamentally altered RTV's approach to voter registration outreach. The organization could exponentially multiply its grassroots registration efforts by allowing any eligible American voter to register online. The OVR tool was also made available to RTV partners, who could personalize the tool to match their websites and company logos. Throughout the 2004 election, the OVR tool was used by over one thousand web partners to register in excess of 1.2 million voters, with a single day record high of forty thousand registrations in late September 2004.[6] When registering to vote, people could authorize RTV to contact them via e-mail or RTV mobile, as well as sign up for RTV's Community Street Teams. The OVR tool added a larger benefit to the organization; RTV now possessed a list of over 1.2 million names with their corresponding e-mail, address, and phone number information.

Traditionally, RTV voter registration efforts drew upon its volunteers to seek out young voters at the places they congregated. The grassroots program relied on face-to-face meetings for recruitment and phone-trees for organizing participation at events. In 2004, RTV changed how it did business by developing its Community Street Team program. Throughout the election RTV's staff oversaw fifty-five Street Teams with more than fifteen thousand members across the nation. CSTs, separated by geographic locations, covered the West Coast, the Midwest, the South, and the East. In order to launch simultaneous national voter registration drives, regional directors were put in place to oversee the efforts of street teams in their geographic areas. RTV staff paid particular attention to developing CSTs in hotly contested states such as Iowa, Ohio, Colorado,

Nevada, and Wisconsin. The CSTs were led by Street Team Leaders (STL) who received directions from their regional directors. The STLs represented the operation's frontline as RTV's foot soldiers, registering young voters and identifying issues important to young people in their communities. The CSTs participated in RTV events and acted at partnering musicians' concerts as liaisons for the national staff.

The program's goal focused on registering new voters and building a platform based upon local area concerns that could then be applied, when possible, to issues that other youths throughout the country shared. The organization hoped to maintain the CSTs following the election. The long-term program sought to create a self-sustaining volunteer network, where the street teams could operate with a certain amount of autonomy to raise funds, organize events, and participate in local politics. The organization envisioned the Community Street Team program as a true realization of its youth empowerment mission. RTV would implement a train-the-trainers formula, where its national staff would teach the CST leaders how to raise funds, lobby local politicians, and implement community youth platforms. The street team leaders would then go and train their teams with these skills. RTV's national staff hoped that the CSTs would eventually rely on the national campaign only for supporting events and partnering with RTV's celebrity sponsors, no longer posing a supply or financial resource burden to the national campaign.

To execute the 2004 strategy and long-term vision, the CST program required a new and dynamic approach to connect and organize the disparate target audience. Engaging young people meant getting to know their minds. This new Internet driven generation was more responsive to online marketing than its costly television alternative. To tap into this, RTV partnered with MySpace and MeetUp to reach its scattered audience. Prior to its major presence on the Internet and its purchase by News Corporation (the parent company for all FOX owned products), the webportal MySpace was used by RTV to reach potential young voters. Rock the Vote's staff was encouraged to not only use their accounts for networking and finding new partners on and off the web, but also to actively blog about issues relevant to young Americans during the election. CSTs could use their individual or their Street Team MySpace pages to post events and workshops, while aggressively recruiting new members.

In conjunction with MTV, Rock the Vote employed MeetUp, a nonprofit networking website where users can locate people in their communities with similar interests and plan face-to-face meetings. MTV advertised the service throughout the election in celebrity endorsed Public

Service Announcements (PSAs) about youth participation's importance in politics. STLs would organize and facilitate the events, and encourage individuals to log onto Rock the Vote's website, use the tools located therein to register voters, join CSTs, and participate in future community MeetUp events.

Rock the Vote's OVR tool and its CST program received additional support from RTV Mobile. The organization's corporate sponsors, Cingular Wireless and Motorola, linked the organization to young Americans in a radically new way. RTV mobile delivered political information and news alerts via text-messages, but the program also became a strategic Get Out The Vote (GOTV) tool. In the election's final days RTV Mobile messaging "included celebrity voicemails that explained how to find a polling place via the web or through an automatic patch through to (800) MY VOTE1."[7] By enlisting over 118,000 young people RTV Mobile developed into a crucial device for organizing the grassroots CST volunteers.[8] Street Team leaders could now connect with their members through text messaging, issuing reminders about events and MeetUps. The combined effectiveness of the web tools and RTV Mobile helped the CST grassroots efforts register more than two-hundred thousand voters throughout the 2004 election.[9]

RTV's effectiveness in using new technology, however, requires a feedback loop, a particular concern in L. von Bertalanffy's *System Theory* when applied to communication reception.[10] Programs like RTV Mobile and the OVR tool elicit one-way communication messages to its audience without ever providing a feedback exchange to determine the input's level of reception or its ability to alter its audience's action. Currently, no research exists that explains the relationship between these one-way messaging systems and their effect in creating participatory action within the receivers. Future research will need to examine the use of these new technologies in electoral politics and decipher whether or not they are true forms of participation, and, ultimately, if they lead to an increased likelihood in voting by their subscribers.

Rock the Vote and Strategic Partnerships

To reach its campaign goals RTV required strategic partners that could contribute the assets necessary to effectively exploit the available technology. The organization enlisted three types of partners: corporate sponsors, media partners, and non-profit organizations. These partners increased RTV's brand visibility and assisted voter registration efforts by adding the OVR tool to their organizations' webpages. However, the partnerships Rock the Vote employed call into question the extent to which its mission and values were compromised through its affiliation with large corporations and, at times, partisan organizations. Throughout the 2004 campaign, RTV tried to limit the concessions it made with these sponsors to protect the integrity of the organization and its mission.

The corporate sponsors were the backbone to the campaign, playing an instrumental role in helping RTV achieve its goals. In 2004, the main sponsors included Ben & Jerry's Ice Cream, Motorola, Cingular, 7-Up, and Sunkist. Each company contributed assets necessary for facilitating key RTV programs that would expand the organization's brand visibility and increase national voter registration efforts.

From the election season's start in 2004, Ben & Jerry's Ice Cream linked a flavor to a cause the company believed in by creating a partnership with RTV and unveiling its new "Primary Berry Graham" flavor. Ben & Jerry's donated a portion from each strawberry cheesecake ice cream pint sold to Rock the Vote throughout the election year. The company also supported RTV's first national voter registration drive of the year on April 27, Earth Day, which Ben & Jerry's ice cream lovers also know as "Free Cone Day." To register voters at each of Ben & Jerry's 200 plus stores, RTV mobilized over one thousand CST members. Additionally, Ben & Jerry's was one of RTV's 2004 Summer Bus Tour sponsors, providing "cool-down" treats at booths near voter registration tables.

RTV's 2004 campaign strategy, as noted, relied heavily on cell phones for its RTV Mobile program and communications. Cingular Wireless and Motorola provided the phones and services necessary for staff communications and the CSTs' organizing demands. The two sponsors were critical in helping develop the services needed to run and operate the RTV Mobile program. In addition to sponsoring RTV's 2004 Summer Bus Tour, staff and CST members were encouraged to take pictures at concerts and events using their cell phones. The media, relayed back to RTV via text-messages, were then posted on RTV's website.

In the spring of 2004, 7-Up and Sunkist joined RTV by sponsoring the Summer Bus Tour. Almost half of RTV's target audience was underage, between eighteen and twenty, which meant that the organization could not schedule its events at popular nightclubs if it wanted to include these young voters. To augment this issue, the Bus Tour traveled to colleges throughout the nation, where alcohol consumption is usually illegal. To help avoid the heat, 7-Up and Sunkist provided free drinks to concertgoers as an alternative to alcohol.

The second partner type that RTV enlisted, media partnerships, were intended to expand the Rock the Vote brand by increasing its visibility and driving young voters to register via the website. The larger media partners like Sony Music Group, Warner Music Group, and the WB encouraged their celebrity talent to participate in RTV's campaign. Bands could promote their new releases in a socially conscious way by playing at one of the organization's concerts. Up and coming talent and musicians with smaller grassroots fan bases signed on to play the Summer Bus Tour for greater national exposure.

The most prolific partner among these media sponsors was MTV. Since Rock the Vote's first nationally recognized campaign in 1992, the RTV brand has been synonymous with MTV. This common misnomer has always had varying effects on RTV's constituency, and the partnership with the media powerhouse during the 2004 presidential election was no different in the strengths and weaknesses it produced. MTV's national broadcasting capability delivered a massive audience to RTV and played an integral role by increasing the organization's brand visibility. Another appealing feature to RTV is the Internet traffic MTV generates on its website—a potential cache of online registrations. In a more strategic sense, MTV could also help instill the importance of civic participation among its younger non-voting audience.

However, partnering with MTV had weaknesses too. Rock the Vote acted as Viacom-MTV's grassroots partner for MTV affiliated marketing and sponsored events. Rock the Vote's CSTs were required to attend these events regardless of conflicting schedules. On several occasions, RTV and its CSTs lacked the human and financial resources to meet MTV's and the organization's other corporate sponsors' demands. In many cases when needs could not be met, it appeared to MTV and the other sponsors that Rock the Vote had disregarded its contractual obligations and commitments. Ultimately, these instances damaged RTV's legitimacy as a grassroots organizer and its credibility among potential sponsors and donors.

Non-profit partners represent the last type of partnership utilized by RTV. Organizations like the League of Women Voters, SEIU, and the New Voters Project offered Rock the Vote outreach opportunities to potential voters it could not reach through corporate sponsored advertising. These partnerships assisted the organization's campaign efforts, unifying the work carried out by similar goal oriented groups. In cases when the organization partnered with partisan organizations, RTV justified the action by maintaining a policy to engage both sides of the political aisle in an effort to remain non-partisan in the relationships. However, in the public's view this was difficult to distinguish when one party might openly embrace a partnership with RTV, which another party might refuse relations with the organization at any level. Nonetheless, the non-profit partnerships became essential, bolstering RTV's credibility among the public, even as it dissipated with MTV and other sponsors.

When partnerships were at their best, Rock the Vote was able to develop and market its brand as the premiere organization for youth empowerment. The organization had all of the attractiveness of an MTV sales campaign, with politics provided in sound bites, and lots of sexy celebrities to wear its message on the red carpet. However, in 2004, several new organizations emerged that appeared more attractive to Rock the Vote's celebrity supporters. The diversity in election issues and the need for specific demographic targets within the youth population required that attention be paid to specific demographic groups that many supporters felt the organization could not reach.

Celebrity Endorsements: The Power Behind the RTV Brand

Star power sells the RTV brand. Since the non-profit's meager beginnings in 1990, the most persuasive feature the organization has possessed is its ability to enlist high profile artists and celebrities to address its youth audience. In 2004, RTV received an unprecedented commitment from a cadre of musicians, actors, and celebrities looking to spread the youth empowerment message. RTV's campaign strategy employed these iconic pop-culture figures in numerous ways; but in the 2004 election, celebrities also had a detrimental effect on the organization and its goals.

Rock the Vote's celebrity partners endorsed the organization's youth empowerment message in three ways. The first method focused on celebrity appearances at RTV sponsored events. These media events, designed to increase RTV's brand visibility, were Hollywood red-carpet parties where fashion magazines and news outlets could snap shots of celebrities posing in front of backdrops adorned with Rock the Vote's and its sponsors' logos. In other instances, celebrities and musicians contributed by performing at RTV's summer bus tour events.

The second technique featured pop icons as RTV spokespeople. These individuals participated in PSAs on television and radio, provided interviews, and spoke at the organization's events. With the help of RTV media partners, cast members of popular television shows like *The O.C.* spread the word about the importance of political participation and the youth vote.

The last area in which celebrities were utilized related to specific RTV programs. Actors, musicians, and other celebrities contributed to programs like RTV Mobile by lending their recognition and voice, reminding people to vote. Rock the Vote also diversified its campaigning to meet smaller audiences through specific programs targeting different demographics. With the support of the Dixie Chicks, RTV launched "Chicks Rock, Chicks Vote." Election and voter research strongly indicated that since the 1984 election women vote more often then men.[11] The "Chicks Rock, Chicks Vote" program was designed to reach out to young American women and encourage their political participation. Following the election, the U.S. Census Bureau reported that "women were more likely than men to vote," comparatively at a rate of 65 percent to 62 percent.[12] RTV's "Do it on Campus" program targeted college students in states where voter registration laws suppressed student-voting rights. At Prairie View A&M University, a small African American college in a predominantly white county near Houston, Texas, for example, the local District Attorney threatened and intimidated students with prosecution if they attempted to claim residency in the county for registering to vote. Rapper Q-Tip (A Tribe Called Quest) and Rap the Vote, a RTV program sponsored by Russell Simmons and Def Jam Records, traveled to Prairie View A&M and launched the "Do it on Campus" campaign, with the support of the Congressional Black Caucus. In the summer of 2004, RTV's Bus tour traveled to universities across the nation to strengthen the program's initiative for student voter rights.

Yet RTV also suffered negative impacts from its celebrity sponsors. On more than one occasion a celebrity spokesperson took the opportunity to speak his or her mind about one of the candidates at an RTV event, calling into question the organization's non-partisan stance. In some of these cases RTV's constituency and sponsors scolded the staff for the organization's failure to stay non-partisan, resulting in RTV severing its ties with the celebrity—no matter what that individual's level of fame or youth appeal. Additionally, organizations like America Comes Together (ACT), New Voters Project, Declare Yourself, and Citizen Change: Vote or Die, materialized during the 2004 election. Some of these new organizations differed from RTV in their ability to advocate for partisan issues and politicians through a loophole in the McCain-Feingold Act by acquiring a 527 tax-status; others duplicated Rock the Vote's mission and strategy. The emergence of these organizations signaled a new approach to targeting youth populations by demographics for voter registration, using RTV as the archetype for their strategies. The new organizations, with their smaller and more targeted audience demographics, competed with RTV for donors and celebrity sponsors and offered greater options to those who wanted their money and efforts to be more focused. This division between RTV and the myriad of new organizations created detrimental effects on RTV's finances and its long-term sustainability.

The 2004 General Election Results and Its Impact on Rock the Vote

Throughout the 2004 election season, hundreds of articles, op-eds, and news stories covered the importance of the youth vote. The media first questioned whether or not America's youth would even vote. At the end of the voter registration period in September, over twenty-one million American youths between eighteen- and thirty-years-old registered to vote. The media quickly changed the story from whether or not young Americans would vote, to whether or not the youth vote would matter. Following the election, the media often divided their opinion about the true impact the youth vote had on shaping the election's outcome. Often, the youth voter turnout percentage would be confused with the youth's share of the electorate. In the 2000 election, the youth voter turnout rate for eighteen- to twenty-nine-year-olds was 42.3 percent, while in 2004 the rate jumped 9.3 percentage points to 51.6 percent.[13] Among this group were eight million new voters, representing 42 percent of the total under-thirty voters and 64 percent of the total thirteen million first-time voters.[14] However, when the youth vote is articulated by its share of the overall electorate it drops to only 16 percent of the total vote.[15]

At the close of the voter registration period in 2004, Rock the Vote maintained that it reached its first campaign goal by registering approximately 1,400,000 young Americans.[16] Pew Charitable Trusts conducted a post-election survey and reported that twenty-one million Americans under thirty voted in 2004, with a 51.6 percent voter turnout.[17] After the election, Rock the Vote commissioned Polimetrix, an online researching firm, to write a follow up report on the organization's Get Out The Vote success. In a 2004 RTV press release, the organization concluded that approximately 1,260,000 of the 1,400,000 who registered through RTV voted, "according to Polimetrix, more than 90 percent of our list turned out to vote."[18] In addition, the Polimetrix study concluded that "72 percent voted for John Kerry, 66 percent are women, 56 percent are under age 25, and 57 percent were first time voters."[19] With over twenty million young Americans voting, Rock the Vote accomplished its second campaign goal and proved itself as a national grassroots organization able to mobilize 90 percent of its constituency. More importantly, the organization's assumption that young voters are more progressive was correct in the 2004 election (if a vote for a Democrat is perceived as more progressive than a vote for a Republican).

Unfortunately, RTV's campaign achievements would not ultimately determine the organization's success in 2004. RTV's leadership and staff knew that the organization's long-term sustainability depended heavily on the election's outcome. RTV indeed needed to accomplish its campaign goals, but more importantly, it required Democrats winning to successfully meet the demands of its donors. A Republican victory would nullify the organization's achievements in the eyes of those who funded it.

Conclusion

In 2004, RTV accomplished its campaign goals of registering one million new voters and mobilizing twenty million young Americans to vote on Election Day, but the organization failed in its mission of youth empowerment through political participation. The new youth voter establishments played a significant role in weakening Rock the Vote as an organization and its 2004 campaign; however, the multiple inconsistencies between the organization's mission, its donor base, and its campaign strategy ultimately led to RTV's failure in shaping the 2004 election.

On February 7, 2006, the *Los Angeles Times* reported that Rock the Vote was $700,000 in debt, and that its staff had been cut to just two members.[20] RTV's debt clearly indicated that the organization had lost donor support. The organization still participated in the 2006 midterm elections, but lacked the visibility it enjoyed during previous campaigns. However, future political campaigns will be dominated by the innovative outreach and organizing tools pioneered by Rock the Vote in the 2004 election. Joe Trippi, the campaign manager who engineered Presidential candidate Howard Dean's Internet fund-raising strategy, noted in an interview, "I think text messaging is going to be more important than ever . . . We may be talking about the Great Text-Messaging Campaign of 2008, not the Great Blog Campaign."[21] In response to other emerging campaign technologies, Trippi stated:

> There are a lot more social networking tools out there than what we were using during the Dean campaign . . . The real issue is how do you translate it into persuasion and into organizing and social networking. We had a glimpse of that in 2003 and 2004 with meetups and offline organizing. Social activities became part of the glue that held the [Dean] meetings together.

Furthermore, politicians campaigned with web-based strategies similar to RTV's in the 2006 midterm election. Facebook.com, a web-portal site analogous to MySpace, allowed politicians to create their own pages. *Time* magazine's Tracy Samantha Schmidt documented the new trend in July 2006, writing, "In the 90's, the message was 'Rock the Vote.' Now it's time to 'Facebook' it . . . They're the new town square—great for any candidate who can figure out the online equivalent of a handshake."[22] Numerous candidates for the 2008 Presidential election have already started to employ the online social networking strategy. "One Facebook group backing Democratic Senator Barack Obama has more than three-hundred thousand members. It was Facebook that helped turn out several thousand people at a rally for the Illinois senator at George Mason University in Virginia."[23] Republican Presidential candidate Senator John McCain is reaching out to young Americans by creating an online networking site "called McCainSpace where supporters can create their own pages and connect with one another."[24]

In future elections Rock the Vote's presence may be more limited than in 2004, but the organization's overwhelming success at linking the nation's youth culture to politics will continue to be copied. Future campaigns and groups will build on the campaigning techniques pioneered by RTV, integrating America's pop-culture with technological advancements, strategic partnerships, and celebrity endorsements to get their messages to resonate with America's young voters.

Notes

1. Rock the Vote, "Rock the Vote Timeline," *Rock the Vote*, http://www.rockthevote.com/rtv_timeline.php (accessed November, 10, 2006).

2. Rock the Vote, "Rock the Vote Timeline."

3. Rock the Vote, "About Us," *Rock the Vote*, http://www.rockthevote.com/rtv_about.php (accessed November 10, 2006).

4. Karen Holder, "Voting and Registration in the Election of November 2004: Population Characteristics," *U.S. Census Bureau* (March 2006): 1-17.

5. Rock the Vote, "Rock the Vote Timeline."

6. Rock the Vote, "Rock the Vote 2004 Election Campaign," *Rock the Vote*, http://www.rockthevote.com/success.php (accessed November 10, 2006).

7. Rock the Vote, "Rock the Vote 2004."

8. Rock the Vote, "Rock the Vote 2004."

9. Rock the Vote, "Rock the Vote 2004."

10. L. von Bertalanffy, "System Theory," *University of Twente: The Netherlands*, http://www.tcw.utwente.nl/theorieenoverzicht/Theory%20cluters/Communication%20Processes/System_Theory.doc/ (accessed November 15, 2006).

11. Holder, "Voting and Registration," 2.

12. Holder, "Voting and Registration," 2.

13. Pew Charitable Trusts, "Youth Voting: Turnout of Under-Twenty-Five Voters Up Sharply," *The Pew Charitable Trusts*, http://www.pewtrusts.com/ideas/ideas_item.cfm?content_item_id=2727&content_type_id=7 (accessed November 10, 2006).

14. Pew Charitable Trusts, "Youth Voting."

15. Center for Information and Research on Civic Learning and Engagement (CIRCLE), "The 2004 Youth Vote: A Comprehensive Guide," *CIRCLE*, http://www.civicyouth.org/PopUps/2004_votereport_final.pdf (accessed November 10, 2006): 1-9.

16. Rock the Vote, "Rock the Vote 2004."

17. Pew Charitable Trusts, "Youth Voting."

18. Rock the Vote, "Rock the Vote's Nine Greatest Strengths," *Rock the Vote* (2004 Press Release).

19. Rock the Vote, "Nine Greatest Strengths."

20. Charles Duhigg, "Rock the Vote is Stuck in a Hard Place," *Los Angeles Times*, February 7, 2006, 1(A).

21. Susanna Schrobsdorff, "Trippi on Web Campaigning," *Newsweek Online*, May 21, 2006, http:www.msnbc.msn.com/id/128 76 663/site/newsweek/ (accessed November 10, 2006).

22. Tracy Samantha Schmidt, "Be My Voter," *Time* 168, no. 3 (July 17, 2006).

23. Associated Press, "Campaigns Focus on Engaging Young Voters," *CNN.com*, March 5, 2007, http://www.cnn.com/2007/POLITICS/03/05/young. voters.ap/index.html (accessed March 5, 2007).

24. Associated Press, "Campaigns Focus."

Chapter 4

"Comic Elections and Real News?" *The Daily Show*, Satire, Public Discourse, and the New Voter

Brian Cogan

In 2004, less than a month before the American presidential election and amidst a rigorous season of political debates among political candidates of all stripes, a momentous event in the history of civic America occurred. Against all odds, a debate containing actual substance occurred, captured live on television, on the nature of civic America, public participation in democracy, and the role of television in maintaining an American version of Jurgen Habermas's Public Sphere. However, this debate was not between Bush and Kerry, or the vice presidential candidates, or even between local candidates in some musty school auditorium in the heartland of America, but between the premier fake journalist in the nation and two of the most acerbic pundits working (at that time) for CNN. Jon Stewart, the host of Comedy Central's popular news spoof *The Daily Show*, made an appearance on CNN's bipartisan debate show *Crossfire* and had the temerity to lecture the hosts on the merits of open debate in constructing a civil society! To the surprise of many, he was allowed to make his case (of course, with many interruptions) for nearly the entire length of the show.

While at first the hosts had lavished Stewart with praise, calling him "the most trusted man in fake news," the tone soon changed. This strange, almost all-too-fitting theme of commonality was not to last, as Stewart made it a point to breach the boundaries of television debate shows by actually asking intelligent and pointed questions: questions not just about partisan political matters, the usual content of the program, but about the usefulness of the very form of such programs, and what Stewart considered the harmful nature of that kind of television.

Stewart first admonished hosts Tucker Carlson and Paul Begala, asking them to "stop, stop hurting America." While this initial volley was just laughed off and Tucker and Begala tried to draw Stewart into a discussion about the merits of the Kerry candidacy, Stewart kept returning to his critique that the rancorous debating style of shows like *Crossfire* were counterproductive to democracy. Jumping in quickly to comment when given a chance, Stewart responded, "I felt it wasn't fair and I should come here and tell you it's not so much that it's bad as it's hurting America." When both Carlson and Begala challenged him and essentially tried to laugh his attack off, Stewart still maintained a calm demeanor and responded, "I'm here to confront you because we need help from the media and they're hurting us." Begala responded to Stewart, asking: "So, the indictment is that *Crossfire* reduces everything to left-right, black-white?"

"Yes," Stewart responded.

"It's because we are a debate show," Begala rebutted. In between Begala's frequent interjections, Stewart finally was able to respond, "No, that would be great, to do a debate would be great, but that's like saying that pro wrestling is a show about athletic competition."[1]

While Stewart's attempt to engage the hosts of *Crossfire* in a productive debate was ultimately futile, it did lead to a flurry of stories about how the fake journalist had come across as having more integrity and more of a commitment to open and civic debate than the real journalists. To many media critics both within and outside academia, this solidified Stewart's role (alongside those of similar satirists such as Bill Maher and Dennis Miller) as one of society's, in the words of Jeffery Jones, "court jesters,"[2] satirically critiquing a world increasingly dominated by journalists and reporters without much apparent credibility and with an obvious interest in maintaining the status quo. To many of the fans of Jon Stewart and other late night emcees, these jesters are the only real providers of not only genuinely biting political satire, but in some cases, of actual news. Earlier that year, much to the chagrin of the regular networks, *The Daily Show*'s coverage of the political conventions outpolled CNN, MSNBC, and Fox News Channel in the Nielsen ratings.[3]

To several critics, this was a positive sign that things were changing and that political discourse had not been lost. Previous critics of television's role in the disappearance of civic life, such as Robert Putnam in *Bowling Alone* and Neil Postman in *Amusing Ourselves to Death*,[4] have suggested that television has usurped the rational print-based world in which political participation was not only a duty, but also a serious obligation. Postman argued, "The epistemology created by television is not only inferior to a print based epistemology, but is dangerous and absurdist and that entertainment is the supra-ideology of all discourse on television. No matter what is depicted or from what point of view, the overarching assumption is that it is there for our amusement and pleasure."[5] It is, to Postman, not only the notion that television creates an absurdist way of presenting information that is dangerous, but that the idea of engagement is less and less likely as one becomes more engaged in a culture defined by television. Critics such as Postman and Putnam, in Jeffrey Jones's view, have argued that television cannot in and of itself lead to any real sense of engagement; instead, it creates a false sensory *feeling* of being engaged.[6]

On the other hand, this contention, that television is a substitute for real involvement instead of a real argument, has been disputed by some.[7] Indeed, a question many were asking after Stewart's appearance and, for that matter, had been asking in the years since he had succeeded original host Craig Kilborn on *The Daily Show*, was, Is this kind of programming and satirical discussion of news events an example of how political discourse has helped to reenergize a demographic unused to participation in political life? Within the context of researchers presenting conflicting reports on how involved eighteen- to twenty-four-year-old voters actually are, some scholars think that satirical programs might help create a newly engaged voter base. In the following pages, I will analyze this ongoing debate about voter participation within the context of a media environment that increasingly merges political discourse and humorous entertainment. As *The Daily Show* points out on a regular basis, there are no easy solutions to complex problems. Accordingly, the enduring debate about civic involvement and entertainment is one that, I will admit at this point, I have still not reconciled in my own mind. Do programs such as *The Daily Show* really engage voters? And, if so, on what level? As I will mention at the end of this chapter, in many ways, the jury is still out on *The Daily Show* and similar vehicles (such as its spin-off, *The Colbert Report*), in relationship to voter engagement.

The Daily Show and Political Engagement

When *The Daily Show* first started in 1996 with then host Craig Kilborn, it represented a pleasant and slightly more intellectual look at contemporary popular culture and politics than usual. As envisioned by creator Lizz Winstead, *The Daily Show* was a spoof of network news with a roving group of correspondents (who eventually included such famous alumni as Steve Colbert, Rob Corrdry, and Steve Carell). When Stewart took over the show after the departure of both Winstead and Kilborn in 1999, the show gradually evolved over the course of several years into a bitingly acerbic look at politics and political foibles—it became more than simply another "Weekend Update"-type skewering of popular culture. Eventually the show began to become more popular, particularly with the attractive younger demographic so craved by advertisers. The 2004 election was a particularly fertile time for *The Daily Show*, with ratings improving to an all-time high and performances leading to an astounding series of major awards, such as five Emmys and a Peabody award.[8] In 2004, the program was also nominated "as one of television's best broadcasts by the TV critics association," and Jon Stewart was named by *Newsday* as the most important newscaster in the country,[9] beating out the anchors of the major cable, network, and public broadcasting stations.

The Daily Show may only be a parody of nightly network broadcasts, but it seems to have taken on, for many critics and fans, elements of legitimacy. Indeed, *The Daily Show* possesses many signifiers of legitimacy in its construction as a news show. As Geoffrey Bayam points out, the show's set, music, and opening all mimic the conventions of regular news broadcasts and contain signifiers familiar to anyone who has regularly watched broadcast news. As Bayam writes, the initial set up of the show, including the opening voice-over announcing the date the show is being broadcast, "borrows a technique from broadcast journalism that seeks textual authority through a claim to immediacy" and the program itself "interweaves at least two levels of discourse, borrowing equally from traditions of authoritative nightly news, and the entertainment talk show."[10] This use of dramatic music and imagery, which is a crucial part of the nightly news broadcast, is as essential in getting an audience to ease into *The Daily Show* as it is in any nightly news broadcast, where no program is complete without "a fancy opening and music sounding as if it was composed for a Hollywood epic."[11] While the indicators might suggest to the audience that the show is merely a parody of news and entertainment talk shows, it seems as though the satire of *The Daily Show* has recently moved to a new level of more serious discourse, mixed in with parody and satire.

A sign of *The Daily Show*'s increasing maturity has been its no-holds-barred analysis of how major networks accept information presented from the government as news, without any suggestion that there might be elements of propaganda present. An example of how *The Daily Show* attempts to dissect network and cable news that simply accepts official government sources verbatim is its analysis of the speech Ayad Allawi, the Iraqi President, gave to the joint session of Congress in 2004. While the major networks and cable channels, in essence, simply reported the speech verbatim, *The Daily Show* analyzed the speech in detail, comparing clips from Allawi's speech to some of Bush's earlier statements on Iraq to demonstrate how the speech was a thinly veiled rewrite of Bush's stump speech. The show's editors presented a montage of matching clips from Bush speeches that contained similarities, then an incredulous-looking Stewart asked, "It's almost like the United States wrote the speech," adding with puzzled ingenuousness, "but . . . that . . . couldn't . . . be?"[12]

This willingness to analyze the standards of nightly news and not simply regurgitate material leads to a "critical distance that cannot be said of the networks."[13] *The Daily Show* uses analysis as opposed to supposed objectivity as its standard. As Colapinto noted in his front-page article on *The Daily Show* in a 2004 issue of *Rolling Stone*, "the target of the show's scorn is not merely the mendacity and incompetence or corruption of our public officials, but the media's refusal to call them on it."[14] According to Bayam, *The Daily Show* has attempted to "revive a spirit of critical inquiry and of the press as an agent of public interrogation that has largely been abdicated by the post-September 11 news media."[15] The new strategy worked, as younger viewers become increasingly attracted to the show, leading to audiences that eclipsed earlier records and soon reached over 1.6 million viewers.[16] With the addition of producer Ben Karlin from the satirical newsweekly *The Onion,* who produced the show for almost seven years, the show solidified its identity, and even became a little afraid of its success and reputation as a source of real news as opposed to a parody of news. With the program growing quickly and becoming popular across the globe in various permutations (including a version on Great Britain's More4 Channel), Karlin once nervously admitted that "We just see the show as a giant, gaping beast and we're trying to feed it as fast as possible so it doesn't devour us."[17]

However, the beast, a la, the American public, seems to be getting something concrete out of *The Daily Show*. Much as Liesbet van Zoonen has suggested, perhaps some forms of entertainment can "provide an environment where citizenship can flourish."[18] While many authors have questioned whether citizens are really "engaged" when being entertained, there are some indications that fans of *The Daily Show* are getting more involved. An Annenberg center study of nineteen thousand respondents revealed that viewers of shows such as *The Daily Show* are "more likely to know the issue positions and backgrounds of presidential candidates than people who do not watch late night comedy."[19] Whether this translates into active involvement is another question, but it does indicate a broader base of knowledge to draw upon when analyzing political issues. As Michael Grabowski argues in Chapter 5, it is unclear how much a de-energized youth voter can be mobilized. Still, it is ironic that Stewart's audience is better informed than most assume, even if they are, in the words of Bill O'Reilly, "stoned slackers" and "dopey kids."[20]

As David Itzkoff wrote in the *New York Times,* "Stewart's point is that in a fevered media environment where the spoils go to whoever can make the loudest and most outrageous arguments, the loser is the American public—and a democracy whose health is dependent on being properly informed by its watchdog media."[21]

This idea of political involvement and watching television, however informative, going hand in hand ties into the notion made by several authors that political involvement and the phenomenon of fandom are not necessarily disconnected; many authors argue that the active nature of fandom and the engagement necessary to be a true fan is akin to the sort of involvement needed to be politically engaged.[22] While it may be unclear as to how "active" all fans of *The Daily Show* are or have been, van Zoonen makes the point that

> Both fans and citizens emerge as a result of performance, of pop-culture and political actors respectively; both fans and citizens seek information about their objects, talk and discuss, try to convince others of their preferences, and propose alternatives; both fans and citizens have a necessary emotional investment in their objects that keeps their commitment going. Thus, the way fans are positioned, the activities they undertake, and the relation they have with their objects is not fundamentally different than what is expected from good citizens in modernist discourse of politics.[23]

The problem is, how does this translate to real involvement? How far should *The Daily Show* go to serve the expectations of their fans is also unclear. As an example, the show was criticized by some critics and even some fans for its perceived welcoming attitude towards Democratic presidential candidate John Kerry during an interview in 2004. Stewart reiterated that looking at *The Daily Show* as anything but comedy shows a fundamental misinterpretation as to what the program is about. According to Stewart, "the idea that somehow we fail when we don't live up to journalistic experience is a misreading of what we are doing."[24] While this may seem a bit disingenuous on Stewart's part, on the one hand, he *is* a comedian; but on the other hand, he does serve a role as a sort of comedic watchdog, one that has a biting edge and is not afraid to lampoon the foibles of the rich and powerful. Stewart clearly takes his responsibility as a watchdog seriously, otherwise the program could have gone back to the frat boy antics of the Kilborn era.

The Daily Show and the Youth Voter

In his book *Entertaining Politics*, Jeffery Jones argues that programs such as *The Daily Show*, Dennis Miller's show, and Bill Maher's various programs have "begun to explore representing politics in imaginative ways, treatments that can offer voices, positions and perspectives not found in traditional television representations of politics."[25] Jones asserts that because hosts such as Stewart talk in language that resembles "more of what would be found in a bar or a basement or barbershop . . . a common vernacular that is accessible and familiar," they offer "a *cultural* site where new issues, languages, approaches, and audience relationships to politics on television are occurring."[26] To Jones, this provides a new open space, where formerly disengaged young voters without much interest in politics can find a voice that engages their participation. If older and more staid political programs that deal with politics are not able to engage the imagination and interest of younger voters, perhaps shows that use satire and engaging wit to skewer the foibles of contemporary politicians can have more of an effect in galvanizing the difficult to motivate younger voting demographic. As Mary Poppins might have put it, a spoon full of sugar helps the medicine go down.

Many scholars, perhaps enraptured by the possibilities provided by the latest communication technologies to engage the public, have argued recently that new forms of technology lead to new forms of political participation. Some have maintained that vehicles such as blogs; celebrity endorsed voting organizations, such as the Citizen Change organization founded by P. Diddy, Russell Simmons's Hip-Hop Summit Action Network, and the Punkvoter.com initiative founded by Fat Mike Burnett of NOFX; and other entities that try similar tacks in motivating and registering youth voters have led to profound change in young voters. Many have lauded these grassroots organizations as helping to not only inform the body politic, but also to radically change the level of discourse and public participation. Although, as mentioned in Chapter 3, these organizations have walked a delicate line between seeming as an "authentic" alternative to mainstream politics and political parties, and seeming to be engaged in the same degree of involvement as any partisan organization and, consequently, "selling out." Strangely enough, programs such as *The Daily Show*, which is carried on a major cable channel owned by the multi-national conglomerate Viacom, do not appear to be subject to the same amount of scrutiny by youth voters, who chafed at any over-involvement of MTV in Rock the Vote but never questioned the ownership of the channels that cablecast television parodies of news. It could be that there is not only a separate way of categorizing news shows parodies by younger voters, but that these programs also serve a different function than the ones organizations that overtly engage in voter registration and awareness campaigns do. Perhaps it is because the programs (at least on the surface—many analysts consider them to lean to the left of the political spectrum) use a veneer of *non-partisanship,* which allows not only a different level of participation by younger viewers, but also a different sort of activity and viewer involvement.

Jones suggests that news parodies actually constitute a sort of space where modern political discourse can occur outside of the regulated discourse that is maintained and solidified by mainstream news organizations and programs such as *Meet the Press*, where the political establishment is legitimized and outside opinions are not given full consideration. It can be argued that these newer shows, with their interactive fan bases and instant response via message boards and viewer participation (at least in the case of Bill Maher's former show *Politically Incorrect*) allow ordinary fans and faux anchors who presumably speak for them to communicate and share feedback as to how the programs affect their lives. The fact that the producers and performers on the programs regularly respond to messages and message threads does indicate a sense of responsibility and ownership on the part of both the fan base and the program, and a sense of involvement, although if this involvement can be labeled political is debatable. Also, it could be that it is only a smaller percentage of active fans who utilize message boards, and some of them may be the most politically active and left-leaning of the viewers, which is ironic given that *The Daily Show* has long portrayed itself as a collection of non-partisan satirists. For example, John Stewart has claimed to talk for the middle, noting, "The point of view of the show is that we are passionately opposed to bullshit. Is that liberal or conservative?"[27]

Voter Involvement

A key question is, Are these shows anything more than a chance for a very limited form of participation, or even a vicarious form of participation? It might well be that Neil Postman was right when he argued that television does not lend itself to serious discussions of important issues such as politics, and that the service provided by shows such as *The Daily Show* provide nothing more than a symbolic way to blow off steam. Even though *The Daily Show* did achieve, for cable, spectacular numbers when covering the political conventions in 2004, the coverage of political conventions had been drastically plummeting for years on most networks and are now mostly watched by only political junkies or insomniacs. This is not to say that *The Daily Show* does not have a significant audience. According to Nielsen, in terms of 2004 ratings, *The Daily Show* with Jon Stewart had, by far, its best ratings ever and its average viewership shattered the one million mark for the first time (1.2 million) in late 2004. By 2006, the average nightly average had risen to 1.6 million nightly viewers.[28]

But is this really civic participation? Most Fox talk or news shows such as *The O'Reilly Factor* (the inspiration for *The Colbert Report*) regularly double on a daily basis the kind of ratings *The Daily Show* produces on its most watched nights. And even if we are not judging by numbers, the question must be asked as to whether this is really civic participation. Douglas Kellner indicates that achieving democracy, even in a minimal sense, requires "greater access to diverse sources of information and participation in social and political processes."[29] While *The Daily Show* is entertaining, what does it mean for over a million Americans to derive their political participation through this program and others like it? Will Hermes in *Spin* noted that "suddenly, even miraculously, it's hip to care about politics."[30] But who is ultimately caring, and is that enough to reenergize a pallid voting base? But then again, what voting base are we talking about? Although many have decried the loss of civic America, this idea of an American public sphere might be just wishful thinking based on some mythical past. As Michael Schudson contends in his article, "Was There Ever a Public Sphere? If so When? Reflections on the American Case," voting rates in America were just as miserable in 1920 as in modern days and even worse during the supposedly golden age of 1790. According to Schudson there was a "golden age of civic participation, but it lasted only from the 1840s to the early part of the twentieth century.[31] Perhaps the real question regards whether anything has substantially changed among young voters since we first began worrying about civic life in the first place. If the young voters of previous generations did not vote with any great regularity, why would we consider it an anomaly that younger voters are not voting in any great numbers to this day? It could be that if *The Daily Show* does have a substantial effect on younger voters, it is not engaging them enough to restore voting levels to the "golden age" of the nineteenth century.

The Daily Show and Serious Civic Discourse

Strangely enough, the place in which both *The Daily Show* and its offspring, *The Colbert Report*, perform especially well, is in the variety of serious chances they provide for the discussion of scholarly and provocative new books. A regular segment, unseen on many late night talk shows, and indeed absent from almost any broadcast outside of NPR and public television (and perhaps *Oprah*), features the regular interviews of authors that Stewart presents. (Colbert does many segments with authors, but these are usually done as Absurdist Theater and rarely performed without tongue planted firmly in cheek—or even occasionally foot planted firmly in mouth.) While it may seem that serious interviews with authors have gone the way of Dick Cavett and David Frost, *The Daily Show* books a wide range of authors, many of whom would find it difficult to find the same kind of exposure and consideration in any other major media platform. Amongst the many heavyweights that Stewart has interviewed in the last two years include Muhammad Yunus, the Bangladeshi Nobel Prize Winner; Vali Nasr, a Middle East expert; Ishmael Beah, the Sierra Leone former child soldier; and many others. Given that this line-up would be impressive for any serious-minded public affairs program, it indicates at least an effort to represent some serious thought amongst the usual levity. Though much consideration has been given to the fact that *Oprah*'s book club can boost the sales of authors such as Cormac McCarthy and William Faulkner, *Oprah* concentrates on fiction (and self help, notwithstanding when the show's host disastrously picked James Frey as a book club author), while *The Daily Show* and *The Colbert Report* often concentrate on weighty tomes about serious topics. As Bossman wrote in the *New York Times*, *The Daily Show* and *The Colbert Report* have "become the most reliable venues for promoting weighty books," according to book publishers.[32]

Despite what one might think, the audience does not seem to tune out these serious discussions, but instead seems to revel in them. The authors' appearances have immensely helped the sales of difficult and serious books. A major reason for this is the lack of any competition for serious discussions of major books on the major networks or other highly-rated cable channels. *Booknotes* on CNN was canceled in 2004, and *The Charlie Rose Show* is not as reliable a venue for featuring authors as it used to be. After being featured on *The Daily Show* the Amazon.com ranking of a book can increase from the upper hundred thousands to the top three hundred, a very respectable increase in sales. Martha Levin of Free Press called *The Daily Show* the "television equivalent of NPR" where "you have a very savvy interested audience who are book buyers, who actually go into bookstores, people who are actually interested in books."[33] While I am not suggesting that by simply promoting books Stewart and his producers are single-handedly changing our culture from a dominant televisual one to one based on literacy, it does seem evident that the serious consideration given to books on politics, government, and civics might help an audience engage in activity outside the parameters of the program. If the increases in sales following an appearance on *The Daily Show* or *The Colbert Report* are any indication, it appears that those who do watch the programs tend to skew towards a more literate audience, and hence are more likely to be of a politically engaged mindset than those who watch only other programs.

Conclusion

In conclusion, it must be queried as to whether programs such as *The Daily Show* and others (such as *The Colbert Report,* Bill Maher's various programs, and the fake news of *Saturday Night Live*'s "Weekend Update") foster genuine political participation or simply create the illusion of participation. Are they funny? Most of the time, yes. Are they relevant? Most of the time, yes. Do they engage in real political issues in a way that carries more substance than most major networks? To a certain extent, yes as well. Does this lead to real involvement or a sense of involvement in younger potential voters that would have existed without the airing of programs such as *The Daily Show*? The answer to this last question is unclear.

Are these programs, as van Zoonen suggests, a way in which entertainment can cultivate real political engagement on a level that has not previously been possible? But then again, before we accept that programs that combine liberal doses of deliberate and calculated entertainment and humor are vehicles for participation, we must ask another question: Should we accept, as Neil Postman indicated, that political participation is cheapened by television and that levels of civic discourse are only possible in a culture defined by the rationality and linearity defined by print culture,[34] and if so, then is it possible for any television program, no matter how politically savvy and intelligent, to foster a real sense of engagement instead of providing passive entertainment?

What is also difficult is that the idea of participation itself is problematic. The term has been used on various levels and with different meanings since at least the time of de Tocqueville; but with so many different ideas and definitions of how to measure real participation, it is difficult to answer the question of what is genuine political participation and how it should be measured. If we are merely to count voters out on the street on election day, we might find that totalitarian counties have the highest levels of political participation, even if the choices are limited or essentially non-existent. And if we are to look at levels of American participation, it seems clear that the most derided forms of political mechanisms, the old "ward" politics, particularly of the Democratic Party in New York City at the turn of the twentieth century, might be seen as a veritable golden age of participation. As Arthur Mann pointed out in his introduction to a revised edition of the classic treatise on political graft, *Plunkitt of Tammany Hall*, the most active voters were not brought to the polls by specific issues and a concern about specific politicians' merits or charisma, but by the ruling Democratic Party machine. To Mann, the proper exchange of influence worked when the voter looked to the district leader for help with political issues and "all he asked for in exchange was your vote."[35] While the idea of political machinery dominance has fallen out of favor, it could be argued that illegal chicanery brought out a steady and far more consistent level of voter turnout than any radio or televised appeal, from FDR's fireside chats to the television commercials of today.

Postman and others have argued that in more literate times, the level of participation was higher; yet it could be argued that the example given above from *Plunkitt* largely signifies that this engagement was based on the specialized needs of immigrant voters who were less aware of the complexities of American political issues. Postman, in his account of the Lincoln and Douglas debates, noted that crowds eagerly stood in fields for hours to cheer their candidate on.[36] Politics served as a form of theater; to Postman, there was a rabid audience for both the entertainment it involved, as well as, it seems, the debate on issues surrounding political campaigns. But do the examples given by Postman and others mean that the mass public was heavily engaged in political displays and engagement, or merely the ardent partisan followers of various candidates? Many even doubt that the form of participation during the "golden age" can be compared to today's idea of involvement. As Michael Schudson explains, golden age politics were "more of a community ritual than an act of individual or group involvement in rational critical discussion."[37] It could be that what Postman argued was involvement was limited to the literate elites, and that literacy rates (which remained very low amongst many immigrant groups, especially, as I have noted in a previous article, nineteenth-century Irish immigrants in New York City, who comprised one of the groups that became heavily involved in ward politics in New York during the "golden age" of civic participation[38]) indicate that class was a dividing factor in the levels of political engagement on display in public.

Was there ever (at least in America) a particularly high level of political participation, particularly amongst younger voters? Perhaps as Michael Schudson ponders, what we need is either a new definition of civic participation, or even more radically, a way to balance both comedy and serious discourse. But Schudson is analyzing a less mediated age; it could also be, as Todd Gitlin notes, "people are pressed to rely on mass media for bearings in an obscure and shifting world."[39] This may mean that political participation and television are intimately connected, even for those who choose *not* to be involved. As Marc Leverette points out in Chapter 10, voter apathy may not be mere apathy, but an equally powerful political act of disengagement from a process seen as corrupt. And as Gitlin adds, "Television has given political discourse and the low involvement viewer access to each other," whereupon, "Those with minimal interest in politics simply opted out of exposure."[40] It could be that some people are unreachable, even through comedy.

Perhaps a show that uses comedy to reach even a million viewers is a way of helping people regain their bearings in a world of noise and confusion. It could also very well be that even though it reaches less people than programs such as *The O'Reilly Factor, The Daily Show*, as Geoffrey Bayam states, "understands the political system ideally to be comprised of individuals engaged in reasoned discussion, a cooperative discourse that seeks to reach a consensual notion of the public good."[41] But the jury remains out as to whether this conversation is actually taking place and to what extent it results in serious discussion of politics and a healthy and vibrant democracy. *The Daily Show* may simply be another way of mocking politics at the expense of real participation. But when Jon Stewart is a lone voice for serious debate in a television landscape that biases the shouting head above the calm call for open debate, perhaps a lone voice *can* be an important start. Maybe instead of questioning whether *The Daily Show* does enough to invite political participation, we should be thankful that Jon Stewart makes a genuine effort. And, in an age in which we are (perhaps) amusing ourselves closer and closer to death, wouldn't it be wonderful if *The Daily Show* helped us amuse ourselves a little bit closer to wakefulness and participation?

Notes

1. Rick Kushman, "Stewart's Crossfire Battle Raises a Valuable Point," *Sacramento Bee*, October 21, 2004, http://ezproxy.library.nyu.2079.universe. document?m=27c2bda91 (accessed March 10, 2007).

2. Jeffery Jones, *Entertaining Politics: New Political Television and Civic Culture* (Lanham, MD: Rowman & Littlefield, 2004). Neil Postman, as will be discussed later, had also made arguments of this nature, although his tone was hardly complimentary.

3. Bruce Fretts, "The News Fakers," *TV Guide*, January 24, 2004, 63.

4. Neil Postman, Neil, *Amusing Ourselves to Death: Public Discourse in the Age of Show Business* (New York: Penguin Books, 1986). While many have dismissed Postman's powerful work as a "jeremiad" or the work of a Luddite, Postman's work is actually a carefully nuanced look at the way in which television has displaced a culture of linearity and thoughtful discourse with the sound bite. The other more recent major work often cited in this category is Robert Putnam, *Bowling Alone: The Collapse and Revival of American Community* (New York: Simon & Schuster, 2001). While Putnam's argument differs from Postman's in many significant ways, the two are sometimes lumped together in terms of their overall argument about the idea of civic involvement and televi-

sion.

5. Postman *Amusing Ourselves*, 87.

6. Jones, *Entertaining Politics*, 8.

7. In particular, this argument has been challenged in many works, but the most cogent argument comes from Liesbet van Zoonen. In her book *Entertaining the Citizen: When Politics and Popular Culture Converge* (Lanham, MD: Rowman & Littlefield, 2005), she argues that although politics and entertainment have become so intertwined, their mixture actually helps to create a symbolic environment that allows greater participation, rather than simply a sense of involvement. The idea that entertainment and politics and popular culture are not compatible may not take into account that people have unique ways of being involved and that championing "serious" discourse as the only entry into political involvement dismisses the majority of ways in which many Americans actually process political involvement.

8. John Colapinto, "The Most Trusted Name in News: How Jon Stewart and *The Daily Show* Made the 'Fake News' a Hit—and more Relevant than the Real Thing," *Rolling Stone*, October 28, 2004, 213.

9. Geoffrey Bayam, "The Daily Show: Discursive Integration and the Reinvention of Political Journalism," *Political Communication* 22: 259-76.

10. Bayam, "Discursive Integration," 262. Although the suggestion of the entertainment talk show might have more to do with camera work and the initial rock music of the opening credits (by Bob Mould) than the actual show itself.

11. Neil Postman and Steve Powers, *How to Watch TV News* (New York: Penguin Books, 1992).

12. Colapinto, "The Most Trusted Name," 213.

13. Bayam "Discursive Integration," 265.

14. Colapinto, "The Most Trusted Name," 213.

15. Bayam, "Discursive Integration," 266.

16. Jaques Steinberg, "The Executive Producer of '*The Daily Show*' and '*The Colbert Report*' is Leaving," New *York Times*, December 2, 2006, www.nytimes.com/2006/12/02/arts/television/02karl.html (accessed December 5, 2006).

17. Dave Itzkoff, "Feeding the Beast on '*The Daily Show*,'" *New York Times*, November 5, 2006, 26(B).

18. van Zoonen, *Entertaining the Citizen*, 4.

19. Brian Long, "Daily Show Viewers are the Best Informed," October 13, 2004, http://www.cnn.com/ 2004/SHOWBIZ/TV/09/28/comedy.politics/index (accessed June 1, 2006). The study goes on to note that viewers of *The Daily Show* are more likely to have detailed knowledge of contemporary politics than not only viewers of Letterman and Leno, but those who watch nightly news broadcasts or read newspapers as well.

20. O'Reilly seemed genuinely indignant when he interviewed Stewart on September 17, 2004. His reaction was priceless.

21. Itzkoff, "Feeding the Beast," 26.

22. John Street, in *Politics and Popular Culture* (Cambridge: Polity Press, 1997), takes an essential look at this intersection. Also John Fiske makes a compelling argument for the importance of popular culture in terms of both everyday life and politics in his *Understanding Popular Culture* (London: Unwin Hyman, 1989). There are also numerous works in cultural studies and popular cultural studies that make the point that the way in which people provide meaning for themselves can in itself provide pleasure and entertainment and that serious discourse does not of itself have to be totally humorless.

23. van Zoonen, *Entertaining the Citizen*, 145.

24. Itzkoff, "Feeding the Beast," 26.

25. Jones, *Entertaining Politics*, 9.

26. Jones, *Entertaining Politics*, 11, 14.

27. Jones, *Entertaining Politics*, 55.

28. Steinberg, "Executive Producer," 2.

29. Douglas Kellner, *Television and the Crisis of Democracy* (Oxford: Westview Press, 1990), 185.

30. Will Hermes, "Life of the Party: Is This the Birth of a New Hipster Political Movement?," *Spin*, October 19, 2004, 100.

31. Michael Schudson, "Was There Ever a Public Sphere? If So When? Reflections of the American Case," in *Habermas and the Public Sphere: Studies in Contemporary German Social Thought*, ed. Craig Calhoun (Cambridge, MA: MIT Press, 1993), 144-63.

32. Julie Bossman, "Serious Book to Peddle? Don't Laugh, Try a Comedy Show," *New York Times*, February 25, 2007, 3 (Weekend sec.).

33. Bossman, "Serious Book," 3.

34. Postman, *Amusing Ourselves*, 29.

35. Arthur Mann, "When Tammany was Supreme," in *Plunkitt of Tammany Hall: A Series of Very Plain Talks on Very Practical Politics*, William Riordan (New York: E. P. Dutton, 1963), xvi-xxix.

36. Postman, *Amusing Ourselves*, 49.

37. Schudson, "Was There Ever," 150.

38. Brian Cogan, "The Irish-American Press as an Agent of Change: The Transformation of the New York Irish 1850-1880," *New York Irish History* 14 (2000): 29-46. The Irish were quickly involved in New York City politics within a few dozen years in the mid-nineteenth century, despite problems in assimilation, such as limited literacy.

39. Todd Gitlin, *The Whole World Is Watching: Mass Media in the Making and Unmaking of the New Left* (Berkley: University of California Press, 1980), 1.

40. Gitlin, *Whole World*, 52.

41. Bayam, "Discursive Integration," 273.

Chapter 5

Lessons in Appealing to the Young Non-Voter: Michael Moore's Slackers Uprising Tour

Michael Grabowski

"Pick nose! Pick butt! Pick Kerry."

Michael Moore's 2004 Slackers Uprising Tour featured these words as its oath. While the phrase does not radiate the presidential campaign aura of "I like Ike" or "It's Morning in America," it seems somehow suitable, given that Moore claimed to be reaching out to one of the hardest-to-motivate populations: politically inactive youth. Moore's Slacker Tour may not have won Kerry the Presidency, but the hastily organized series of events certainly drew the attention of both his supporters and detractors and inspired at least three documentary films.[1] More importantly, the tour brings to mind serious questions regarding political participation and polarization. This chapter examines Moore's rhetoric during the tour, responses to it through blog postings and media coverage, and Moore's own responses to this feedback. Ultimately, the 2004 Slacker Tour complicates the notion of youth mobilization campaigns and redefines political engagement, contributing to an environment that many scholars claim is becoming increasingly polarized[2] and offering implications for future presidential elections.

Beginning with his first feature documentary film, *Roger and Me*, Moore has built a career upon critiquing corporate and government policies of globalization and deregulation. In *Roger and Me*, Moore attempts throughout the film to ask General Motors CEO Roger Smith about the effect of his shutting down the company's plant in Moore's hometown of Flint, Michigan. After the successful commercial release of this film,[3] Moore continued to critique corporate abuses with *TV Nation*, a television program first shown on NBC, then picked up by Fox after NBC cancelled the program. When Fox also cancelled the program, Moore renamed the comedic investigative series *The Awful Truth*, which then aired for two seasons on cable network Bravo (two years after canceling the program, Bravo was purchased by NBC, an irony that sort of supported Moore's warning about corporate consolidation).[4]

Though Moore had highlighted the hypocrisy of politicians in general and the nefarious relationship between politics and corporate money, he had not explicitly attacked a President until the publication of *Stupid White Men*. The book was exceptionally critical of the 2000 presidential campaign, election, post-election, and the corporate interests that Bush serves. Its publisher, Regan Books,[5] withheld its release on its scheduled debut date of October 2, 2001, because it felt that a critical book about Bush was not appropriate in the wake of the terrorist attacks on September 11. Moore and his publisher agreed to delay the book's release and update it to reflect the recent events; but his publisher then asked Moore to be less critical of the President and help pay for the production of the new edition. Incensed by the threat of censorship, Moore, as the keynote speaker at a meeting of New Jersey Citizen Action, spoke about his publisher's demands. A librarian in the audience, Ann Sparanese, notified other librarians through e-mail listervs about this prior restraint and, together, they led a public outcry that resulted in the publishing of the uncensored text.[6] The post-9/11 environment that quashed political dissent riled Moore; the Bush administration's subsequent campaign for the war in Iraq, along with the granting of no-bid contracts to Halliburton, Vice President Dick Cheney's former employer, motivated Moore to make *Fahrenheit 9/11*, a documentary/polemic that Moore publicly hoped would help to convince voters to oust Bush in the 2004 election.

It was within this atmosphere, as polls showed Bush and Democratic challenger John Kerry in a extremely close race, that Moore announced in the early fall of 2004 that he would travel to various college campuses toward the end of the 2004 presidential campaign to register young people to vote. Combining celebrity status and comic appeals, Moore made his pitch through his self-entitled, "Slackers Uprising Tour." The expressed purpose of the tour was to register young people to vote; but the tour itself became an entertainment-driven event that promoted Michael Moore himself as much as his particular cause. Like other youth voter mobilization efforts, the Slacker Tour combined celebrity appearances, music, and vigorous speeches, but differed from these other movements in its positioning of itself as an "anti-effort," claiming to appeal to youth who had no interest in voting. An amalgamation of humor, prizes, and self-effacing identification seemed to paint Moore as an older brother who was asking his younger siblings for a big favor, one that he expected they would not do, but also one that would really help him, and them, out of a bad situation. Slackers, indeed, but they could change the world just this once.

Slackers Uniting

The very setup of this youth mobilization campaign seemed to be antithetical to any other organized effort that promoted the election of a particular candidate, party, or even a non-partisan civic goal of high voter turnout. In his book, *The Good Citizen*, Michael Schudson explores changes in how American society has construed and solicited political participation. He writes, "Eighteenth-century American political authority was rule by gentlemen; the nineteenth century brought rule by numbers, majorities of associated men organized in parties; and twentieth-century American politics is rule by everyone, and no one, all at once."[7] Likewise, Robert Putnam explores the history of civic participation in American society in search of the cause of its decline. He discusses key groups that have helped to influence participation, including religious affiliations, workplace associations, and informal social networks, and personal factors such as educational levels and age. Ultimately, Putnam places much of the blame on the rising use of media technologies, which, he claims, have served to isolate people. He concludes by suggesting a challenge "to restore American community for the twenty-first century through both collective and individual initiative."[8] Moore, in appealing to a post-twentieth-century America, seemed to rise to this challenge. He moved beyond traditional participation power brokers, such as political parties, mass media, or political campaigns themselves, and personalized the voter drive by seeking out others who are supposedly just like him: slackers.

Moore labeled his campaign a "Slacker Uprising Tour," but alternatively referred to it simply as a "Slacker Tour" and promoted the tour with the slogan "Slackers Unite." The campaign's title and promotion painted the tour as a type of last-minute, unpolished, do-it-yourself appeal, one that could attract young people accosted and numbed by well-planned advertising campaigns vetted by focus groups and test marketing. By using the slacker label, Moore identified with a group of young people who may reject traditional mobilization campaigns. As advertisers struggled to cut through promotional clutter by placing ads in unusual venues,[9] integrating advertising and program content,[10] and producing viral advertising campaigns intended to be distributed by consumers rather than advertisers themselves,[11] any attempt to mobilize young voters risked having its message lost in the din of saturation marketing. To make itself heard, the Slacker Tour, in a sense, was an anti-campaign.

Despite his slacker stance, Moore actively appealed to a demographic group that typically has not exercised its right to vote. Pollsters have mapped out in great detail how youth voter participation has declined over the past three decades.[12] In response to this trend, organizations like Rock the Vote have built substantial networking infrastructures and media campaigns to inspire young people to become more active in the political process. Voter registration drives, rallies, petition campaigns, and issues information sessions have become a staple on college campuses during the presidential campaign season.[13] These traditional mobilization campaigns were likely to reach those who initially had little vested political power but were interested in participating in the political process if they were shown a path to effective participation.[14]

Rather than demonstrating the civic responsibility of voting or engaging those who are more likely to become involved in the political process, Moore distinguished his from the other campaigns by appealing to those voters he thought were least likely to vote. These youth, according to Moore, have dropped out of the political process because they feel as though they have no voice in this process, in effect creating a self-fulfilling prophecy. Contributing to their lack of interest is the tendency for youth to perceive that the mass media coverage of the political campaigns is relatively less engaging than other mediated and interpersonal communication, including entertainment culture, their own schoolwork, and other participatory and passive diversions. Moore writes: "As 'non-voters' you have been written off. But if only a few thousand of you vote, it could make all the difference. You literally hold all the power in your hands. That's even cooler than holding a TV remote."[15] As discussed below, whether this group of non-voters is the one he reached is questionable.

By labeling this series of events a "slacker tour," Moore attempted to inject some humor into the serious youth voter mobilization campaign, and to position his campaign as opposing those other more established mobilization efforts like Rock the Vote. He was demonstrating to these young people that, by voting, their identity as anti-authoritarian individuals who reject the hypocrisy of establishment politics is not threatened. Moore assured audiences that he was not asking them to commit to a lifestyle change or philosophical shift, but merely participate in a single event that may pose as a momentary inconvenience. A message he posted on his website during the tour read:

> I tell these slackers that I understand and respect why they think politicians are not worth the bother. I tell them that I may have been the original slacker, and that I do not want them to change their slacker ways. Keep sleeping 'til noon! Keep drinking beer! Stay on the sofa and watch as much TV as possible! But, please, just for me, on 11/2, I want you to leave the house and give voting a try—just this once.[16]

Moore promoted the tour through his website, mass e-mails, and traditional media outlets. Over the course of the tour, Moore sent out e-mail messages to people who had signed up to receive updates about the tour, *Fahrenheit 9/11*, and the upcoming election. His website and blog, www.michaelmoore.com, showed pictures from many stops, and included short commentaries on both the tour and the presidential campaign. Throughout the tour, Moore promoted an atmosphere of victory, maintaining that, despite the apathy voters felt toward Kerry, Bush must and would be voted out of office. In Seattle, he chanted: "Two more weeks. Two more weeks. It will be all over."[17]

The stops on the tour were structured as a form of entertainment. Showing clips from his films and parodies of President Bush's campaign commercials, Moore made videos an integral part of these live events. Though audiences purchased tickets to attend a communal gathering not unlike a concert, the video screen was omnipresent. Some events included short comic videos produced specifically to entertain the crowd while reinforcing the message of electoral regime change. Deleted scenes from *Fahrenheit 9/11* added a sense of exclusivity to the entertainment, allowing fans to consume content as yet unavailable to others.

At many venues, Moore arranged for available celebrities to appear with him, adding an incentive for students to attend the event and news media to cover it. At the University of Southern California, Rage Against the Machine's Tom Morello sang anti-Bush folk songs, while Linda Ronstadt, who had been ridiculed for dedicating her song "Desperado" to Moore at a performance in Las Vegas, made an appearance at the tour's stop in Tucson. Though they did not perform, members of REM joined Moore onstage in Cincinnati,[18] and Gloria Steinem and the music group Anti-Flag joined Moore at the University of South Florida.[19] Much like that at any other live entertainment, every effort was made to create a festive atmosphere. In Jacksonville, Florida, Moore enthusiastically told students, "This is the first rally we've had that's actually been a party."[20]

While Moore's mobilization campaign resembled other youth get-out-the-vote campaigns by bringing in performers and other celebrities to attract young people, Moore's purpose throughout the tour was to commit enough students to vote to guarantee that Bush would be voted out of office. Teaching these students the virtues of political engagement was a secondary motivation, if it was present at all. The overall tone of his tour was temporary and finite: he wanted people to vote just that one time. He expressed little interest in creating life-long voters, and in fact, talked with audiences about his own general lack of interest in politicians and political campaigns.

Covering the Slackers

News coverage of the Slacker Tour demonstrates Herbert Gans'[21] criticism of political balance in journalism. He notes that mainstream news coverage tends to identify dominant or extreme positions of an issue and represents these positions as binary conflicts. In *Dirty Politics*, Kathleen Hall Jamieson explores how news media, using preexisting schema to cover political campaigns, emphasize drama and stereotypes in their coverage.[22] Both authors discuss the power and limitations of journalists in their attempts to cover political campaigns. The Slacker Tour presented a new challenge for reporters, as Moore himself was not running for office. Indeed, news coverage of the tour followed the traditional framing of political campaigns models as citied by Gans and Jamieson (among others) by presenting Moore as a proxy candidate for Kerry, without necessarily the consent of the Kerry campaign.

Network newscasts did not broadcast a single story about the tour,[23] but local newspaper and television reports did mention it, particularly when Moore prepared to visit each city. Local television coverage tended to mention the tour either on the day of the event, using file footage of Moore, or the day after, showing footage from the event in that city. Longer television news stories strained to balance their portrayal of the tour, interviewing both supporters and critics of Moore.[24] Local coverage of the Slacker Tour intensified on October 6, when the Michigan Republican Party asked several prosecutors throughout the state to file charges against Moore for attempting to buy votes with his offer of clean underwear and Ramen noodles.[25] Beautifully demonstrating the blending of politics, news, and entertainment, the entertainment and celebrity news syndicated program *Inside Edition* included the tour in its October 5 broadcast as a related story to its coverage of the release of *Fahrenheit 9/11* on DVD.

Newspaper reporting of the tour provided more in-depth coverage, though these stories also attempted to achieve balance by highlighting an equal number of supporters and detractors in each story. Major newspapers, unlike network television newscasts, covered stops on the tour, especially when controversies over the tour's funding erupted. The *Washington Post* focused on George Mason University's decision to cancel the tour's stop at that school after officials received complaints regarding using state money to fund Moore's appearance.[26] The *San Diego Union-Tribune* referenced the controversy of another cancellation when it wrote that Moore attracted a crowd of ten thousand at his stop there, "attracting ten times the audience he would have had if he had not been banned from Cal State San Marcos."[27] Although it led with a description of how Moore adapted the tour during his stop in Minneapolis by conducting a live play-by-play commentary of the presidential debate, the *Minneapolis Star Tribune* included within its coverage questions posed during a news conference that speculated how much profit the tour might generate for Moore, as well as his angry reply to the mention of a Minnesotan's documentary response titled, *Michael Moore Hates America.*[28] The *Seattle Times* mentioned the Michigan controversy in its coverage of the tour's stop at Seattle's Key Arena, as well as the protesters outside the venue. Illustrating the spectacle of personal conflict throughout news coverage of the tour, reporter Tyrone Beason wrote, "Moore wears his detractors' hostility like one of his signature baseball caps."[29]

Given that Moore attempted to make each stop of the tour on or near a college campus, student newspapers dutifully covered the event and controversy surrounding it. Most student publications attempted, sometimes painfully, to provide balanced coverage. Usually, after describing the event, student newspapers concluded each article with short quotes from one student supporter and one detractor at the event. For example, Ohio University's *The Post Online* reported that a political science major who planned to vote for Bush "says Moore's films are fictitious and the director's extreme views inspired a lot of tension during the event," while a student who planned to vote for Kerry described the event as "entertaining" and the statistics Moore cited as "particularly striking."[30] Focusing on student protesters who interrupted Moore several times with chants of "four more years," the *Arizona Daily Wildcat* framed its story as a question of the effectiveness of protests: "Some students on campus have defended the Moore protesters' actions as a demonstration of free speech, while others criticized them for being disruptive." In the story, each quote supporting the protesters was paired with another that condemned them.[31] Even when no students were interviewed for a story, college publications sought balance. A short story in the University of Michigan's *The University Record* accompanied the piece about the tour with two photos, one of Moore onstage, and another of Bush supporters protesting Moore's visit.[32]

Whether they appeared within professional or student publications, stories about the tour tended to focus on students with strong political opinions, both supporting and protesting Moore and his tour. One supporter, a high school student who wore a "Michael's Hot" T-shirt, told a reporter for the *San Diego Union-Tribune*: "He's my hero. . . . He's one of the few people who can stand up to Bush, and what he says goes around the world."[33] At Moore's stop in Pittsburgh, another student stated, "I'm here because I'm sick and tired of Michael Moore. . . . I have seen *Fahrenheit 9/11*. Quite frankly, he lied the whole way through it."[34]

Jamieson argues that news media cover candidates by grouping and identifying them in a way that discourages political discourse. She writes, "Visceral identifications and appositions that are the raw stuff of campaigns simplify the world into Manichean dualities and, in their use of the evocative and the visceral, merchandise our hopes and fears. At the same time, they offer ways of seeing that occlude rather than clarify our vision."[35] Though Moore was not a candidate, the coverage he received followed that of a candidate because the news media did not have another frame in which to construct the narrative of the tour. Yet this framing of supporters and detractors that is typical of campaign coverage in general did not allow for more in-depth discussion of the issues that had motivated him to work to oust Bush from office. Then again, Moore himself, throughout his celebrity career, has played into this framing by giving news media the sound bites and actions to cover.

Partying without Parties

Though Michael Moore positioned his tour as a simple and last-minute appeal to young people to exercise their right to vote, it is no real secret that Moore had a political agenda for the tour. His goal, which he overtly stated at each stop, was to oust President Bush from office. Moore engaged in a type of voter participation that scholars describe as a benefit approach. According to Steven J. Rosenstone and John Mark Hansen, "Each form of citizen participation in politics offers a unique mix of collective and selective benefits. Citizens find each combination of benefits more or less worthwhile depending on their interests, preferences, identifications, and beliefs."[36] Thus, citizens are more likely to participate in the political process if they desire a particular political outcome. On its surface, then, the tour would appear to be more effective than a traditional voter mobilization campaign, but at the risk of jeopardizing its claim to non-partisanship.

In fact, under pressure from conservative critics, several colleges and universities prohibited their funds from being used to bring Moore to their schools, and a few barred the event from taking place on campus whatsoever. Alumni from several schools threatened to cut off donations after learning that Moore would speak at their alma maters.[37] Alan Merten, the president of George Mason University, called the school's invitation to Moore "a mistake" and cancelled the tour's stop at the school after conservative state lawmakers in Virginia openly criticized the use of state funds to pay for the visit.[38] Republican Virginia State senator Mark Obenshain inferred that Moore was nothing more than a con man stealing tuition dollars from the university, saying, "Michael Moore is trying to make money wherever he can; he's trying to see if anyone is foolhardy enough to pay his $35,000."[39] Moore responded by demanding his fee and offering it to fund a scholarship to promote free expression at the school. A private coalition paid Moore's fee to attend the University of Minnesota after school officials received pressure from the school's College Republicans to withhold student fees for the event. Countering the perception that he was profiting from the tour, Moore asserted that the entire fee was used to pay the university rent for the college's arena.[40] In San Diego, California State University at San Marcos' president Karen Haynes rescinded the University's invitation to host the tour. She claimed that the tour was a partisan activity, prohibiting the university from using state funds to pay for the event. After the school's student government raised private funds to bring the tour to a location off-campus, Moore announced that he would use the fee to create a "hell-raiser" scholarship for the school that would be awarded to student dissenters.[41]

To be sure, despite his non-partisan claims for the tour, Moore openly advocated for voters to elect Kerry. In Pittsburgh, for example, Moore admitted to Carnegie Mellon University students, "I'm hoping the majority of you vote for John Kerry."[42] However, Republican attempts to dismiss Moore as a partisan profiteer detracts from the fact that both the tour and Moore operated independently of the Democratic Party. Certainly, those who supported Bush's reelection campaign had no reason to differentiate Moore from the campaign of the Democratic opposition, as they were both threats to their goal. Yet, to group the Slacker Tour with other Democratic efforts misses a key development during the 2004 campaign. Like MoveOn.org and many other 527 groups, Moore was not a member of or worked with the Party whose candidate he supported. These independent groups shared the goal of removing Bush from office, but their methods for doing so could not, by law, be coordinated.

Not that Moore had any desire to coordinate his tour with the Kerry campaign. Rather, Moore passionately stated his position that he was not at all happy with the Democratic candidate. Declaring himself an Independent voter, Moore confessed in Florida that Kerry was not his perfect choice for President, but mobilizing voters to choose him was the most likely way of unseating Bush.[43] At the University of Oregon, Moore conceded that the Democratic candidates "aren't everything we want them to be," but he insisted, "We're facing a nightmare here and we've got to remove George W. Bush from the White House."[44] Moore used slightly different language at Syracuse University to describe his position when he stated, "Bush and Kerry both suck; that's why I'm voting for John Kerry."[45]

As someone who had endorsed Ralph Nader and the Green Party in the 2000 election, Moore felt that Nader had betrayed him and the American people by breaking his promise to avoid campaigning in swing states. Throughout the tour, Moore expressed his concern that Nader would again split the vote in 2004, and he appealed to Nader supporters to vote for Kerry.[46] At the University of South Florida, Moore stopped security officials from ejecting two women holding a Nader sign and pleaded with them, "Don't vote for Ralph this year. . . . Just join with us in removing George Bush from the White House this year. Just this once. Just this once, please."[47] In New Mexico, he congratulated Nader supporters for moving the Democratic Party toward more liberal positions, but then added, "Declare victory and go home."[48]

Moore's own declarations during the tour demonstrate that he was more interested in mobilizing a strategic vote to remove the neoconservative wing of the Republican Party from power as opposed to supporting the platform of Kerry and the Democratic Party. His insistence that slackers needed to step up this one time only, without having to participate in the activities of any political party, further promoted the atomization of the public sphere, where the most visible option for improving conditions is through the election of the least objectionable representatives. Facing the persistent problem of non-participation, Moore advocated an attempt to rally youth to perform this one joint political act before retreating again to their individual pursuits.

Moore himself viewed his push as promoting the democratic ideal of political participation. During the tour, he made several references to the cyclical problem of non-participation: representatives will address the concerns of only those who vote, further discouraging non-voters from participating. He advised the audience in Pittsburgh: "The 50 percent who don't vote generally are not the wealthy and the powerful. They are the working class, the single mothers and young people, and this is your election. . . . You can make a difference."[49] Without asking too much, Moore reasoned, he could persuade slackers to perform a single act that would help their politically active peers achieve what they could not otherwise. Yet, despite his desire to motivate the working class, on his tour, Moore targeted college campuses, where youth were more likely to participate. A Harvard study notes that, though youth voter turnout did increase significantly during the 2004 election, the gap in participation between college and non-college educated youth continued to widen, further disenfranchising less-educated youth.[50] As many studies cite personal contact with potential voters as the best predictor for voting, an event like the Slacker Tour offered an opportunity for that contact to happen. However, working-class youth will benefit from contact only if an outreach effort extends beyond college campuses to their own social networks. Though political party leaders recognize the need to connect with youth, their increasing focus on immediate election turnout over long-term party building activities, as well as their perception of the difficulty in motivating this group, discourages them from working harder to increase young participation in their parties.[51] Ignored by both parties and political candidates, disenfranchised young people may have had little reason to respond to Moore's appeal "to leave the house and give voting a try."

Slackers Blog Back

Moore exerted a significant amount of time and energy touring the country to motivate a strong youth voter turnout. In past elections, audiences had little opportunity, other than responding to polls and actually voting, to offer feedback to mobilization campaigns. In 2004, however, both political parties and traditional media outlets recognized the increasingly important role of bloggers and other forms of online participation. Howard Dean's run for the Democratic nomination created a new campaign model that incorporated organizing and fund-raising via the Internet.[52] Bloggers became a new, alternative source of information at both the Democratic and Republican Party conventions,[53] and blogs competed with broadcast and cable television network news coverage on election night.[54]

Like they did for the rest of the 2004 Presidential campaign, bloggers of all varieties of influence reported and commented on the Slacker Tour. Many of these bloggers, unlike traditional media coverage, eschewed any attempt at political balance in their posts, instead either cheering Moore on or attacking him for any of a number of offenses, though some simply reported their experience of observing or participating in one of the tour's stops. These bloggers had, and have, no specific geographic center, whether from Salt Lake City, Ames, Jacksonville, or Philadelphia.

Just as Moore publicized his tour online, several anti-Moore websites posted comments that derided him and his tour. Many of these sites emerged to refute claims Moore made in *Fahrenheit 9/11* and his earlier film, *Bowling for Columbine*. It is immediately obvious from their sites' titles, like moorelies.com and mooreexposed.com, as well as their depictions of Moore,[55] that some bloggers sought to discredit Moore at every opportunity. A few sites, like michaelmoorehatesamerica.com and shootingmichaelmoore.com, promoted books or films that attacked Moore. One site critical of Moore, moorewatch.com, often reposted articles and e-mails with commentary. For instance, reprinting Moore's defiant response to Michigan Republicans who wanted to arrest Moore for buying votes, moorewatch.com prefaced the post with: "Moore seems to be playing the 'it's just a joke, it's just underwear' card. The law says 'anything of value' Mr. Moore. Even if it's of value only to a slacker."[56] A post in moorelies.com quoted a *Tucson Citizen* article about a book signing by David T. Hardy, a Moore critic. The article used the opportunity to critique Moore as a profiteer:

Hardy is scheduled by the Associated Students of the University of Arizona to speak at UA at 7 p.m. Oct. 7, though the author said he has not been told where the talk will take place. It will be an unpaid appearance. Moore is scheduled by ASUA to speak at 7 p.m. Oct. 11 at McKale Center. ASUA will pay Moore $27,500 to appear.[57]

Moorelies.com also posted e-mails from readers. Nick D., college student from Iowa State University, reported on Moore's stop there:

> He showed up one hour and forty-five minutes late, during wich [sic] about one thousand students walked out. Before he would go on stage a lady came out and asked what was left of the crowd to fill the seats behind hime [sic] so in the video clips and photos it looked like a full crowd. I thought this was kind of bogus since he was just going to build this into another one of his lies. . . . Oh well, just thought id [sic] let you in on this—I was really apalled [sic] at the camera tricks he uses to make it look like he has a LOT of supporters.[58]

The casual tone of these posts, as well as direct addresses to Moore in some of them, was typical of these blogs and infers a conversation among a small group that mirrors interpersonal, face-to-face communication.

Certainly, anti-Moore websites were only a part of the online communication about Moore and the Slacker Tour. Numerous bloggers wrote about the tour with enthusiasm, many of whom identified themselves as liberals or supporters of the Kerry campaign. For example, Connie Wilson, the daughter of a Democratic County Treasurer whose blog is affiliated with Leftyblogs.com, wrote about the same Slacker Tour stop in Iowa from a different perspective:

> Michael Moore had some difficulty getting to Iowa State University in Ames on Sunday, October 17, to continue his Slacker Tour 2004. His plane was delayed in Wisconsin; then, the airport in Ames wouldn't let the plane land (he had to drive in from Des Moines). Once inside Hilton Coliseum, Moore hit the ground running and kicked b-tt . . . two things that are hard to do simultaneously. . . . The faithful stayed and were not disappointed.[59]

Wilson continued to provide a thorough description of the event, including a moment when hecklers interrupted Moore:

> There were detractors when Moore finally appeared onstage. In the up-

per balcony to his right, young male Bush supporters, testosterone rag-
ing, were heckling Moore. . . . Michael sent someone up to the vocal
boys with enlistment paperwork for Iraq, telling them to sign on the
dotted line NOW. He added, "Ain't no weapons of mass destruction
back at your fraternity house." The Republican faithful slunk away,
never to be seen again.[60]

Like Wilson, many bloggers who supported Kerry wrote more detailed
posts than those attacking Moore. Many of these blogs sought to propa-
gate messages Moore articulated during the tour, including statistics that
reflected negatively on Bush and his campaign.

Unlike conservative blogs, those from the left were more varied in
their tone. Some took issue with the fact that Moore supported a candidate who had not campaigned against the Iraq War, while others accused
Moore of becoming yet another corporate profit-seeker. Thus, Moore
endured attacks from both the right and the left. Even bloggers who professed their support for Moore did not shrink from criticizing the manner
in which he conducted the tour. Despite acknowledging having a good
time at the tour's stop in Camden, NJ, a blogger for *The Long Cut* wrote:

Last night's lecture was a case of preaching to the converted. That's the
biggest problem. Worse, Moore is not a very good preacher. Moore is
very funny but he's all over the place, rarely looking at his notes and
often screaming obscenity-laced anti-Bush slogans. We who have no
problem proudly calling ourselves liberals eat this stuff up. But it does-
n't attract those on the fence.[61]

This post acknowledges that the tour, in fact, functioned more as a rally
for the political base than an attempt to persuade undecided voters.

The comments that readers posted to blogs tended to reinforce the
posts themselves, suggesting that readers of these blogs supported the
same political point of view as the bloggers. Moorewatch.com, one of the
more prominent anti-Moore websites, attracted many vitriolic comments.
Commenting on the report of Michigan Republicans asking prosecutors
to charge Moore with buying votes, a video store clerk identified as
sustinererex wrote: "Moore just makes me more and more sick. Ugh and
today I have to go to work and rent F9/11 to people. Man do I hope they
issue a warrant for his arrest, I would laugh myself silly." Others more
eloquently called Moore to task for hypocrisy and corruption of the
democratic system, like Camkrisand:

He adopts tactics right out of a political machine in a big city . . . and then expects people to be hoodwinked by his feeble attempts to downplay what he really has been doing. Here is a prime example of bending and breaking election laws from the man who has been crying foul for three and a half years about the "stolen" election in 2000. I hope he has stuck his neck out too far with this stunt. But he'll try to play the martyr for his righteous cause and claim the laws designed to protect the citizen from corruption in elections are wrong if that means that they can't go out and motivate the slackers to vote.

Though some websites disabled the ability to comment on posts, many bloggers on them quoted e-mails they had received from friends and other readers. A Washington Redskins fan, judging from his posts, who professed he would be voting for Kerry, posted an e-mail from a friend he identified as EL:

> So (we) went downtown (N-ville) last night to Michael Moore's Tennessee stop on his Slacker Uprising Tour. I was a little anxious to see what the crowd, if any, may look like. Along with the pink-haired obvious green party guys and gals, there were almost fifteen thousand mad as hell Southern Democrats that are sick of W's sh*t. It was awe-inspiring and another piece of evidence that the pendulum that's been over to the right for so long is swinging our way.[62]

Whether they were from a liberal or conservative perspective, these comments never suggested that the posters had been swayed after attending the tour. Overwhelmingly, conservative posters characterized the tour negatively, dismissing Moore's comments as lies or distortions, offering evidence to refute facts Moore stated during the tour, or caricaturing the tour and Moore's supporters as a liberal delusion. Though some liberal posters critiqued Moore's style of rhetoric or conciliatory appeals to vote for Kerry over a third-party candidate, no one suggested that the event convinced them to change their vote.

Bloggers did not accept Moore's surface claim that the Slacker Tour was a non-partisan mobilization campaign. If anything, the tour functioned to help hold the liberal fringe of the Democratic Party, even as it also energized his opponents. Because the tour seemed to draw out those who were either already supporters or vocal critics, it is questionable whether the tour mobilized the apathetic young audience Moore claimed he was trying to reach.

Indeed, the blogosphere just as likely dissipated, rather than propagated, the message of the tour. Unlike traditional media, which often adhere to the journalistic principle of the summary lead, many bloggers seldom stayed on message. Chuck Pennacchio, a Philadelphian who attended the tour's stop at Temple University, focused his post more on the evils of the ticket sales and distribution company Ticketmaster than the Bush administration:

> (We) wanted very much to go and show our support and see our fellow twenty-somethings joined together in deposing W. So I clicked through to the Ticketmaster site to buy some tix. They are $5-$15. I was looking at the $15 seats for us. With stupid surcharges and "convenience fees" the total was like $48. That is fucking insane. I'd think that Moore would've been able to work something out and not have to go through the horrible Ticketmaster, but he did and ti [sic] sucks. So, then I thought, how about I just take a trip up to the box office at Temple and buy my ass some tickets? But the box office has some asinine hours: 10am-5pm. How the hell are non-Temple students going to get tickets? Arg. I think we may just head up there as soon as I get out of work and see if there are any extra tickets available, in the $5 range, I guess. I refuse to let Ticketmaster get the best of me.[63]

Finally, many bloggers simply recorded the event as another aside in their lives, presented in all the unordered glory of this non-linear medium. Laurie Mann, from Mount Lebanon, Pennsylvania, wrote about the tour's stop in Columbus, Ohio, but seemed to be more interested in the actor who played Aragorn in the film version of the *Lord of the Rings* trilogy and appeared with Moore at the event:

> I am a huge fan of Viggo's, and a moderate fan of Michael's. I thought about seeing Michael when he was on tour in Pittsburgh a few weeks back, but he was in town during one of my trips out of town.

Within the same post, Mann drifted from the Slacker Tour to her work on the Kerry campaign and football:

> After spending yesterday just hanging out, resting, and staying pretty glued to the Internet, today I was awake enough to rake my front yard and then go work for Kerry/Edwards. I leafleted a friendly Squirrell Hill neighborhood with Tracey, a woman who lives in DC but who's spending the next few days helping out in Pittsburgh. Then we walked from headquarters (with a third person, whose name was Cliff, I think) across town to Heinz field for a little visibility before the Steeler game. The weather was perfect for the walk, and we spent some time waving to the crowd. Now, I'm home watching the Patroits [sic] playing the Steelers. Talk about your mixed feelings! I like the Steelers, but the Pa-

triots are having a great year.[64]

These posts illustrate the problem that mobilization campaigns face in controlling their message within a participatory, hyperlinked environment. While campaigns may seek to harness the power of viral messages that spread throughout the Internet, there is no guarantee that those messages will reproduce without mutations, digressions, or inversions. Furthermore, it becomes difficult to target a message to a narrow audience without that message leaking to other, unintended audiences, likely creating unintended outcomes along the way. The emergence of social networking and video sharing websites, linked seamlessly with blogs, only exasperates the difficulty.

Political Entertainment or Entertaining Politics?

A question many readers of this chapter may have is: Was the Slacker Tour a success? Though quantitative methods, such as exit polling and surveys, may attempt to isolate variables to determine whether more young people voted for Kerry after learning about or attending the tour, an answer to this question is nearly, if not certainly, impossible to obtain. Another question may elicit a more fruitful answer: What was the purpose of the Slacker Tour? The answer to the latter question may make the former question irrelevant, as the tour pursued many goals, and achieved only some of them. A primary purpose of the tour was to remove Bush from office, and the surest way to do that, in Moore's view, was to mobilize votes for Kerry. However, a closer examination of the tour and responses to it suggests that the tour's specific purposes became muddled, partly as a result of the participants' desire to generate interest within a media-saturated environment. In the end, one may question whether the tour sought more to register young people or generate news coverage about itself. How did Moore use this event as a live opportunity to connect with potential youth voters, and how did he use mediated communication to promote the tour and its purpose? As a media event, how much of this tour was a political rally, a civic mobilization effort, or an entertaining pseudo-event?

Over four decades ago, the historian and former Librarian of Congress Daniel Boorstin defined and critiqued the purpose of the pseudo-event in his book *The Image*. For Boorstin, the main characteristics of a pseudo-event are that they are planned, created for the purpose of cover-

age, and "its relation to the underlying reality of the situation is ambiguous."[65] Though Moore hastily announced and planned the tour, adding
dates and venues throughout the month before the election, his Slacker
Tour was integrated into the publicity campaign for his film *Fahrenheit
9/11*. In addition to showcasing clips and deleted scenes from the film at
each event, Moore attracted audiences who had seen and responded to
the film. Furthermore, traditional news accounts and blogs often mentioned both the tour and film within the same articles or posts. In this
light, it is possible to view the tour as an extension of the film itself, a
type of interactive, recursive, multi-media making. Although Moore often stated his goal passionately and sincerely in using the tour to achieve
a political end, it was hard to distinguish where the entertaining promotion ended and the voter registration drive began.

Then again, *Fahrenheit 9/11* and its promotional campaign can easily be perceived as voter mobilization tools themselves. Moore encouraged audiences to copy the film and pass it along to others, and created a
"Fahrenheit for Free" day, which involved him encouraging video stores
to offer to rent the film to patrons for free on October 26, a week before
the election.[66] Yet, even considering *Fahrenheit 9/11* and the Slacker
Tour as an integrated media campaign to achieve a political end, one can
conclude that the entire enterprise could not escape the pattern it set as a
form of entertainment designed to generate press coverage.

Modeling a political mobilization campaign as a form of entertainment may allow the campaign to more easily integrate with an entertainment-driven, celebrity-saturated culture, but it also creates a problem
by constraining the form that the campaign takes. Entertaining images
displace substantive discussion, and emotion-laden slogans and sound
bites masquerade as rational arguments. One consequence of Moore's
appeal was the reversal of political patronage. Rather than political
bosses promising favors to constituents in exchange for money and
votes, Moore basically asked constituents to vote as a favor to him. Trading his celebrity status and entertainment for votes, Moore offered up a
show to attract the politically uninterested. He parodied vote-buying by
giving away clean underwear and Ramen noodles to anyone who registered to vote. Moore then used Republican accusations of vote buying as
a form of entertainment itself. In the Moore campaign, political participation is reduced to an entertaining consumer act.

Four years later, entertainment is becoming an even more inherent
component of Presidential politics. Hillary Clinton, competing for the
Democratic nomination, created a video parody of *The Sopranos* season

finale that starred herself and her husband, the former President. Its intent was to drive viewers to her campaign website, where they could discover another entertaining enterprise, a vote for her official campaign song. The performance and vote contained no substantive political discussion, yet they dominated media coverage for several days and circulated on YouTube, the popular video-sharing website. The generation of viral videos and other forms of user control offer an unprecedented level of voter participation in political campaigns, but to what effect? If the power of social networking is used to simply promote more pseudo-events like the Slacker Tour, both political and non-partisan voter mobilization campaigns risk reducing political participation to discrete consumer acts, ultimately stripping constituents of political power. Simultaneously, Moore and his Slacker Tour illuminate the phenomenon of entertainment becoming increasingly politicized. The 2008 Presidential candidates will likely have to consider celebrity and entertainment culture as a space to make political stands. The future suggests an environment in which slackers and activists, as well as entertainment and civic action, are impossible to differentiate. As Moore often stated during his tour: "Sleep until noon, drink beer and vote."

Notes

1. *This Divided State*, DVD, directed by Steven Greenstreet (New York: The Disinformation Company, 2005) documents the controversy over inviting Moore's Slacker Uprising Tour to Utah Valley State College, and *Manufacturing Dissent*, DVD, directed by Rick Caine and Debbie Melnyk (Toronto: Persistence of Vision Productions, 2007) follows Moore during the Slacker Tour, *Roger & Me*-styled. At this writing, Moore has completed editing his own documentary, *The Great '04 Slacker Uprising*, but is holding back its commercial release so that it does not interfere with the summer 2007 release and promotion of *Sicko*, his documentary on the health care crisis. He has already shown a work-in-progress of *The Great '04 Slacker Uprising* at the 2006 Toronto International Film Festival (Thom Powers, "An Evening with Michael Moore," *Toronto International Film Festival*, 2006, http://www.e.bell.ca/ filmfest/2006/films_schedules/films_description.asp id=355 (accessed January 25, 2007), and confirmed to me that he will make this documentary available after the release of *Sicko*.

2. The Pew Research Center concludes that "partisan differences are deeper now than at any point since 1987." Andrew Kohut, "Political Polarization: Reality, Not Myth," *Washington Post*, December 10, 2003, 30(A). The

114 *Michael Grabowski*

increasing political party polarization in the House of Representatives is documented in Jeffrey M. Stonecash, Mark D. Brewer, and Mack D. Mariani, *Diverging Parties: Realignment, Social Change, and Political Participation* (Boulder, CO: Westview Press, 2002). Tom Rosenstiel argues that polarization has contributed to a mistrust of campaign coverage in a news environment he describes as "an ecosystem in distress," in Tom Rosenstiel, "Political Polling and the New Media Culture: A Case of More Being Less," *Public Opinion Quarterly* 69, no. 5 (2005): 698-715. An overview of the limits of political communication's influence on increasingly polarized voter attitudes can be found in Chapter 7 of William H. Flanigan and Nancy H. Zingale, *Political Behavior of the American Electorate*, eleventh ed. (Washington, D.C.: CQ Press, 2005).

3. *Roger & Me* was sold to Warner Bros. for $3 million, the biggest deal for a documentary at the time. Moore claims that *Roger & Me* earned more than $25 million at the box office, but his producer's representative for that film, John Pierson, believes the revenues to be half that. Despite this discrepancy, *Roger & Me* was the highest-grossing documentary film up to that time. See John Pierson, *Spike, Mike, Slackers & Dykes* (New York: Miramax Books, 1995).

4. Allison Romano and John M. Higgins, "Bravo! NBC Has a Cable Net," *Broadcasting & Cable*, November 11, 2002, 12.

5. Regan Books was an imprint of HarpersCollins, which is owned by Rupert Murdoch's News Corporation. Five years after Regan attempted to censor Moore, Murdoch fired Regan Books head Judith Regan and closed down the imprint over her planned publication of *If I Did It*, O. J. Simpson's controversial account of how he would have killed his ex-wife. See Josh Getlin and Scott Timberg, "HarperCollins Axes Regan Imprint: ReganBooks' Century City Office Is to Close," *Los Angeles Times*, January 18, 2007, 1(C).

6. Ann Sparanese, "Activist Librarianship: Heritage or Heresy?" *Progressive Librarian* 22 (Summer 2003), http://libr.org/pl/22_Sparanese.html (accessed January 25, 2007).

7. Michael Schudson, *The Good Citizen: A History of American Civic Life* (Cambridge, MA: Harvard University Press, 1998), 7.

8. Robert D. Putnam, *Bowling Alone: The Collapse and Revival of American Community* (New York: Simon & Schuster, 2000), 403.

9. That same year, Sony and Major League Baseball reached an agreement to advertise the film *Spiderman 2* by placing ads on the bases at selected fields. After an outcry from fans, the ads were placed merely on the on-deck circles. See Gary Silverman and Peter Thal Larsen, "Diamond not an Advertiser's Best Friend: Plans to Advertise a Movie on Baseball Fields Have Outraged the Public," *Financial Times*, May 8, 2004, 7.

10. Suzanne Vranica, "Product-placement Sheds Its Cozy Trappings," *Wall Street Journal*, September 23, 2004, 1(B).

11. Eric Pfanner, "Viral Ads: Marketing Tightrope on Advertising," *Inter-*

national Herald Tribune, May 3, 2004, 9.

12. A good summary of this trend, and its reversal in the 2004 election, can be found within the Center for Information and Research on Civic Learning and Engagement's website: http://www.civicyouth.org/quick/youth_voting.htm.

13. Evelyn Nieves, "College-Age Voters Feel Tug of Recruiters," *Washington Post*, September 26, 2004, 11(A).

14. Writing about the apathy of young people during the 2000 election, Julia Spiker et al. discuss how young people have a low sense of political power but feel that participation is important. The authors conclude that to get young people more involved in the political process, they need to be provided with more information about candidates and more contacts with politicians. See Julia A. Spiker, Yang Lin, and Scott D. Wells, "The Voice of Young Citizens: A Study of Political Malaise in Campaign 2000," in *The Millennium Election: Communication in the 2000 Campaign*, ed. Lynda Lee Kaid et al. (Lanham, MD: Rowman & Littlefield, 2003), 254.

15. Michael Moore, "Michael Moore on Tour: Slackers of the World, Unite!" *Michaelmoore.com*, September 25, 2004, http://www.michaelmoore.com/words/message/index.php?messageDate=2004-09-25 (accessed January 25, 2007).

16. Michael Moore, "Republicans, Out of Ideas, Ask Prosecutors to Arrest Michael Moore," *Michaelmoore.com*, October 6, 2004, http://www.michaelmoore.com/words/message/index.php?messageDate=2004-10-06 (accessed January 25, 2007).

17. Tyrone Beason, "Moore Urges Voter Turnout," *Seattle Times*, October 20, 2004, 3(B).

18. Denise Smith Amos, "Filmmaker Moore Brings Anti-GOP Show to Town," *Cincinnati Enquirer*, October 28, 2004, http://www.enquirer.com/editions/2004/10/28/loc_michaelmoore28.html (accessed January 25, 2007).

19. "Past 'Slacker Uprising Tour' Appearances," *Michaelmoore.com*, http://www.michaelmoore.com/words/mikeinthenews/index.php?id=170 (accessed January 25, 2007).

20. Tiani Jones, "Michael Moore's 'Slacker Tour' Visits Jacksonville to Rally Voters," *First Coast News*, in Michael Moore, *Michaemoore.com*, October 3, 2004, http://www.michaelmoore.com/words/mikeinthenews/index/php?id=185 (accessed January 25, 2007).

21. Herbert Gans, *Deciding What's News: A Study of CBS Evening News, NBC Nightly News, Newsweek and Time* (New York: Random House, 1979).

22. Kathleen Hall Jamieson, *Dirty Politics: Deception, Distraction, and Democracy* (New York: Oxford University Press, 1992).

23. A search of the Vanderbilt Television News Archive, which records news programs from the broadcast and cable news networks, produces no news stories of the tour. The only mention of it can be found during one commercial, broadcast on October 9, 2004, over the Nashville cable system's local feed of CNN, advertising the tour's stop at Vanderbilt University.

24. For example, Katie Nielsen, *News 4 Arkansas Weekend Edition*, KARK-TV, October 3, 2004; Amy Speropoulos, *NewsChannel 3*, WREG-TV, October 8, 2004; Joe Fryer, *KARE 11 News*, KARE-TV, October 8, 2004; *Channel 2 News*, KATU-TV, October 19, 2004; *Eyewitness News Daybreak*, KSL-TV, October 21, 2004; Angie Lau, *Good Morning Cleveland*, WEWS-TV, October 25, 2004; Cyndy McGrath, *Fox 53 News*, WPGH-TV, October 26, 2004.

25. *Action News Midday*, WXYZ-TV, October 6, 2004; *Fox 8 News at 6*, WJW-TV, October 6, 2004; *Fox 2 News at 6*, WJBK-TV, October 6, 2004.

26. Amy Argetsinger and Leef Smith, "Moore's GMU Booking Called 'a Mistake,'" *Washington Post*, October 2, 2004, 5(B).

27. "'Slacker' Tour Attracts Thousands," *San Diego Union-Tribune*, October 17, 2004, 1(B).

28. Jeff Strickler, "Moore Calls the Political Plays," *Star Tribune*, October 9, 2004, 1(B).

29. Beason, "Moore Urges."

30. Kyle Kondik, "Filmmaker Addresses Voters," *The Post Online*, November 1, 2004, http://thepost.baker.ohiou.edu/articles/2004/11/01/news/10903.html (accessed January 25, 2007).

31. Natasha Bhuyan, "Political Visits Stir Student Protests," *Arizona Daily Wildcat*, in *University Wire*, October 21, 2004.

32. "Photos: Michael Moor's 'Slacker Uprising Tour' Hits Hill Auditorium," *The University Record Online*, October 8, 2004, http://www.umich.edu/~urecord/0405/Oct04_04/11.shtml (accessed January 25, 2007).

33. Lisa Petrillo and Michael Burge, "'Slacker' Tour Plays Fairgrounds," *San Diego Union-Tribune*, October 13, 2004, 1(B).

34. Bill Zlatos, "Moore Visit Raises Questions over Cost of Controversy," *Pittsburgh Tribune Review*, October 27, 2004.

35. Jamieson, *Dirty Politics*, 101.

36. Steven J. Rosenstone and John Mark Hansen, *Mobilization, Participation, and Democracy in America* (New York: Macmillan, 1993), 17-18.

37. Associated Press, "Iowa State Alumni Upset over Filmmaker Michael Moore's Campus Appearance," *WCF Courier*, http://www.wcfcourier.com/articles/2005/02/20/news/breaking_news/doc416a8f7c09b92209720364.txt (accessed January 25, 2007).

38. Argetsinger and Smith, "Moore's GMU Booking."

39. Johanna Cluver, "GMU Cancels Moore Visit," *The Cavalier Daily*, October 5, 2004, http://www.cavalierdaily.com/CVArticle.asp?ID=20829&pid=1194 (accessed January 25, 2007).

40. Strickler, "Moore Calls."

41. Petrillo and Burge, "'Slacker' Tour."

42. L.A. Johnson, "Filmmaker Moore Regales CMU Crowd," *Pittsburgh Post-Gazette*, October 27, 2004, 14(A).

43. Kathy Steele and Mark Holan, "Bush, Kerry Allies Hit Area," *Tampa*

Tribune, October 4, 2004, 1.

44. Parker Howell, "Moore Bush-Bashing," *Oregon Daily Emerald,* October 19, 2004, http://media.www.dailyemerald.com/media/storage/paper859/news/ 2004/10/19/News/Moore.BushBashing-1969117.shtml (accessed January 25, 2007).

45. Dana Moran, "Filmmaker Rehashes Politics in Dome Speech," *Daily Orange*, September 23, 2004, http://media.www.dailyorange.com/media/storage/paper522/news/2004/09/23/Pulp/Filmmaker.Rehashes.Politics.In.Dome.Speech-728133.shtml (accessed January 25, 2007).

46. Matthew Chavez, "Moore Calls on Slackers to Vote," *Daily Lobo*, October 11, 2004, http://media.www.dailylobo.com/media/storage/paper344/news/ 2004/10/11/News/Moore.Calls.On.Slackers.To.Vote-749055.shtml   (accessed January 25, 2007).

47. Kevin Graham, "Filmmaker Makes Plea to Students for Kerry," *St. Petersburg Times*, October 4, 2004, http://www.sptimes.com/2004/10/ 04/Tampabay/Filmmaker_makes_plea_.shtml (accessed January 25, 2007).

48. Chavez, "Moore Calls on Slackers."

49. L.A. Johnson, "Filmmaker Moore."

50. Thomas E. Patterson, *Young Voters and the 2004 Election* (Boston: Joan Shorenstein Center on the Press, Politics, and Public Policy, 2005), http://www.ksg.harvard.edu/presspol/vanishvoter/Releases/Vanishing_Voter_ Final_Report_2004_Election.pdf (accessed January 25, 2007).

51. Daniel M. Shea, "Throwing a Better Party: Local Mobilizing Institutions and the Youth Vote," *Circle Working Paper 13*, April 2004, http://www.civicyouth.org/PopUps/WorkingPapers/WP13shea.pdf   (accessed January 25, 2007).

52. Maura Keefe, "Dean's True Legacy," *Washington Post*, February 19, 2004, 23(A).

53. Matthew Klam, "Fear and Laptops on the Campaign Trail," *New York Times Magazine,* September 26, 2004, 43.

54. Greg Gatlin, "Early Returns Show Bloggers Taking Lead," *Boston Herald*, November 3, 2004, 37.

55. Many sites exaggerate Moore's weight, and show him in an angry pose with his mouth open, either eating or shouting uncontrollably. Moorewach.com depicts Moore with flapping jowls, and mooreexposed.com uses a photograph of Moore with his lips puckered and shows the cover of the book *Michael Moore Is a Big Fat Stupid White Man*, which depicts Moore as eating the dome of the U.S. Capitol building.

56. Paratrooper, "Moore Responds," *Moorewatch.com*, October 6, 2004, http://www.moorewatch.com/index.php/moore_responds/ (accessed January 25, 2007). It is interesting to note that, despite the numerous posts on this site regarding *Fahrenheit 9/11* and the 2004 election, relatively few mentioned the Slacker Tour itself.

57. Paul L. Allen, "Anti-Moore Author to Sign Book," *Tucson Citizen*,

September 30, 2004, http://www.tucsoncitizen.com/intucson/living/ 093004a4_
hardy, in Jason, "If You're in Tucson: Meet David Hardy Tonight!" *Moore-
lies.com,* September 30, 2004, http://moorelies.com/2004/09/30/tucsonmeet-
david/ (accessed January 25, 2007).

58. Jason, "Slackers Continue to Rise Up—against Moore," *Moore-
lies.com,* October 29, 2004, http://moorelies.com/2004/10/29/slackersuprise/
(accessed January 25, 2007).

59. Connie Wilson, "Michael Moore's 2004 Slacker Tour Visits Ames,"
Blog for Iowa, October 17, 2004, http://www.blogforiowa.com/blog/Connie
WilsonMisc/_archives/2004/10/20/162898.html (accessed January 25, 2007).

60. Wilson, "Michael Moore's 2004."

61. "Presidental [sic] Ticket," *The Long Cut,* September 21, 2004,
http://frymax.typepad.com/longcut/2004/09/presidental_tic.html (accessed January 25, 2007).

62. "Report from the Field," *ETJB,* October 11, 2004, http://etjb.
blogspot.com/2004_10_01_archive.html#109754156234221552 (accessed January 25, 2007).

63. Chuck Pennacchio, "Michael Moore: Slacker Uprising Tour in Philly,"
Philly, October 19, 2004, http://dragonballyee.blogs.com/philly/2004/10/
michael_moore_s.html (accessed January 25, 2007).

64. Laurie Mann, "Viggo Mortensen Joined Michael Moore's Slacker Tour
in Columbus Ohio on 10/30!" *No Longer the World's Slowest Blog,* October 31,
2004, http://dpsinfo.com/blog/2004_10_01_lastmonth.html (accessed January
25, 2007).

65. Daniel J. Boorstin, *The Image: A Guide to Pseudo-Events in America*
(New York: Atheneum, 1987), 11.

66. "Moore Launches 'Fahrenheit for Free' Campaign in Madison," *WISC-
TV,* October 18, 2004, http://www.channel3000.com/news/3829157/detail.html
(accessed January 25, 2007).

Chapter 6

Screening Abu Ghraib, Reelecting the President: The Symbolic Politics of Torture in Fiction Film and Television, 2003-2005

Marco Calavita

Young people, many of you are looking to make a difference, to challenge the status quo. Well, the way Dr. Martin Luther King opposed authority was revolutionary. And I think we can do better. He accomplished so much by refusing to engage in violence. Doesn't it stand to reason that we can accomplish so much more by refusing to engage in anything at all? . . . Young America, it is time to go beyond passive resistance to pure passiveness. And you're off to a great start. In almost four years of war, there have been no rallies, there have been no actions in the street. . . . But you can do less. So get up out of your chair right now, and lie down on your sofa.
—*The Colbert Report*, 1/15/07

[Brigadier General Patrick Finnegan] has for a number of years taught a course on the laws of war to West Point seniors—cadets who would soon be commanders in the battlefields of Iraq and Afghanistan. He always tries, he said, to get his students to sort out not just what is legal but what is right. However, it had become increasingly hard to convince some cadets that America had to respect the rule of law and human rights, even when terrorists did not. One reason for the growing resistance, he suggested, was misperceptions spread by *24*, which was exceptionally popular with his students. As he told me, "The kids see it, and say, 'If torture is wrong, what about *24*?'"
—Jane Mayer, "Whatever It Takes" *The New Yorker*, 2/19/07

When George W. Bush won the 2004 Presidential Election, beating John Kerry to gain a second term in the White House, political analysts and pundits had their ready-made explanations—including the notion that "morality" and "values" had driven Americans to reelect the President. In retrospect, however, it seems indisputable that the primary explanation of Bush's victory over Kerry was how many Americans regarded each as leaders, and specifically as prosecutors of the "War on Terror."

Despite a life of great privilege and enabling, despite revelations of his spotty National Guard record during the Vietnam War, and despite evidence of serious intelligence agency, military, and Administration deceptions and failures in his first term, Bush was still regarded by most Americans as strong, decisive, and effective, a Real Man intent on protecting America from another 9/11 by any means necessary. Kerry, on the other hand, was regarded by many Americans as a soft, elitist, intellectual flip-flopper, one whose preferred vacation sport—surfing in whichever direction the wind takes him—seemed all-too-revealing. (This despite Kerry's actual record as a war hero.)[1] Bush critics trotted out all manner of logical, fact-based arguments against reelection, those cited above among them.[2] But while some of these attacks may have dented Bush's armor, and his standing, to these critics' great confusion and consternation he was still the preferred President, Commander-in-Chief, and Terror Warrior of most American voters on November 2, 2004. In keeping with longstanding voting trends toward young adults supporting Democratic presidential candidates, the only major age group that did not support Bush over Kerry was eighteen- to twenty-nine-year-olds, 45 percent of whom voted for Bush.[3]

There are many possible explanations for Bush's reelection amidst the "War on Terror," but for a scholar of mass media and popular culture, a particularly intriguing avenue of thought concerns what Murray Edelman called the "symbolic uses of politics." For Edelman, the tangible stuff of politics can at times pale in significance compared to the *symbolic meanings of politics that are used and understood by the public.*[4] Take the issue of torture, the focus of this chapter. To a Bush critic, the scandals that arose in 2004 involving Abu Ghraib and to a lesser extent Guantanamo Bay were proof positive that President Bush was not fit for the office. For the ostensible purpose of information gathering, Americans acting on direct orders and (more often) tacit guidance from the Bush Administration and the Pentagon were perpetrating forced nudity, sexual humiliation, sleep deprivation, stress positions, starvation, water-boarding, denial of medical care, or worse against "terror captives," all in defiance of international and American law.[5]

And yet, if we examine more closely the potential *symbolic meanings* of the torture revelations that year—especially for Americans paying only scattershot attention to mainstream news media that were superficially critical of the scandal but still solidly on board with America's "War on Terror"[6]—they may suggest something altogether different. Given the election results and the majority of Americans who continued throughout 2004 to proclaim their faith in Bush as Commander-in-Chief and Terror Warrior, and however counterintuitive it may seem, it is *possible* that these revelations may have actually benefited Bush in 2004, or at the very least may not have damaged him to the extent one might assume.

No particular symbolic meaning of any kind was inevitable, of course. Depending on the nature of the audience/public (especially its partisan preferences), and on exactly how news of the torture scandals/policies was reported and framed, the symbolic meanings of America's engagement in torture as part of the "War on Terror" could vary considerably. That said, reasonable generalizations can be made about what *predominant* symbolic meanings of torture may have been activated in 2004, and how. Despite oft-repeated assumptions about America's intense ideological divide in 2004, most Americans did not have perfectly clear and fixed attitudes about President Bush, about exactly how the "War on Terror" should be waged, or about how—if at all—torture should be used in that war (if they even knew what constituted torture).[7]

Given the combustible and controversial nature of such issues in the post-September 11 era, and in an election year, it might be an exaggeration to characterize Americans' views on these subjects as, in the words of Philip Converse, "non-attitudes." But political science research has demonstrated for decades that Americans' attitudes and opinions on many issues can be highly unstable and dependent in large part on contextual factors, including the nature of a people's shared myths and predispositions, and more specifically of the current information environment.[8]

Most political communication and political psychology research interprets the term "information environment" to mean the diffused output of news and public affairs media.[9] But in a nation so immersed in varied entertainment media, and given the growing awareness of the political implications of such forms, a broader view that includes our *cultural* environment is vitally necessary. Most specifically, examining the representations of torture in fictional film and television can give us a better sense not only of what predominant symbolic meanings of torture were most likely to be activated in that context, but also, of course, what these films and shows were saying to their audiences relatively *directly*.

The year 2004 was a high-water mark for the discussion and popular analysis of entertainment media's political/ideological messages and meanings—of films like *The Passion of the Christ, Fahrenheit 9/11*, and *The Day After Tomorrow* in particular—as well as for the focus on the political implications of youth-oriented entertainment like *The Daily Show* and *South Park*, as other chapters in this book make clear.[10] But on both counts, the significance of entertainment media representations of torture in 2004 and its aftermath went largely unnoticed, despite the prevalence of such representations in American fiction film and television produced between 2003 and 2005—the majority of which had youth audiences as their targeted (and actual) market demographic.[11] The other element most of these televised and cinematic representations of torture during this period had in common was their essential characterization of torture: it's an admittedly ugly business, but in these unprecedented times it's also *an extra-legal necessity* if we want justice, security, and vengeance against the evil that surrounds us. This representation of torture, which fed quite naturally into the symbolic politics of the Bush agenda during this same period, can be seen in varied forms in *Man on Fire* (2004), *Kill Bill* (2004), *Saw* (2004), *The Punisher* (2004), *Sin City* (2005), *The Devil's Rejects* (2005), *Lost* (2004), *24* (2003-2005), and, paradoxically, *The Passion of the Christ* (2004).

I will begin by discussing the historical context of the post-1960s (and post-9/11) era in which 2004's eighteen- to twenty-nine-year-old young adults were born and came of age, and in particular the "lawless justice" films and shows of the 1970s and since. These entertainment products simultaneously emerged from and fed a decades-long conservative backlash against a social construction of crime and, to a lesser extent, against America's "Vietnam Syndrome." In other words, I will be arguing that these films and shows had a constitutive relationship with the times in which they were made, and further that they are the ideological, myth-making ancestors of the 2003-2005 film and television torture representations. I then turn to readings of the specific films and shows listed above, all but one of which (*The Passion of the Christ*) was predominantly geared toward young adults and depicted torture as an understandable, necessary, and effective method of achieving justice, security, and vengeance. I conclude by first considering counterexamples and counterarguments to my analysis, and then speculating about the possible political implications and effects of these films and shows in 2004 and beyond, for their young adult audiences in particular. One of the possible influences may at first glance seem counterintuitive—that young adults, who voted in greater numbers for Kerry than Bush, were yet more likely to support and vote for Bush than they would have been otherwise had they not been immersed in cinematic and televised torture. In this sense, ideological messages can translate into real world practices at the polls.

Conservative Backlash and "Lawless Justice" Film and Television

Americans who were eighteen to twenty-nine years of age during the 2004 election year were born between 1975 and 1986. In addition to being the exact period of fear, panic, and Othering that Philip Jenkins has referred to as the "decade of nightmares"—a time when the more liberal political values of the 1960s changed into those of the 1980s and since[12]—those years were also, not coincidentally, a prime stretch for television and especially film representations of vigilantism, revenge, and lawless justice in general. These products (and shapers) of post-1960s backlash conservatism began in earnest with the immensely popular 1970-1971 cinematic triumvirate of *Joe* (1970), *The French Connection* (1971), and *Dirty Harry* (1971), and have continued mostly unabated throughout the entire life-spans of today's young adults.[13] Such diverse films as *Walking Tall* (1973), *Death Wish* (1974), *Taxi Driver* (1976), *The Exterminator* (1980), *An Eye for an Eye* (1981), *The Star Chamber* (1983), *Vigilante* (1983), *Cobra* (1986), *The Untouchables* (1987), *Falling Down* (1993), *Ransom* (1996), and *In the Bedroom* (2001) all follow a similar lawless justice script. In these films the criminals are typically the Other, carrying out decontextualized acts of degradation and violence against defenseless members of civilized society, White women and children worst of all. When our White male heroes look to the law for justice—they are themselves sometimes members of law enforcement—they find it at best ill-equipped for the job and at worst siding with the criminals rather than the victims. This forces the good guys, as a matter of common sense, to go beyond the law in order to rid society of this menace, achieve justice, and have their vengeance.

This 1975-1986 "decade of nightmares," and specifically the years 1983-1986, also produced a war film subgenre with similarities to the lawless justice films. In these films, which include *Uncommon Valor* (1983), *Missing in Action* (1984), *Rambo: First Blood, Pt. II* (1985), and *Iron Eagle* (1986)—the last three of which, like many popular lawless justice films, spawned sequels—too many wimps and bureaucrats in the military have ruined things for the real warriors, who must take matters into their own hands when fellow soldiers or loved ones are taken captive by our dreaded enemies.[14] These warriors are decided underdogs but their desire for justice and vengeance, and their improvised, highly individualistic approach to warfare, carries them through. Without going through proper channels, without sticking to the rules, and by shooting first and asking questions later, these men *get the job done*. In the "Return to Vietnam" films in particular, these men also get *payback* for what was (ostensibly) done to them, and for the "Vietnam Syndrome" of weakness and defeatism with which America has apparently been saddled. The illogic of *America* wanting revenge for a war that *it* pursued with such ferocity, and justice for a cadre of live POWs that likely *did not exist* by the 1980s, was not nearly as important as the restorative symbolic power of Rambo's exploits.[15]

On television, meanwhile, representations of justice (and vengeance) also went through significant changes in the post-1960s era. As Elayne Rapping has observed, coexisting with popular cop shows such as *Dragnet* (1952-1970), *Ironside* (1967-1975), and *Hawaii Five-O* (1968-1980) from the early 1960s to mid-1970s were many shows about (often socially conscious) defense attorneys, among them *Perry Mason* (1957-1966), *The Law and Mr. Jones* (1960-1962), *The Defenders* (1961-1965), *Judd for the Defense* (1967-1969), *The Lawyers* (1969-1972), *Storefront Lawyers* (1970-1971), and *Owen Marshall* (1971-1974). But by the late 1970s such defense attorney shows had virtually disappeared, as private detective shows, paramilitary action shows, cop shows, and shows about criminal prosecutors continued to thrive (the last two types especially in the 1990s and beyond).[16] For instance, the number of these types of shows on network television fall schedules between 1979 and 1984 rose from fifteen to twenty-one, while the number that made the top twenty-five in the ratings rose from three in 1979 to ten in 1984. In addition, the heroes of these crime shows often had little in common with by-the-book types like Joe Friday from *Dragnet*, even aside from the fact that so many of them were not official agents of the law, and so were not bound by its strictures. *Eischied* (1979-1983), *Walking Tall* (1981), *Today's FBI* (1981-1982), *Airwolf* (1984-1986), *Miami Vice* (1984-1989), and *Hunter* (1984-1991) were just some of the shows during this period in which laws needed to be massaged or broken to punish the bad guys. (The following year promptly saw the premiere of *The Equalizer* [1985-1989], which was exactly what it sounds like.) During this same five-year span, 1979-1984, there were no longer any shows about defense attorneys on network television.

These films and shows did not emerge from a vacuum, of course. They were directly connected to the social realities of the 1970s and 1980s (and since), and even more so to the predominant myths and discourses about crime in the post-1960s era of backlash conservatism. Violent crime in particular was and is a real and terrible social problem (although it has declined significantly since the early 1990s). Relatedly, the simultaneous decay of urban America, faltering American economy, budget cuts, and prominent moments of public unrest and protest—some of it sparked by the first war that America would more or less *lose*— understandably gave many Americans the sense that the country was emasculated and out of control.[17] Looking to the criminal justice system for law and order, many saw crime-fighters rendered ostensibly impotent or worse by the (Warren) Supreme Court's expansion of defendants' and prisoners' rights.[18]

Still, those actualities and attendant developments did not dictate, a priori, how Americans would come to talk about and portray crime, in the process defining what crime is, where crime comes from, who commits crime and why, and most significantly, how to respond to it. (Much the same could be said about terrorism in the post-9/11 era.) This was the stuff of ideology-laden myths and discourses, which could be found in: the political rhetoric of conservative politicians and pundits (including presidential candidate George Wallace and Presidents Nixon and Reagan); the nascent "Victim's Rights" movement; news media biases, preoccupations, and narrative devices, especially those of the crime-heavy local television newscasts that sprouted up in the early 1970s[19]; and in a growing list of extant popular films and TV shows like *Dirty Harry, Death Wish, Rambo, Hunter,* and *The Equalizer.*

In other words, these lawless justice films and shows were mutually embedded in the realities, and even more so the myths and discourses, of the post-1960s era in which today's young adults have been born and come of age—just as the torture films and shows of 2003-2005 have been mutually embedded in the realities, myths, and discourses of the post-9/11 era.

Torture as Lawless Justice in Fiction Film and Television, 2003-2005

Although many films (and shows) represented torture as necessary and effective between 2003 and 2005, including *The Punisher* (2004), *Kill Bill* (2004), and *Sin City* (2005), the revenge thriller *Man on Fire* (2004) manages to stand apart. Directed by Tony Scott and starring Denzel Washington as a bodyguard who scorches Mexico City looking for the kidnappers and murderers of the nine-year-old American girl he was hired to protect, it debuted in American movie theaters on April 21, just days before the Abu Ghraib torture scandal broke. Despite the painful irony of that timing, few if any serious examinations have been undertaken of *Man on Fire*'s agenda and its eerie parallels with the cultural-political context of 2004.

John Creasy (Washington) is a washed-up and haunted alcoholic, a former Special-Ops killer whose old friend Rayburn (Christopher Walken) helps him find work protecting Pita (Dakota Fanning). The film's first third is devoted to the platonic love that develops between Creasy and the preternaturally cute (and very White) Pita. She awakens his soul and inspires him to stop drinking; he protects her, coaches her to success as a swimmer, and becomes the father figure her self-absorbed Mexican stepfather has failed to be. But, with tragic inevitability, and despite Creasy's valiant efforts, Pita is taken by the crooked cops and other scum from "La Hermandad," a brotherhood of organized crime specializing in kidnapping. Shot several times and left for dead, Creasy awakens days later to discover that the ransom exchange for Pita was botched, and that she was murdered. Its revenge story and representations of torture don't kick in until this point—fully half-way through the film—but *Man on Fire* makes up for lost time.

With weapons provided by Rayburn, drips of information provided by journalist Mariana (Rachel Ticotin) and A.F.I. Chief Manzano (Giancarlo Giannini), and further spurred by Pita's heartbroken American mother (Radha Mitchell), Creasy becomes a driven, systematic, one-man wrecking crew, a Warrior. His trail of torture and murder through the Mexico City underworld begins with Jorge (Mario Zaragoza), the crooked cop who drove the kidnappers' car. Killing two birds with one stone, Creasy tortures this man both for information and for revenge. Stripped to his underwear in the driver's seat of his car, Jorge's hands are duct-taped to the steering wheel—the better for Creasy to cut off his fingers while interrogating him, then use the car's cigarette lighter to stop the bleeding. After Creasy learns all there is to know he promptly kills Jorge with a shot to the head, then turns him and his car into a spectacularly fiery wreck. This is the film's first object lesson in that staple of so many lawless justice films of the last thirty-five years, the absolute necessity of going beyond the law if you truly want justice (and vengeance). As Rayburn later explains to A.F.I. Chief Manzano: "He'll deliver more justice in a weekend than ten years of your courts and tribunals. Just stay out of his way."

Creasy goes on to torture and kill other members of La Hermandad—most imaginatively, in one instance, by stripping a man down, tying him to a car bumper, shoving an explosive charge up his anus, and then questioning him as seconds tick off the clock timer. (The man explodes soon enough.) Eventually, Creasy reaches the brother and wife of the kidnapping ringleader, and is then put in phone contact with "The Voice" himself, Daniel. When Daniel is not forthcoming over the phone, Creasy shotguns his brother's hand off and threatens to kill the whole family. Daniel finally caves, as they all have, and gives Creasy some shocking news: if Creasy will spare his family's life and turn them over along with himself, Daniel will produce Pita, who was never actually murdered. She is still alive, and okay. Creasy is floored by this news, consents to the deal, and goes off to meet his maker—he was dying of his earlier wounds anyway—while Pita tearfully reunites with her thankful mother. That same day, apparently inspired by Creasy, the previously by-the-book Manzano finds and kills Daniel, in cold blood.

This bears repeating: the supposed murder of Pita, the sad stimulus to Creasy's rampage, *never actually happened*. His bloody trail of torture and murderous revenge was predicated on a lie (although of course he didn't know that). Given this fact, *Man on Fire*'s parallels with the contemporaneous Abu Ghraib torture scandal become even more distinct. Just as Creasy tortures and kills to avenge a death which never took place, the U.S. went to war in Iraq based on lies and miscalculations about the existence of WMD, spreading democracy, and Iraq's role in 9/11—and then tortured (and in some cases killed) countless detainees who turned out *not* to be insurgents or terrorists. Such acts are egregious enough, but a perhaps even more revealing and disquieting parallel is what happens in the aftermath of the truth being revealed. Are those responsible overcome with regret, or anger, or shame, for having perpetrated such acts based on misinformation? Does *Man on Fire*, or do the political architects of American military and intelligence policy, pause to consider the mistakes made and wonder what they/we have become? Of course not.[20] Creasy is a haunted man and dies at the end of *Man on Fire*, and the actual individuals who tortured detainees at Abu Ghraib may very well be haunted as well, but in a broader sense neither that film nor mainstream American political culture grapples seriously with the implications not simply of torture, but of *torturing innocent men* (although in *Man on Fire* the kidnappers are guilty of other crimes). Failing to do so suggests that this is, in the grand scheme of things, not a cause for concern, especially if they are foreigners of color. As the sayings go: War isn't pretty, you can't make an omelet without breaking some eggs, and men have to do what they have to do.

What of women? In the lone example from all these films and TV shows of a *female* main character doing the torturing and killing, the vengeance-seeking "Bride" returned in Quentin Tarantino's *Kill Bill: Vol. II* (2004)—just five days before *Man on Fire* was released in that same, very busy, month of April 2004. Introduced in the previous year's *Kill Bill: Vol. I*, the Bride (a.k.a. Beatrix Kiddo) was, like John Creasy, a former assassin before a child (in this case her unborn child) turns her life around. But, as was the (apparent) case with Creasy, the light of Beatrix's life is taken away from her, and Beatrix is left for dead. She proceeds to recover, track down those responsible for her unborn child's death, and do whatever's necessary to get her extra-legal revenge and justice. The trail will be a bloody one, including dozens of dead villains and others with eyes gouged out or lost limbs, but Beatrix eventually arrives at her ultimate target: Bill. Then, as in *Man on Fire*, she too learns that the death that (partially) inspired her rampage did not take place after all—her child is alive and well, living with Bill. Too busy for soul-searching at that point, both Beatrix and the film itself have to carry on with the inevitable killing of Bill and the happy reunion of Beatrix and her daughter. As in *Man on Fire*, the slate is (mostly) wiped clean, and the dead and dismembered are forgotten.

Opening on the very same April day as *Kill Bill: Vol. II* was *The Punisher* (2004), another film depicting torture and murder as extra-legal vengeance and justice. Based on the comic book of the same name, *The Punisher* in question is Frank Castle (Thomas Jane), a former Delta Force specialist and current FBI undercover officer who is the lone survivor of a murderous attack on his beloved family orchestrated by

Howard Saint (John Travolta), a powerful gangster. His family gone, and his body shattered, Castle begins a long road toward physical recovery and revenge and justice for the loss of his family. Castle has spent his whole life till this point observing the dictates of the law, but he comes to realize—quite appropriately, this and other films and TV shows imply—that the law is not an effective vehicle for justice, even less so for vengeance, and that it can in fact put you at a disadvantage in a battle against evil forces who think nothing of fighting dirtily, criminally, immorally. So, like Creasy and Beatrix, Castle puts all his skills to use in a masterful plan to kill off the guilty parties one by one, gathering information along the way, until he arrives at Saint. Castle tricks Saint into killing both his wife and best friend, reveals that fact to him, and then ties him to the bumper of a car and has him dragged around a parking lot before a series of exploding parked cars (!) eventually kill him—though not before he has suffered through some intense pain, of course. That, apparently, is appropriate punishment.

The month before *The Punisher* was released in theaters—along with *Kill Bill: Vol. II* and *Man on Fire*—another film based on a comic book went into production. Like the three films discussed above, *Sin City* (2005) was geared predominantly toward the teen and young adult demographic, and presented torture (and murder) matter-of-factly as a vehicle for information-gathering, revenge, and justice—at least when used by a good guy. In *Sin City* torture is utilized so much it's almost a hobby, especially for the sadistic child molesters and cannibals who make up the worst of the film's villains. Among the ostensible good guys, though, the true master of torture is Marv (Mickey Rourke), a hulking palooka who meets the woman of his dreams one night, sleeps with her, and then wakes to find her dead in bed beside him. As with all the other films already discussed, Marv is himself wronged and abused, but the real stimulus for his journey to vengeance and justice is the loss of a (preferably young, White, female) loved one. Barely escaping hordes of cops who think he's the culprit, Marv quickly sets off to find and punish those responsible for killing "my Goldie."

Befitting its origins in Frank Miller's violent pulp-noir comic book, *Sin City* is a dark film of over-the-top extremes, and Marv is no exception. Sporting plenty of scars, a huge, ugly mug, and muscles upon muscles, he freely admits in his good-natured voice-over that he's going to Hell in a hand-basket. But given the universe of the film, the cruel frame-up perpetrated against him, and in particular the heinous forces arrayed against all the decent folk of Basin City, the audience is clearly being encouraged to cheer Marv on, regardless of his methods. And Marv's methods, we come to learn, are torturing anyone he thinks might be even tangentially involved and/or have information to give up. Marv will shoot and wound men as he interrogates them, he'll relentlessly stuff them down a (non-flushed) toilet during questioning, and he'll drag their faces on the street as he drives his car at high speeds, waiting for them to talk. Luckily, as Marv says of one dirtbag, "Conley talks. They *all* talk." The implication of Marv's methods (and their results) is obvious; only guilty people who know something get tortured (and killed), and the torture always works. (Marv confesses to his three most recent torture-murders and his overall torture modus operandi when he visits a corrupt, sadistic priest—just before killing him, too.) When Marv eventually finds Goldie's killer, the beyond-creepy Kevin (Elijah Wood), he ties him to a tree, cuts off all his limbs, and, for good measure, feeds him to a rabid dog while he's still alive.

Although topping the sadism on display in *Sin City* is a tall feat, three other films during this period give it a strong run for its money—*Saw* (2004), *The Devil's Rejects* (2005), and *The Passion of the Christ* (2004). Released in theaters four days before the 2004 election, *Saw* is the only film or television show discussed in this essay to feature an ostensible *villain* using torture to pursue what he sees as extra-legal justice. But "Jigsaw" (Tobin Bell), much like Hannibal Lecter, is not really someone we are invited to hate and root against in an uncomplicated way. Instead, especially in later films when his character is further fleshed out, Jigsaw receives the audience's (perhaps unconscious) respect for his cleverness, his principles, and for at least *taking stands and doing things*, however bizarre and inhuman. Jigsaw is terminally ill with cancer, and the gift of that disease has made him see the world more clearly, he says. There are too many people living among us who, in Jigsaw's simultaneously warped-and-ostensibly-keen-eyed view, deserve to suffer terribly for the way they have lived their lives (or, alternately and unconvincingly, because they need to appreciate life more). With echoes of the serial killer John Doe (Kevin Spacey) in *Se7en* (1995), Jigsaw sets about righting these wrongs in elaborate, torture-filled fashion. So it is that a variety of average people are trapped and forced to set themselves on fire, cut themselves to death on razor wire, saw off their own feet, and so on. A low-budget independent film without big stars, *Saw* has nevertheless spawned three other box office hits that are particularly popular with youth audiences: *Saw II* (2005), *Saw III* (2006), and *Saw IV* (2007).

The Devil's Rejects is itself a sequel, to *House of 1000 Corpses* (2003). A pastiche of 1970s horror films like *Last House on the Left* (1972) and *The Texas Chainsaw Massacre* (1974), but with even more gore and nihilism, *Rejects* follows the travels of the Firefly clan, who have for many years been torturing and murdering those unfortunate enough to cross their path. But when the more-than-a-little-loony Sheriff Wydell (William Forsythe) catches their scent and decides he must avenge the death of his brother at their hands, they will soon be in for tastes of their own medicine. Wydell catches them, ties them up, tortures them with sharp instruments, and then sets the house on fire and leaves them to burn. From the tone of the film and the nature of its (a)moral universe, it's unclear whether audiences are supposed to feel happy, sad, angry, or indifferent when the Firefly family manages to escape and Wydell's neck is soon snapped.

On the other hand, there is no confusion whatsoever about how audiences are invited to feel while watching the first entry (chronologically) in this period's torture films. If one is to grapple with cinematic representations of torture during the momentous 2003-2005 period, there is no avoiding the box-office dynamo and cultural firestorm that was Mel Gibson's *The Passion of the Christ* (2004),[21] which debuted two months before *The Punisher, Kill Bill: Vol. II, Man on Fire*, and the breaking of the Abu Ghraib torture story. On the face of it, *Passion* does not seem to fit the pattern of the torture films discussed above, because it is only Jesus who gets tortured throughout the film, and we are meant to feel his pain and suffer with him. In addition, unlike the other films and TV shows discussed in this essay, it was not predominantly geared toward—and did not to a much greater extent reach—youth audiences. That all said, *Passion* still demands attention as a politically charged torture marathon, one that was no doubt seen by tens of millions of young adults.

Much of *Passion*'s running time is devoted to long, grotesque scenes of Jesus being beaten, whipped, flayed, and crucified. In fact, as critic A. O. Scott noted in his *New York Times* review of the film, "the film is so relentlessly focused on the savagery of Jesus' final hours that this film seems to arise less from love than from wrath."[22] That wrath, and the focus of Mel Gibson's and the audiences (anticipated) righteous anger, is the key to understanding *Passion*'s cultural and ideological significance in the context of 2004 America. The villains of the film—the ostensible authors of Christ's torture and death—are the bisexual King Herod, a soft-on-crime governor who frees the notorious murderer Barabbas, a mass of drunk soldiers with bad teeth, and, most notoriously, Jews, all of whom are presented as an arrogant elite. In post-1960s and then post-9/11 America, that roster is a virtual who's who for backlash conservatism's misplaced anger and aggression—the so-called Liberal Elite in particular.[23]

Even when the pieces of the puzzle don't fit together in any rational sense (Jews had nothing to do with 9/11; some Jewish pundits and officials have been cogs in the neoconservative movement), seeing that crowd order such vicious, sadistic, inhumane treatment of Jesus Christ is *all about* "wrath"—God's, the audiences', and, symbolically, the Bush Administration's in the "War on Terror." Look at what "they" did to family values, morality, decency, and law & order, look at what "they" did to us on 9/11, and look at what "they" are doing to Jesus Christ! The fact that Jesus responds with non-violence to the prolonged and horrific torture only feeds the audiences' empathy, anger, and desire to step up and avenge him—ideally with a disproportionately powerful counterattack against their mortal enemies on the screen and in the world, whether at Guantanamo, in Iraq, or elsewhere. It in fact is very similar to the many lawless justice films Gibson himself has starred in and/or produced—*Lethal Weapon I* (1987) and *II* (1989), *Ransom* (1996), *Payback* (1999), *Paparazzi* (2004), and so on—only with the vengeance left up to the audience. The parallels with President Bush, his loyal followers, and that post-9/11 historical moment are all-too apparent. "After 9/11," Frank Rich has written, "[President Bush's] view of faith as a Manichaean scheme of black and white to be acted out in a perpetual war between good and evil was synergistic with the violent poetics of popular culture favored by his religious-right political base," including "Mel Gibson's gory cinematic blockbuster *The Passion of the Christ*."[24] Given this interpretation of what was done to Jesus, and of the historical moment—the world hangs in the balance, Godly America must prevail against the evils of terrorism and liberalism, *and* we deserve some *payback*—is it any wonder that so many care so little about America's illegal uses of torture?

Although there was indeed ample representation of torture on movie screens between 2003 and 2005, torture representations on television sprang up with even greater regularity. According to a study done by the organization Human Rights First, before 9/11 fewer than four acts of torture appeared on prime-time television each year. Since then, there have been more than one hundred per year, and the makeup of the torturers has changed significantly. Before the 9/11 attacks, one could count on the torturers to almost exclusively be villains; since 9/11 the torturing is often carried out by the shows' heroes—or, at the very least, the shows' protagonists.[25] In some cases, such as the compellingly corrupt cop Vic Mackey (Michael Chiklis) on *The Shield* (2003-2005), or the vigilante-serial-killer-cop Dexter on the more recent Showtime series of the same name (2006), the main character may utilize torture but actually be a very complicated *anti-hero*.

Quite often, however, the 2003-2005 representations of torture on shows like *Lost* and especially *24* proceeded according to the extra-legal justice, vengeance, and information-gathering trend. Although *Lost* would complement some of its depictions of torture with serious counterarguments and soul-searching, it also set up situations in which torture seemed like the necessary course of action. The most (in)famous torture scene in the first season took place in the episode aired on November 10, 2004, the week after the presidential election. As the young, pretty, and blonde Shannon (Maggie Grace) begins to suffer from increasingly bad asthma attacks, the heroic doctor Jack Shepherd (Matthew Fox) decides that the outlaw Sawyer (Josh Holloway) has her remaining inhalers in the secret stash of goods he has stolen from the rest of the castaways. With the help of Sayid (Naveen Andrews), a former interrogator in the Iraqi Republican Guard, Jack ties Sawyer up and demands to know where the inhalers are. When Sawyer refuses to divulge anything—despite not actually having the inhalers—Jack instructs Sayid to torture Sawyer. Sayid sticks sharpened bamboo shoots under Sawyer's fingernails, but Sawyer does not break. Although the torturing further poisons Sayid's soul, and ultimately does not work, the audience is still invited to feel that given the extraordinary circumstances—Shannon might die otherwise!—it certainly made sense to try.

Then there is *24*, a hugely popular show on television and then DVD, particularly among young people. Taking place squarely in the context of the "War on Terror," and consisting of nothing *but* "extraordinary circumstances," *24* has been the very embodiment of the Bush Administration's symbolic politics (and tangible agenda), especially between 2003 and 2005. And while its focus on one tough, individualistic, straight White male's heroic efforts to save America from all manner of terrorist threats is itself quite significant ideologically, representations of torture in particular have been the bloody beating heart of the show's Bush-friendly political meanings.

For the uninitiated, each season of *24* is devoted to one comically momentous day in the life of "Counter-Terrorism Unit" expert Jack Bauer (Kiefer Sutherland), who inevitably finds himself at the center of efforts to stop terrorists from setting off weapons of mass destruction in a major American city—*that very day*. Each episode equals one hour in real time, and a clock often ticks on the screen, the ominous, thumping sound effects bringing us one second closer to annihilation. In other words, in the context of the "War on Terror" and understandably voluminous public fears of terrorist attacks in the post-9/11 era, every season of *24* in one way or another replays the hoary "ticking time-bomb" storyline. Given that fantastical narrative structure—we're facing a veritable Armageddon, the evildoers will stop at nothing, and time and information are of the essence—the good guys' use of torture is framed in a very particular (and unrealistic) way. As David Luban has written in "Liberalism, Torture, and the Ticking Bomb," an incisive essay about loaded and simplistic torture discourse in post-9/11 America, the "ticking bomb" scenario is a Trojan horse for radical redefinitions of what we find morally, ethically, and legally acceptable.[26] Sure, we may be squeamish about the use of torture in general, this trope concedes—it is illegal, after all, no matter what the circumstances—but if we know that in this one specific situation that torturing this one specific terrorist will keep this one specific nuclear bomb from going off and killing millions of Americans, don't we have to do it? One might be able to have a legitimate argument about such a dilemma, Luban writes, but it elides the basic fact that *torture doesn't work that way*. Nevertheless, many politicians and pundits (and entertainment producers) attempting to make sense of torture still skip over its realities and latch onto this one hypothetical scenario so rare as to be virtually irrelevant. In doing so, they play a part in normalizing America's use of torture in the public mind.

As a consistent purveyor of the "ticking bomb" torture trope and a self-identified "patriotic" show with several Bush Administration and right-wing agenda-setting admirers—Karl Rove, Lynne Cheney, Michael Chertoff, Rush Limbaugh, and Ann Coulter among them[27]—*24* is a perfect example of media representations that both emerge from, and return to further shape, our political culture and society. Tellingly, the talk and use of torture was rare in the first season of the show (2001-2002), which was fully planned and partly shot before 9/11. But beginning in its second season (2002-2003)—beginning in fact in the *very first scene* of that season, when a terrorist is tortured into revealing that a nuclear bomb is set to go off in L.A. *that day*—drastic times have called for drastic measures. In the three seasons that follow, examples abound of Bauer and other Americans torturing terrorists and their enablers in the hurried, desperate interest of national security. (Throughout the torture Bauer or another American present can be expected to scream at the captive: "Tell me where the bomb is!"; or "Where's the bomb?!"; or "Those men will kill your family if you don't tell me where the bomb is now!") The conscious and stated purpose of that torture is always the same—straightforward information gathering on impending terrorist threats—and this framing of torture as a necessary measure *that works* is in itself significant. (While observing a torture session that he himself has authorized, even the liberal and level-headed President Palmer [Dennis Haysbert] notes that "Everybody breaks eventually.") But there is also a giddy and vengeful sadism involved in *24*'s use of torture. One indicator of that unstated and perhaps unconscious component of *24*'s American-authored torture is its impressive variety: captives have been beaten, cut, injected with harsh chemicals, electrocuted, shot, subjected to sensory deprivation, denied medical care, tricked into believing their children have been murdered before their eyes, and so on.

What, it must be asked, are the implications and effects of these and other torture representations for their predominantly young adult audiences in particular? I have examined this issue in observations and asides throughout my discussion of these representations, but it is to some concluding analyses and speculations that I now finally turn.

Conclusion

Before considering the political implications and effects of these films and shows, for young audiences in particular, it would be wise to consider some possible counterexamples and counterarguments to my analysis thus far. There are, to be sure, depictions of torture in fictional film and television during this period which do not fit the torture-as-lawless-justice paradigm. In *Syriana* (2005), for example, the CIA operative played by George Clooney is tortured in a brutal scene that likely elicits disgust, sympathy, and a disquieting sense that this constitutes American foreign policy chickens coming home to roost. *Law & Order: Criminal Intent*, meanwhile, has in several instances expressed significant criticism of the idea that torture is a viable, ethical method of interrogation. In 2005 alone an episode included Detective Barek

(Annabella Sciorra) mentioning matter-of-factly that torture was not an effective method of acquiring information, while another episode revolved around the psychological trauma and unexpectedly deadly repercussions of torture methods the U.S. has been using at Guantanamo.

The popular horror film *Hostel* (2005) could also be interpreted as critical of torture and American foreign policy, or at the very least as an example of what Robin Wood called an ideologically "incoherent text."[28] On the one hand, the torture that two young American men abroad suffer through at the hands of rich foreigners paying for the right to torture will most likely elicit sympathy for their plight. On the other hand, the audience is also introduced to a scarily eager-to-torture American man who seems to symbolize bloodthirsty capitalism, and even the young guys themselves are represented as ignorant, sexist, entitled Americans who may be reaping what their country has sowed. That all said, it may be more likely that *Hostel* isn't a counterexample to the above torture films and shows so much as it is part of what could be a counterargument to their supposed ideological moorings and significance.

Hostel is quite clearly an exploitation film, and like some of the *Saw* films, *House of 1000 Corpses*, and the more recent *Turistas* (2007), it may actually have little on its mind other than a desire to provoke, to up the sensationalism ante in an era when it takes more to stand out from the crowd. One could argue, in other words, that *Hostel* and many of these other films and shows are primarily about shock value and the need for attention, often on low budgets—especially at a time of rapid technological change and migrating audiences. (This is not to say, however, that such films are not also rooted in contemporary anxieties and desires; those roots may just be more strictly emotional than ideological.) These developments are particularly noticeable in the media usage and consumption of the prized demographic of young people, especially young males,[29] and it may not be accidental that so many of the films and shows discussed above are primarily geared toward them. Alternately, the fact that torture films from Australia (e.g., *Wolf Creek* [2005]), Japan (e.g., *Audition* [1999], *Living Hell* [2000]), and South Korea (e.g., *Oldboy* [2003]) are popping up in recent years is another possible counterargument to the idea that recent American torture films are specifically rooted in the ideology of the post-9/11 period. If that were so, what would explain such films in countries which were not attacked on 9/11, and which have not had their own Abu Ghraibs?

That all said, it seems more than reasonable to conclude that something politically significant was going on with American fiction film and television torture representations between 2003 and 2005. As I argued above, these films and shows have a constitutive relationship with the particular times in which they were made; that is, they are mutually embedded in some of the predominant myths and discourses about torture, terrorism, war, and crime from the post-9/11 period in particular (*Man on Fire* and *24* being the most poignant examples), but from the overall post-1960s era as well. Furthermore, as texts themselves their dominant (or "preferred") meanings typically speak to the necessity and effectiveness of torture in the pursuit of security and lawless justice—not to mention the (perhaps unconscious) satisfaction to be derived from vengeful violence against an Other that started the whole thing with a deadly, unprovoked, sneak attack. This last meaning and mythical element has deep roots in American history, from attacks on Native Americans as part of "Manifest Destiny" to the Vietnam War,[30] but its echoes are particularly strong in the post-9/11 period.

Returning to the question of how these 2003-2005 torture representations may have played a part in activating certain kinds of symbolic political meanings (and political behavior) in that informational and cultural environment, for eighteen- to twenty-nine-year-olds or anyone else, it is difficult to answer with much certitude. But there is no question that these films and shows were at least *conducive* to Bush-and-America-friendly interpretations of the 2004 torture scandal in ways direct—if, as was often the case for this age group, the specific shows and films were actually seen—and/or ecological. The most consequential of these symbolic torture meanings and interpretations are: 1) The "War on Terror" is not something we asked for, but now that we've been stirred to anger and committed ourselves *we have to do what we have to do*—including torture—to survive this unprecedentedly scary and dangerous fight (if it weren't unprecedented, we wouldn't be engaging in torture); 2) Our captives, *as stand-ins for our terrorist enemies generally*, are de facto guilty, evil, and subhuman (if they weren't, we wouldn't be engaging in torture); and 3) In this frightening zero-sum game against self-evidently guilty and evil foes bent on our annihilation, *President Bush is absolutely certain of what he is doing and of America's rightness,* and is single-mindedly focused on protecting us, wimpy ACLU lawyers, un-American international treaties, and flip-flopping Senator Kerry be damned (if President Bush weren't, we wouldn't be engaging in torture). Ergo sum, President Bush and his policies look relatively more attractive—and Kerry and his policies less—than they would otherwise.

Of course, even if an American young adult were to see these specific films and shows, and even if the larger cultural environment is affected by them, there is no guarantee of what political effects and implications there might be for an individual's beliefs and behavior. (For what it is worth, the eighteen to twenty-nine American demographic *was* in one prominent 2004 poll the most supportive of torture as part of the "War on Terror"—21 percent thought torture was "often justified" and 24 percent thought it "sometimes justified.")[31] It is highly unlikely, for instance, that a young leftist would interpret the torture and civil liberties scandals of 2004 as symbolic confirmation of Bush's strength and effectiveness just because she had seen *Man on Fire* and *The Punisher* in recent months. Furthermore, even a devout young conservative, Bush supporter, and *24* fan would not *necessarily* regard the torture revelations as symbolic confirmation of President Bush's strength and convictions, the country's rightness, and the enemies' subhuman evilness.

That said, I would argue that along with the broadly cultural ecological and contextual importance of these shows and films (and their lawless justice predecessors, complete with significant mythical meanings), at a micro-level they probably have what has been described as "political uses and effects."[32] This theory posits that media uses and (sought-after) gratifications are tied in to a variety of effects, both expected and not, including knowledge, attitudes, and perceptions of social reality. How much of that process is based on selectivity, as compared to the interpretation of polysemic content, is hard to say, but it is easy to imagine both scenarios, especially for moderates and conservatives who see these films and shows.

As for how exactly such young adults might be affected politically, one could claim that arguing that these torture representations incline one toward Bush and away from Kerry flies in the face of data showing young adults voting for Kerry over Bush on election day. While this is true, this neglects the possibility that young adults would have been that much more likely to support Kerry over Bush were it not for the immersion of so many in this kind of popular culture. After all, the Iraq War, the national debt, gay marriage, and a whole host of other issues might have conceivably given Kerry an even more lopsided margin among young adults were it not for distorted entertainment media representations of torture. (Not to mention that, as other chapters in this book detail, Kerry also benefited from the efforts of several liberal leaning [although officially identified as non-partisan] pop culture-related groups and icons such as Rock the Vote and Citizen Change, as well as, arguably, Michael Moore.) The previously noted fact that young adults were more likely than any other age group to support the use of torture lends credence to this possibility.

The two epigraphs at the beginning of this essay speak to two other related possibilities (although there are, to be sure, countless others). With respect to the Colbert quote in particular, I suspect that the greatest power of these torture representations may lie in the way they may blunt the potential shame and outrage young adult Americans might—should—feel when they learn of what is being done in their name. In such a scenario, apathy and indifference would amount to extremely significant political effects, for those individuals and for the political system as a whole. One can imagine as one hypothetical a moderately liberal young woman who, partly because of these torture representations, votes for Kerry but does not raise her public voice or expand her level of political engagement beyond voting. Alternately, not seeing sufficiently stark moral and ethical differences between Bush and Kerry, she might not vote at all.

As I write these words, the *New York Times* is reporting today on a new film about a young, pretty, blonde woman who is kidnapped, held captive, and tortured. Taxi and billboard ads for *Captivity* (2007) have apparently sparked so many complaints from New Yorkers that the ads will soon be pulled (although not before attracting publicity, of course).[33] The ads in question feature four grisly images complete with captions: "Abduction," "Confinement," "Torture," and "Termination," the latter of which shows the character with her head thrown back, seemingly dead. Although the broader themes and messages of the film—if any—are not yet clear, in any event it makes a certain superficial sense that the captive is played by actress Elisha Cuthbert, best known as Jack Bauer's daughter on *24*.

Notes

1. In a September 2004 survey, President Bush bested Kerry 54 to 30 percent on the question "Who can best handle terrorism?" Bush also bested Kerry 63 to 23 percent as the man more aptly described as "willing to take an unpopular stand," and 54 to 28 percent as the man more aptly described as a "strong leader." Pew Research Center for the People & the Press, "Bush Widens Margin Again, Despite Vulnerabilities," September 28, 2004, http://people-press.org/reports/display. php3?ReportID=226 (accessed March 1, 2007). Also

see John Clifford Green, Mark J. Rozell, and Clyde Wilcox, eds., *The Values Campaign?: The Christian Right and the 2004 Elections* (Washington, D.C.: Georgetown University Press, 2006); Evan Thomas, *Election 2004: How Bush Won and What You Can Expect in the Future* (New York: Public Affairs, 2005); Kathleen Hall Jamieson, ed., *Electing the President 2004: The Insiders' View* (Philadelphia: University of Pennsylvania Press, 2006).

2. See Eric Alterman and Mark Green, *The Book on Bush: How George W. (Mis)Leads America* (New York: Viking, 2004); John W. Dean, *Worse Than Watergate: The Secret Presidency of George W. Bush* (New York: Little, Brown, 2004); Mark Crispin Miller, *Cruel and Unusual: Bush/Cheney's New World Order* (New York: Norton, 2004).

3. See Paul Abramson, John Aldrich, and David Rhode, *Change and Continuity in the 2004 Elections* (Washington, D.C.: CQ Press, 2005); http://www.civicyouth.org.

4. Murray Edelman, *The Symbolic Uses of Politics* (Urbana: University of Illinois Press, 1964).

5. See Mark Danner, ed., *Torture and Truth: America, Abu Ghraib, and the War on Terror* (New York: New York Review Books, 2004); Seymour Hersh, *Chain of Command: The Road from 9/11 to Abu Ghraib* (New York: Harper Collins, 2004); Karen Greenberg, ed., *The Torture Debate in America* (New York: Cambridge University Press, 2006).

6. See Frank Rich, *The Greatest Story Ever Sold: The Decline and Fall of Truth from 9/11 to Katrina* (New York: Penguin, 2006); J. David Slocum, ed., *Terrorism, Media, Liberation* (New Brunswick, NJ: Rutgers University Press, 2005).

7. See Pietro Nivola and David Brady, eds., *Red and Blue Nation?: Characteristics and Causes of America's Polarized Politics* (Washington, D.C.: Brookings, 2006); Morris Fiorina, *Culture War?: The Myth of a Polarized America* (New York: Longman, 2004); Greenberg, ed., *The Torture Debate*.

8. See Philip Converse, "The Nature of Belief Systems in Mass Publics," in *Ideology and Discontent*, ed. David Apter (New York: Free Press, 1964); David Sears, "Symbolic Politics: A Socio-Psychological Theory," in *Explorations in Political Psychology*, ed. Shanto Iyengar and William J. McGuire (Durham, NC: Duke University Press, 1993).

9. See Iyengar and McGuire, eds., *Explorations in Political Psychology*; Doris Graber, *Processing the News: How People Tame the Information Tide* (Lanham, MD: University Press of America, 1993); W. Lance Bennett and Robert Entman, eds., *Mediated Politics: Communication in the Future of Democracy* (New York: Cambridge University Press, 2001).

10. See Jeffrey Jones, *Entertaining Politics: New Political Television and Civic Culture* (Lanham, MD: Rowman & Littlefield, 2004); Terry Christensen and Peter Haas, *Projecting Politics: Political Messages in American Films* (Armonk, NY: M.E. Sharpe, 2005); Liesbet van Zoonen, *Entertaining the Citizen: When Politics and Popular Culture Converge* (Lanham, MD: Rowman

& Littlefield, 2005).

11. See Motion Picture Association, "2004 U.S. Movie Attendance Study," 2005, http://www.tvtracker.com/daily_ratings.php (accessed February 28, 2008).

12. Philip Jenkins, *Decade of Nightmares: The End of the Sixties and the Making of Eighties America* (New York: Oxford University Press, 2006).

13. On the post-1960s conservative backlash, see Michael Kazin, *The Populist Persuasion: An American History* (Ithaca, NY: Cornell University Press, 1998), 245-66; Alan Crawford, *Thunder on the Right: The "New Right" and the Politics of Resentment* (New York: Pantheon, 1980); Sidney Blumenthal, *The Rise of the Counter-Establishment: From Conservative Ideology to Political Power* (New York: Harper Perennial, 1988). On these films, see David A. Cook, *Lost Illusions: American Cinema in the Shadow of Watergate and Vietnam, 1970-1979* (Berkeley, CA: University of California Press, 2000), 188-97.

14. See Stephen Prince, *Visions of Empire: Political Imagery in Contemporary American Film* (New York: Praeger, 1992), 66-69, 127-35; William Palmer, *The Films of the Eighties: A Social History* (Carbondale, IL: Southern Illinois University Press, 1993), 87-96.

15. See H. Bruce Franklin, *M.I.A. or Mythmaking in America: How and Why Belief in Live POWs Has Possessed a Nation* (New Brunswick, NJ: Rutgers University Press, 1993); James William Gibson, *Warrior Dreams: Violence and Manhood in Post-Vietnam America* (New York: Hill and Wang, 1994).

16. Elayne Rapping, *Law and Justice as Seen on TV* (New York: New York University Press, 2003); Earle Marsh and Tim Brooks, *The Complete Directory to Prime Time Network and Cable TV Shows, 1946-Present* (New York: Ballantine, 2000).

17. See the Bureau of Justice Statistics, "National Crime Victimization Survey: Violent Crime Trends, 1973-2002," http://www.ojp.usdoj.gov/bjs/glance/tables/viortrdtab.htm (accessed February 28, 2007); Thomas Byrne Edsall and Mary Edsall, *Chain Reaction: The Impact of Race, Rights, and Taxes on American Politics* (New York: W.W. Norton, 1992), 49-52, 110-13; Barry Bluestone and Bennett Harrison, *The Deindustrialization of America: Plant Closings, Community Abandonment and the Dismantling of Basic Industry* (New York: Basic Books, 1982); Kenneth Jackson, *Crabgrass Frontier: The Suburbanization of the United States* (New York: Oxford University Press, 1987), 272-96. Although these phenomena had their own concrete and tangible realities (and effects), it is also virtually impossible to separate them from the way they were talked about and represented, especially in the news media. For example, the significance of urban riots and myriad protests and clashes during this period was of course inextricably bound up with the particular ways in which they were covered in the news—on this point see for instance Barbara Ehrenreich, *Fear of Falling: The Inner Life of the Middle Class* (New York: Harper Perennial, 1989), 97-101; Todd Gitlin, *The Whole World Is Watching: Mass Media in the Making and Unmaking of the New Left* (Berkeley: University

of California Press, 1980); Ronald Jacobs, *Race, Media and the Crisis of Civil Society: From Watts to Rodney King* (New York: Cambridge University Press, 2000), 54-80.

18. See David Bodenhamer, *Fair Trial: Rights of the Accused in American History* (New York: Oxford University Press, 1991), 108-27. For a right-wing perspective on the Supreme Court's "judicial activism" throughout history, see Mark Levin, *Men In Black: How the Supreme Court Is Destroying America* (Washington, D.C.: Regnery, 2005).

19. See Lawrence Friedman, *Crime and Punishment in American History* (New York: Basic Books, 1993), 294-323. On mythology and misinformation about crime and criminal justice, including the extent to which the public shares such beliefs, see Victor Kappeler and Gary Potter, *The Mythology of Crime and Criminal Justice* (Prospect Heights, IL: Waveland Press, 2004); Julian Roberts and Loretta Stalans, *Public Opinion, Crime, and Criminal Justice* (Boulder, CO: Westview Press, 2000). On the Victims' Rights movement, see Robert Elias, *The Politics of Victimization: Victims, Victimology, and Human Rights* (New York: Oxford University Press, 1986); Ezzat Fattah, ed., *From Crime Policy to Victim Policy* (London: Macmillan, 1986). On media biases, preoccupations, and narrative devices, see Jeffrey Scheuer, *The Sound Bite Society: Television and the American Mind* (New York: Four Walls, Eight Windows, 1999); Steven Stark, *Glued to the Set: The 60 Television Shows and Events That Made Us Who We Are Today* (New York: Delta, 1997), 235-43; Leonard Downie, Jr. and Robert Kaiser, *The News About the News: American Journalism in Peril* (New York: Vintage, 2003), 157-94; Joel Best, *Random Violence: How We Talk about New Crimes and New Victims* (Berkeley, CA: University of California Press, 1999), 1-47; Travis Dixon and Daniel Linz, "Overrepresentation and Underrepresentation of African Americans and Latinos as Lawbreakers on Television News," *Journal of Communication* 50 (2000): 131-54; Franklin Gilliam and Shanto Iyengar, "Prime Suspects: The Influence of Local Television News on the Viewing Public," *American Journal of Political Science* 44 (2000): 560-73; Mira Sotirovic, "Affective and Cognitive Processes as Mediators of Media Influences on Crime-Policy Preferences," *Mass Communication & Society* 4 (2001): 11-29.

20. Michael Isikoff and David Corn, *Hubris: The Inside Story of Spin, Scandal, and the Selling of the Iraq War* (New York: Crown, 2006); Thomas Ricks, *Fiasco: The American Military Adventure in Iraq* (New York: Penguin, 2006); Rich, *The Greatest Story*; Danner, ed., *Torture and Truth*.

21. See Jorge Gracia, ed., *Mel Gibson's Passion and Philosophy: The Cross, the Questions, the Controversy* (Chicago: Open Court, 2004).

22. A.O. Scott, "Good and Evil Locked in a Violent Showdown," *New York Times*, February 25, 2004, 1(C).

23. See Thomas Frank, *What's the Matter with Kansas: How Conservatives Won the Heart of America* (New York: Metropolitan, 2004).

24. Rich, *The Greatest Story*, 144.

25. Jane Mayer, "Whatever It Takes," *New Yorker*, February 19 & 26, 2007, 66-82.

26. David Luban, "Liberalism, Torture, and the Ticking Bomb," in *The Torture Debate in America*, ed. Karen Greenberg (New York: Cambridge University Press, 2006), 35-83.

27. Mayer, "Whatever It Takes."

28. Robin Wood, *Hollywood from Vietnam to Reagan and Beyond* (New York: Columbia University Press, 2003).

29. See Sharon Waxman, "Study Finds Men Attending Fewer Films," *New York Times*, October 8, 2005, 17(A); Laura Holson, "Caught on Film: A Growing Unease in Hollywood," *New York Times*, August 19, 2006, 1(B).

30. See Richard Slotkin, *Gunfighter Nation: The Myth of the Frontier in Twentieth Century America* (New York: Harper, 1992); Tom Engelhardt, *The End of Victory Culture: Cold War America and the Disillusioning of a Generation* (Amherst: University of Massachusetts Press, 1998).

31. Pew Research Center for the People & the Press, "Foreign Policy Attitudes Now Driven by 9/11 and Iraq," August 18, 2004, http://www.people-press.org/reports/display.php3? ReportID=222 (accessed March 1, 2007).

32. See Alan Rubin, "Media Uses and Effects: A Uses-and-Gratifications Perspective," in *Media Effects: Advances in Theory and Research*, eds. Jennings Bryant and Dolf Zillmann (Mahwah, NJ: Lawrence Erlbaum), 417-36; Marco Calavita, "Idealization, Inspiration, Irony: Popular Communication Tastes and Practices in the Individual Political Development of 'Generation Xers,'" *Popular Communication* 2, no. 3 (2004): 129-51.

33. Lawrence Van Gelder, "Horror Film Ads Prompt Outrage," *New York Times*, March 21, 2007, 2(B).

Chapter 7

Cast a Vote, Yo: Targeting the Hip-Hop Generation through Popular Culture

Tony Kelso

The event that triggered my interest in writing this chapter was my viewing of a commercial produced by the liberal-leaning 527 MoveOn.org for its "Don't Get Mad, Get Even!" advertising initiative. MoveOn's idea was to run one new commercial per week for the final ten weeks of the 2004 U.S. presidential campaign season. The commercial that caught my attention was the first installment of the ten-commercial series entitled "Everybody." Aired on MTV and BET, the commercial attempted to reach members of the hip-hop generation—and young African Americans in particular—and encourage them to vote in the coming election. For me, it served as a springboard for delving into a more general concern—the intensifying effort to mobilize the hip-hop generation through political advertising and marketing efforts that appropriate elements from the realm of popular culture. Can such an endeavor play an effective role in activating young African-American voters, whose participation in the election process, just like that of other eighteen- to thirty-year-olds, until recently, had diminished over the past few decades? Or are campaigns designed to engage African-American youth doomed to carry about as much significance as a new series of commercials hawking the latest redesigned SUV? This chapter is meant to trigger discussion on the subject by evaluating the methods used to reach Black voters during the most recent presidential election season and discussing their long-term significance.

Although hip-hop culture—and rap music in particular—has often received a bad rap, from the outset, my attitude toward this expression is not alarmist. Indeed, I would argue that we must recognize hip hop and rap's significance within the cultural landscape. Now roughly thirty-years-old, with precursors that extend much further back, rap, the best-selling musical genre in the country, has forever undermined the notion that it is just a passing fad. Moreover, despite its consistent use of vulgar, misogynistic, homophobic, or otherwise offensive language; association with images of violence, gangs, and gyrating booties; and elevation of bling-bling as a preeminent value, rap is a multifaceted phenomenon with the potential to promote positive social change, as I hope to illustrate below.

Before proceeding, a definition is in order—what does the term *hip-hop generation* signify in this chapter? I draw upon the work of Bakari Kitwana, who contends in his book, *The Hip Hop Generation*, that the phrase "is used interchangeably with Black youth culture."[1] Distinguishing this group from so-called Generation X, which, Kitwana maintains, applies more to whites, he specifically yet somewhat arbitrarily identifies the hip-hop generation with those Blacks born between 1965 and 1984. Other authors link the concept with youth culture in general, especially given that non-blacks account for the vast majority of rap music purchases. Still, when one considers the extent to which rap performance in the United States is dominated by African Americans and how central hip hop is to the identities of many young Blacks, then Kitwana's definition no longer seems unjustified. In this essay, then, the focus will be on Black youth.

Thirty-Second Rap Video

To help frame the discussion, a description of the spot by MoveOn that sparked this investigation is in order. The commercial opens with a young Black man talking on his cell phone to an unidentified person, ending the call with, "No, it ain't goin' down like that." Next, he begins walking through the "hood," rounding up a "posse" along the way. At this point, the commercial is playing on the stereotype of "dangerous Black youth." At the end of the story, however, the tables are turned: When the man, along with his recruits, arrives at his final destination and is confronted by a police officer who asks if the group is looking for trouble, the young man replies that, no, "we're here to vote."

Performing a textual analysis by looking at the commercial's rhetorical argument is simple: it encourages young African Americans to vote. But as Glenn Richardson asserts in his book, *Pulp Politics*, a full critical reading of a political advertisement involves going beyond a summary of its overt theme by taking a holistic approach. He explains that many political advertising campaigns resonate with meaning because of the way in which, through their visual and aural production techniques, they articulate with elements of popular culture and evoke certain associations with genres found in other forms of media.[2] In this spot, we can see how it closely mimics the conventions of a rap video—complete with its implied reference to the police brutality many African Americans face in their neighborhoods, which in this case, the young citizens turn on its face by demonstrating their determination to not be deterred from the polls as others had allegedly been in previous elections. Indeed, several weeks after this commercial was scheduled to run, the notorious rap artist Eminem released a scathing anti-Bush video that promoted a similar message. While it favors stylistic scenes that incorporate animation techniques over the more naturalistic shots of the commercial just described, nonetheless, Eminem's piece, in its tone and plot, mirrors MoveOn's advertisement, which was directed by Benny Boom, an artist known for his work on rap videos. Referring to the "Everybody" spot for MoveOn, Boom used language that is commonly linked with hip hop to describe his motivation for directing it and belied its purportedly "neutral," pro-vote message: "I'm more passionate about being opposed to Bush," he said. "George Bush is probably the first real gangsta we have had in office. John Kerry needs to be a little bit more of a gangsta himself."[3]

But the MoveOn spot was but a blip on the map in relation to efforts to stir members of the hip-hop generation to vote in the 2004 presidential election. Consequently, it needs to be considered within a wider context. Some of the more well-known initiatives included the rap artist and entrepreneur P. Diddy's Citizen Change campaign, which featured its fashion line of "Vote or Die" T-shirts; the hip-hop mogul Russell Simmons's Hip-Hop Summit Action Network; a spin-off of the Rock the Vote program suitably entitled "Rap the Vote"; the first ever National Hip-Hop Political Convention; as well as other media campaigns designed to mobilize potential youth voters in general. As with the MoveOn ad, these activities were positioned as non-partisan, get-out-the-vote drives; but even a cursory survey of the websites connected with these campaigns revealed a pro-Kerry bias. All of the initiatives appeared to be partly inspired by the idea that the youth vote in general and the hip-hop vote in particular could make the difference in the coming election.

What Do the People Think?

For much of the rest of this chapter, I would like to group these various yet similarly themed events and campaigns together as a collective "text" and conduct a textual analysis that attempts to illuminate their significance in striving to rouse the hip-hop voter into action through expressions of popular culture. My approach is based on the qualitative model of Alan McKee, who argues that "[w]hen we perform textual analysis on a text, we make an educated guess at some of the most likely interpretations that might be made of that text."[4] In other words, the emphasis is not on producing a scholarly, arcane reading far removed from the lives of everyday people, but in generating defensible interpretations that reflect the possible readings of the text's actual audience. One of the central tactics the researcher can use to construct plausible, popular interpretations is to consult what McKee terms "intertexts," that is, "publicly circulated texts that are explicitly linked to the text you're interested in."[5] For this case study meant to provide insight into a more general phenomenon, I examined dozens of intertexts that put me in touch with the hip-hop generation, including political websites that feature blogs and articles composed by fresh writers aligned with this audience such as "Pop and Politics," "Wiretap," and "Yo! Youth Outlook"; articles and editorials in college newspapers published in historically Black colleges and universities such as Howard, Florida A&M, and North Carolina Central; as well as recent books by hip-hop generationers. The question that guided my exploration was, How were the popular culture political campaigns aimed at the hip-hop generation during the 2004 campaign season actually read by their intended audience? After looking at the results from 2004, I will turn to a brief assessment of hip-hop related activities that occurred in the run-up to the 2006 midterm elections. Finally, I will reflect on the implications of the findings for future elections within the context of youth culture and the political process in general.

One theme that emerged in the intertexts was the possibility that youth voters would be turned off by the heavy-handed, paternalistic provoting messages that were perceived as not only issuing from popular rappers, but from other behind-the-scenes adults outside the hip-hop generation. "As for this bunch of clowns, I find it distasteful at best that they have decided to use the term 'Hip-Hop' for a political movement. . . . fuck 'em—they are trying to buy their way into the hip-hop consciousness and all we can hope for is they fuck off," blogged a writer, who goes by the name of Mink-C, on the Hip Hop Central website.[6] A number of published authors from the hip-hop generation, including Yvonne Bynoe, Jeff Chang, and Bakari Kitwana, illustrate there is a generation gap among African Americans that is reminiscent of the one widely discussed during the 1960s between adults and youth at large.[7] Many younger African Americans in fact respect the political fights that were waged by the civil rights generation—yet they are tired of being labeled as apathetic or out of touch with communal cultural integrity in comparison with their elders. Rather than trying to understand their children on their own terms, many parents of hip-hop generationers often provoke feelings of alienation by reflexively decrying rap music and other forms of popular culture that cut to the core of youth identity. Consider this recent comment by the great civil rights leader Julian Bond as he reminisced on the movement that reached its heyday over forty years ago— before the hip-hop generation was even born: "Now, those were the days when women and men of all races and creeds worked together in the cause of civil rights. Those were the days when good music was popular and popular music was good."[8] His attitude exemplifies the type of sentiment that can spark youth resistance.

Moreover, another important point related to this issue is raised by producers Goodman and Dretzin, in their PBS documentary, *Merchants of Cool*, and Thomas Frank, in his book, *The Conquest of Cool*.[9] They reveal how savvy companies and interest groups marketing to younger people increasingly keep in mind a tacit guideline that can be summed up in the simple phrase: "Never let your marketing show." In short, young people do not want to be preached to. And the political initiatives of P. Diddy et al., in spite of their integration with the accoutrements of hip-hop culture, smacked of moral didacticism. Perhaps this is why the audience broke into a chorus of boos when Vanessa and Alexandra Kerry promoted voter registration at that year's MTV Video Music Awards. Commenting on the event on the website "Pop and Politics," Philip Herrick wrote the following about an appearance by John Mellencamp, who is most definitely *not* a hip-hop generationer: "[W]hen the heartland rocker came out on stage to introduce an award and ended up quickly plugging voting, you just knew the crowd was rolling their eyes and thinking, 'Dad, stop nagging me already.'"[10]

Not surprisingly, perhaps the most prevalent interpretive position I discovered in the intertexts centered on whether the hip-hip political programs primarily signified superficial flash or represented earnest and substantial attempts to empower young Black voters. Many writers in the articles, blogs, and books at least partially took a critical stance toward the voter mobilization drives. To start, several authors questioned the credibility of the rappers encouraging young citizens to register for the vote. Some of the celebrities admitted that they themselves had never voted in the past—why should anyone, then, take their directives seriously? Not only that, why would a performer within the realm of popular culture carry any political authority to begin with? A student at Howard University contended that African-American communities are too driven by celebrities. "Why do we need entertainers to get us involved in something that we should have always been a part of?" she asked.[11] Furthermore, a number of the commentators wondered if high-profile rappers such as P. Diddy and Eminem really cared about increasing voter registration or were merely in it for the bling. For example, mourning on the day after the election, Moya Bailey scoffed, "P. Diddy's death threats weren't enough to turn out the youth vote. Not that he cares; he made a grip on those $30 'Vote or Die' T-shirts."[12] Several people suggested that the hip-hop initiatives trivialized politics by turning politicians into commodities. "Voting was sold to young people like Nike or Sprite is sold to the masses," Raj Jayadev complained after November 2.[13]

But for some, the problem was not just a matter of shallow marketing campaigns directed toward the hip-hop generation; it was the product that was being sold. Let me put it this way: if you are not already, imagine yourself as a twenty-two-year-old African American lover of hip-hop culture who has experienced first-hand the institutionalized racism that still exists in many Black neighborhoods, including police brutality, an alarmingly high rate of incarceration for African-American men, and conditions of poverty. Then bring to mind the stiff- and awkward-looking face of John Kerry, which is the solution being pitched to you as a means of gaining political empowerment. Need I say more? Numerous hip-hop critics maintained, just as many of their progressive, non-hip-hop counterparts did, that an anti-Bush position was not enough; the Democrats had to offer a viable alternative. In short, John Kerry did not resonate with many African-American voters. In addition, as further evidence of a generation gap among Blacks, various writers elucidated that people should not assume that young African Americans will automatically vote Democratic. "And although voting age blacks are being registered by the masses in an effort to expire Bush's Oval Office occupancy," the editorial board of Florida A&M's campus newspaper wrote on October 1, "they still remain skeptical of Kerry."[14]

One point that was uttered again and again by the writers leery of the hip-hop events was that they focused too much on voter *registration* and not enough on voter *education*; therefore, their impact was bound to be short lived. As the editors at Howard put it, "we hope that these artists are doing their part to truly educate these young voters so that they understand their vote and not just vote because 'Diddy said it was what's up.'"[15] Jimi Izrael, whose commentary made it into the *Los Angeles's Times* op-ed section, agreed. "[A]ctivation without proper education won't bring about the long-term effects needed for the hip-hop generation to become a political force."[16] Some authors also indicated that just because a young person is offered the opportunity to painlessly register to vote at a hip-hop concert does not guarantee she will take the extra step and brave the lines on November 2nd.

An extension of this theme, which, again, many critics articulated, was that P. Diddy, Russell Simmons and their cohorts might prove instrumental in promoting voting as "sexy"—but for the hip-hop generation to achieve lasting political gains, it must mount a sustained movement that goes beyond mere voting. In her book, *Stand and Deliver*, Yvonne Bynoe eloquently outlines the argument in an especially biting manner. Positioning hip-hop activism—or raptivism—as a misnomer, she declares that "while Hip Hop culture may espouse political viewpoints, the bulk of its political activism is limited to artists lending their support and talents to a particular protest record . . . or a live performance, rather than endeavors with real influence on policy." Consequently, she continues, "Hip Hop culture, as we currently know it, cannot adequately foster a political movement."[17] In sum, what happens once the mad beats at the show stop and the people in the crowd go their separate ways? How does hip hop maintain that momentum and mobilize young adults into a 24/7 political presence? Can a dope rhyme or a dance move substitute for good old fashioned strategic planning and grassroots organizing?

Yes, But

Still, overall, most of the bloggers and other writers I surveyed, even when somewhat critical, expressed support for the hip-hop initiatives. Many of them seemed to suggest that maybe the hip-hop, get-out-the-vote drives did put too much emphasis on voting as a fashion statement, serve the cynical interests of the artists behind them, and represent a trendy episode that would likely be short lived; but in the end, they at least raised awareness about a very important election. Put simply, they did more good than harm.

After all, as Jesse Cottrell noted on "Wiretap," "hip-hop has been political in nature since its birth in the youth subculture of the Bronx during the late 1970s."[18] It would probably be more accurate to say that *some* hip-hop expression has had a political element. In his book, *Can't Stop Won't Stop*, Jeff Chang provides a history of the hip-hop generation; along the way, he underscores the variety of rap genres that have emerged, some of which have directly promoted or implicitly conveyed political messages—from Public Enemy's resurrection of Black Panther radicalism, to gangsta rap's anti-American Dream depiction of life in the 'hood, to Mos Def's "conscious" rap. Once Corporate America discovered rap's ability to reach not only angry, African-American youth, but disaffected, white suburbanites as well, it quickly co-opted the genre and strove to replace any remnants of political energy with the glamour of female-ass-grinding and gold-chain-wearing consumerism.[19] But business can never fully drain the meaning from a form of culture. And so rap's potential remains.

Moreover, a considerable amount of hip-hop inspired activity during the 2004 election season indeed extended beyond mere registration drives and expressions of popular culture. For example, in June 2003, roughly three thousand delegates and participants gathered together in New Jersey for an historic event entitled the National Hip-Hop Political Convention, which blended performance, film panel discussions, and rallies. With an emphasis on raising awareness on the issues that matter to mostly young African Americans, as well as promoting an "Intergenerational Dialogue" between people who came of age during the Civil Rights struggles and today's Black youth, the convention resulted in the formation of a national agenda that included reparations for African Americans and Native Americans and an end to the War on Youth. At Howard University, the first ever Hip-Hop Caucus met, whose primary goal, according to Michael Ivey in the campus's newspaper, was to educate Howard students, as well as visitors from nearby colleges and universities, about the electoral process and major political issues facing young voters.[20] At Florida A&M, a student quoted in the school's paper suggested that the university's own mobilizing efforts gained momentum from the buzz instilled by P. Diddy's Citizen Change and Russell Simmons's Hip-Hop Summit.[21] On October 28, Simmons visited North Carolina Central University not to simply put on a show but to deliver a lecture and participate in a panel discussion.[22] At Prairie View A&M University, members of the Congressional Black Caucus engaged with students in a town hall meeting hosted by Rap the Vote's parent organization, Rock the Vote.[23]

Overall, it appears as though the so-called fashion statements associated with the national hip-hop initiatives *did* resonate with many Black college students in a way that went beyond trendy display. "P. Diddy and his shirts, and students like myself reaching out to Black neighborhoods to educate others show how our community have [sic] really taken it to heart," said Howard sophomore Sonja Cajuste.[24] "[M]any people are rocking the 'Vote or Die' tees," observed Florida A&M writer Diamond Washington.[25] Yet she also noted how they were attending rallies and candidate debate forums. At North Carolina Central University, about twelve hundred students marched two miles to cast early ballots. On their way, "students sported 'Vote or Die' T-shirts and sang 'Amazing Grace' and 'We Shall Overcome,'" described student Carolyn McGill.[26] Prairie A&M writer Matthew Jackson stated that "Vote or Die" shirts were seen all over campus. But the students bearing the slogan did not spend their time laundering their T-shirts on election day—they turned out in large numbers to cast their ballots.[27]

In the end, over four million more young people (eighteen to twenty-nine) voted in 2004 than in the previous presidential election—an almost 10 percent increase. Yet many mainstream pundits expressed "disappointment" toward young voters' supposedly less than stellar participation at the polls. Why the disparity? It turns out that the youth vote did not have an appreciable impact on the election because turnout went up across the board. Still, is this a sign of youth apathy? After all, the number of young voters actually exceeded the goal of MTV's "Choose or Lose" campaign. On top of that, according to the Choose or Lose team's analysis, these voters represented the only age group to support John Kerry over George Bush, by a margin of about 10 percent, a number confirmed by the Center for Information & Research on Civic Learning & Engagement.[28] Had young people showed up on election day to the same extent as they did in 2000, instead of a narrow win, George Bush would have enjoyed a larger victory.

I would argue, based on my survey of intertexts and polling data, that the major hip-hop initiatives *did* have an impact on mobilizing young Blacks to vote—although, given all the variables, determining to what extent they influenced them is grounds for speculation and cannot be solved here. Even if it were true that P. Diddy, Russell Simmons, Eminem, and other high-profile rappers advocated voting primarily as a way of fattening their own wallets, that does not mean that the audience inevitably internalized the producers' intentions and responded with cynicism. Instead, there is good reason to believe many young Black people, so to speak, read these artists' texts and decoded a pro-vote message that they took to heart. At the same time, I agree with the many writers who contended that the various celebrity-driven, get-out-the-vote drives will represent only a chic episode if they do not ultimately lead to a sustained political movement.

Rap and the 2006 Midterm Elections

The role of rap in politics can be further examined through an analysis of the youth vote—and the black youth vote in particular—during the 2006 midterm elections. It appears that the increase in youth participation in 2004 was not a passing fad—the share of total votes cast by voters between eighteen and twenty-nine rose from the previous midterm elections, with an estimated increase of two million young people.[29] Indeed, turnout for voters under thirty was higher than it had been for a midterm election in at least twelve years.[30] No doubt these young citizens had a significant impact on the outcome, given that the Democrats regained control of both the House and Senate and that voters under thirty favored Democrats by over a 20 percent margin.[31] Moreover, despite (Democratic Party) fear that Black voters, disillusioned over various allegations of efforts to suppress Black participation—or even not count actual ballots cast by Blacks—in 2000 and 2002, would turn out in low numbers, African Americans actually made a good showing on election day.[32] Moreover, African-American young voters, with 13 percent of the youth vote, in fact outpaced the overall Black vote, which represented 10 percent of the total electorate.[33]

This should not be surprising. In a study completed by the Center for Information and Research on Civic Learning and Engagement, released in 2006, the researchers concluded that, when it comes to young people of voting age, African Americans are "the most likely to vote regularly, belong to groups involved with politics, donate money to candidates and parties, display buttons or signs, canvass, and contact the media." African-American youth, the study claims, "are the most politically engaged racial/ethnic group."[34]

Still, the impetus behind young African Americans' participation in the 2006 political process can hardly be attributed to hip-hop culture. True, in the run-up to the midterm elections, various political groups used elements of popular culture to further their causes or encourage voter registration. The World Wrestling Entertainment launched its "Smackdown Your Vote," which unveiled an innovative drive to register voters through the use of cell phone text messaging.[35] Music for America continued its attempt to reach young people through concerts—as many as three to eight a night—that featured rap as well as other genres of popular music.[36] The League of Young Voters, as always, employed strategies rooted in the arts, including rap and other music.[37] Some similarly minded organizations, such as the Hip-Hop Caucus Institute, specifically turned to hip hop to stir political interest. Rap entered into political commercials as well. Alana Clark won a contest sponsored by the National Coalition on Black Civic Participation for her entry, "The Movement," which was incorporated into a radio public service announcement that encouraged people to vote and was broadcast in eight states.[38] The web master for the California Nurses Association, Colette Washington, released a rhyme, in support of Proposition 89, that was turned into a sixty-second television commercial, as well as a longer video that received over ten thousand hits on YouTube.[39] Meanwhile, the rap quintet Jurassic 5 created a music video for its song, "Work It Out," which sardonically lampoons a bumbling George W. Bush.[40]

Yet it can easily be argued that these activities represented but a blade of grass in the meadow in comparison to the full range of organizing ventures conducted on behalf of reaching young African-American voters, which overshadowed the kind of popular culture tactics exploited in 2004. This time, Russell Simmons's Hip-Hop Summit Action Network was nowhere to be found. Mr. Diddy had moved on to other money-making enterprises, including the release of his first studio album in five years.[41] It appears that although the youth participation of 2004 was no trendy affair, the "Vote or Die," "Rap the Vote," "Choose or Lose" spectacle most certainly was. Instead, traditional grass-root measures, it seems, ruled the day. "You won't see rap artist Diddy in a 'Vote or Die' T-shirt or any other signs of MTV's 'Rock the Vote' campaign at Arizona State University in coming weeks," reported Chris Ramirez in a newspaper article that was subsequently posted on the website of the school's chapter of Student Public Interest Research Group (Student PIRG). "Research has indicated that voter turnout among college-age adults generally is better if they are urged by peers to register."[42] The New Voters Project, sponsored by Student PIRG at large, reported that students "engaged in old fashioned shoe leather and clever visibility tactics" to register over seventy-five thousand young citizens and promote voter turnout.[43] According to Young Voter Strategies, 46 percent of those young people surveyed by the bi-partisan polling team of Ed Goeas and Celinda Lake said they had been contacted by a political campaign or organization during the 2006 campaign—usually by phone, mail, or face-to-face—and that this proved to be a key factor in driving them to the polls.[44] "eighteen- to twenty-nine-year-olds were compelled to vote because of one of the oldest media tactics," wrote Joe Garofoli of *The San Francisco Chronicle*. "Somebody asked them, often in person." Goeas's and Lake's first post-election Young Voter Battleground Poll also revealed that 58 percent of young voters had talked with family and friends about the election.[45] Although The New Voters Project indeed integrated the occasional "party at the polls" or "X-Games at the Polls" into its tactical plan, these entertaining events were by no means its central thrust. It was not about tapping into youth culture per se, but about creating a "voter culture," stated Sarah Clader, a campaign coordinator for the New Voters Project at Rutgers University.[46]

Meanwhile, the second National Hip-Hop Political Convention (NHHPC) was held in Chicago in July 2006. Yet under the theme of "Money, Power, Respect," it functioned more as a conference presenting a diverse array of panels, workshops, and, yes, concerts, than as a mechanism for triggering buzz about the upcoming elections. Reporting on the event for the website "Hip Hop DX," Cherryl Aldave seemed to take a dismissive stance toward the recent "odd monstrosities like Diddy's 'Vote or Die!' campaign or Russell Simmons' [sic] 'Hip-Hop Summit Action Network.'" Indeed, Diddy and Simmons did not attend the gathering. Yet she focused on putting the lie to the assumption that Hip Hoppers are somehow apathetic or lazy and described a number of actions they were instituting at the local level, including a "Stop the Violence" campaign in Milwaukee, Wisconsin.[47] On "Wiretap," Malik Cooper discussed how the Convention has spawned various LOCs, that is, Local Organizing Committees, such as the one established in the Bay Area, which had held its own Hip Hop Summit in 2005 that included a speech by Representative Barbara Lee.[48] No doubt, the energy behind the NHHPCs and their local offshoots are a legitimate expression of hip-hop, political engagement. But whether these vehicles constitute the seeds of a full-fledged movement, only time will tell. It is clear, however, that the NHHPC's impact on the 2006 midterm elections was negligible.

Hip Hop and Future Elections

Can hip hop be a central element in a protracted, grassroots affair that has a bearing on future elections and stirs social reform? I would answer no, but add that the very expectation that hip hop could be is misguided. Was Jimi Hendrix a fundamental figure in bringing an end to the Vietnam War through his Woodstock version of the National Anthem? Did the rock group Ten Years After, producers of the hit single, "I'd Love to Change the World," play an instrumental role in implementing progressive change?

Still, although culture cannot single-handedly engender social transformation, it can serve as a tool of power. As hegemony theory reminds us, governments and other state-supported institutions disseminate ideology through culture. But everyday people can too. By itself, rap music can accomplish little. But it can inspire, it can raise political awareness, it can facilitate bringing people together in a spirit of activism to engage in the fund-raising, organizing, planning, and myriad activities required to launch and maintain a movement capable of generating political gains. "The role of the artist in a movement is to support the people in the frontlines," asserts hip-hop generation artist Rha Goddess.[49]

Yet if hip hop is to assist in a movement that picks up where the Civil Rights Movement left off, it will need to exploit the full resources of the new media. Between the 2004 Presidential and 2006 midterm elections, Internet phenomena such as MySpace and YouTube dynamically worked their way into public consciousness. It has become almost cliché to point out that in today's mediated environment, the traditional top-down model is being at least partially usurped by a paradigm in which everyday people can participate not only as consumers but as producers of content. Then again, although the observation is obvious, how this democratic potential ultimately unfolds is in no way apparent. It could very well play out that MySpace and other social networking sites will be nothing more than that—social networking sites. Similarly, YouTube and its inevitable spin-offs could evolve into a fragmented labyrinth of never-ending amusement. Certainly, backed by Ruppert Murdoch's acquisition of MySpace, Google's purchase of YouTube, and the corporate realm's nearly inexhaustible supply of resources, if the advertisers and other marketers have their way, any expression of grassroots, political energy will be muted. But fortunately, the future is never carved in stone. With a home video camera and a novel idea, anybody can make a political commercial that resonates. Moreover, cell phones that double as recorders of moving images are moving us closer to a full-blown surveillance society—but instead of Big Brother scornfully viewing the feeble herd, this scrutinizing culture is about everybody keeping tabs on one another. At first glance, such a prospect is terrifying. On the other hand, citizen, cell-phone journalists signify a powerful means of holding politicians more accountable. Just ask former Virginia Senator George Allen, who transformed his certain re-election into a startling defeat when he repeatedly uttered during a campaign speech the odious epithet, "macaca," in reference to a non-supporter of color in attendance, while, unbeknown to him, his performance was being captured by cell phone and later exposed on YouTube. "We live in a world in which everybody has the power to capture and then broadcast," explains Matthew Gross, the Internet strategist for John Edward's 2008 presidential campaign.[50]

One of the salient issues that will shape the future of the Internet— and the hope of fuller democratic engagement—is whether or not "net neutrality" remains a guiding principle. Should the online sphere become the two-tiered system that privileges those entities that pay for speedier distribution to users, which the cable and telephone industries advocate, the Internet could merely reproduce the commercially driven structure of the traditional mass media, rendering the voices of those less-moneyed groups and individuals marginalized. The implications for hip-hop activism are clear. As Angela Woodson, the co-chair of the first National Hip-Hop Political Convention puts it, "There are three worlds of hip hop. There's the corporate world, the political world—and the stupid world," the latter referring to rap music centered on gansta expression and bling.[51] On a pay-to-play information highway, the corporate world would most likely leave the political one far behind. Conscious rappers such as Rhymefest and Dead Prez would be hard pressed to compete with the artists bankrolled by the major record labels.

But even before speculation yields to concrete manifestations, I would concur with some of the earlier mentioned writers who declared that for the hip-hop generation to realize any of its agenda, it must do more than enter a voting booth every four years. In his classic text, *A People's History of the United States*, Howard Zinn demystifies the popular perception of voting as an almost sacred act. Instead, he counters, elections perhaps function to merely perpetuate the status quo as they diffuse much of the energy everyday citizens might use to join grassroots organizations or channel toward ongoing, political operations.[52] "There, I've voted—now I can go back to my Grand Auto Theft video game and plug into my iPod." If the most significant act of democracy for many women and men can be reduced to choosing every four years between two deeply entrenched, highly affluent, corporate-friendly figureheads of huge political parties, then maybe it is time to remind ourselves of what democracy means. As Public Enemy once so eloquently put it in its rap, "Fight the Power," "You gotta go for what you know, make everybody see, in order to fight the powers that be."

Notes

1. Bakari Kitwana, *The Hip Hop Generation: Young Blacks and the Crisis in African-American Culture* (New York: Basic Civitas Books, 2003), xiii.
2. Glenn Richardson, *Pulp Politics: How Political Advertising Tells the Stories of American Politics* (Lanham, MD: Rowman & Littlefield, 2003).
3. Howard Kurtz, "MoveOn, Mobilizing the A-List Against W," *Washington Post* (Final Edition), August 24, 2004, 1(C).
4. Alan McKee, *Textual Analysis: A Beginner's Guide* (London: Sage, 2003), 1.
5. McKee, *Textual Analysis*, 97.
6. Mink-C, Posted on *HipHop-Central.com*, August 16, 2004, http://www.hiphop-central.com/index.php?act=Search&nav=&CODE=show&searchid=38dbac1fa2c2504a93704afc39a6b3cc&search_in=posts&result_type=posts&hl=&st=225 (accessed March 21, 2005).
7. Yvonne Bynoe, *Stand and Deliver: Political Activism, Leadership, and Hip Hop Culture* (Brooklyn, NY: Soft Skull Press, 2004); Jeff Chang, *Can't Stop Won't Stop: A History of the Hip Hop Generation* (New York: St. Martin's Press, 2005); Kitwana, *The Hip Hop Generation*.
8. "Campaign for America's Future 'Take Back America' Conference," June 2, 2004, http://rocky.iona.edu:2087/universe/document?_m=dlc1655al92154e2d41e5ef4d4ba395d&_docnum=38&wchp=dGLbVib-zSkVA&_md5=ea53ca76e9b9d899d239618571563903 (accessed March 17, 2005).
9. Barak Goodman and Rachel Dretzin, producers, *Merchants of Cool* (Boston: WGBH Boston, broadcast on February 27, 2001); Thomas Frank, *The Conquest of Cool: Business Culture, Counterculture, and the Rise of Hip Consumerism* (Chicago: University of Chicago Press, 1997).
10. Philip Herrick, "Rocking the Vote at the VMAs," *Pop and Politics*, September 1, 2004, http://www.popandpolitics.com/articles_detail_archived.cfm articleID=1245 (accessed March 17, 2005).
11. Tracey Jordan, "Vote or Die: Fashion Statement or Political Stance?" *Hilltop Online*, October 15, 2004, http://www.thehilltoponline.com/global_user_elements/printpage.cfm?storyid=754620 (accessed March 19, 2005).
12. Moya Bailey, "Where Have All the Progressives Gone?" *Pop and Poli-*

tics, November 3, 2004, http://www.popandpolitics.com/articles_detail_archived .cfm?articleID=1314 (accessed March 17, 2005).

13. Raj Jayadev, "Imagining a Real Youth Movement," *Pop and Politics*, November 9, 2004, http://www.popandpolitics.com/articles_detail_archived. cfm?articleID=1351 (accessed March 17, 2005).

14. "Black Leaders Become," *Famuan Online*, October 1, 2004, http:// www.thefamuanonline.com/global_user_elements/printpage.cfm?storyid=73 8562 (accessed March 20, 2005).

15. "Rock the 'Vote' or Die," *Hilltop Online*, September 14, 2004, http:// www.thehilltoponline.com/global_user_elements/printpage.cfm?storyid=717710 (accessed March 19, 2005).

16. Jimi Izrael, "Hip-Hop Needs More than a Good Beat to Be a Political Force; Bling-Bling and Ching-Ching Are No Substitutes for a Civic Education," *Los Angeles Times* (Home Edition), August 27, 2004, 13(B).

17. Bynoe, *Stand and Deliver*, x-xi.

18. Jessie A. Cottrell, "Mobilizing the Hip-Hop Generation," *Wiretap*, April 24, 2003, http://www.wiretapmag.org/stories/15691/ (accessed March 18, 2005).

19. Chang, *Can't Stop*.

20. Michael Ivey, "First of its Kind Hip-Hop Caucus Comes to Cramton Auditorium," *Hilltop Online*, September 14, 2004, http://www.thehilltoponline. com/global_user_elements/printpage.cfm?storyid=717764 (accessed March 19, 2005).

21. Mike Cooper, "Coalition Educates," *Famuan Online*, October 13, 2004, http://www.thefamuanonline.com/global_user_elements/printpage.cfm?storyid= 751189 (accessed March 20, 2005).

22. Kristen Hunter, "Hip-Hop Mogul to Visit," *Campus Echo Online*, September 22, 2004, http://www.nccu.edu/campus/echo/archive4-0405/c-simmons.html (accessed March 24, 2005).

23. "The Panther's Top Stories," *Panther Online*, December 1, 2004, http:// www.pvpanther.com/global_user_elements/printpage.cfm?storyid=818297 (accessed March 24, 2005).

24. Brittney Johnson, "Political Junkies Sad at End of 2004 Campaign," *Hilltop Online*, November 2, 2004, http://thehilltoponline.com/global_user_ elements/printpage.cfm?storyid=791399 (accessed March 19, 2005).

25. Diamond Washington, "Students Place New Focus on 'Politickin,'" *Famuan Online*, October 15, 2004, http://www.thefamuan.com/global_user_ elements/printpage.cfm?storyid=754537 (accessed March 20, 2005).

26. Carolyn McGill, "NCCU Students Exercise Right to Vote," *Campus Echo Online*, October 6, 2004, http://www.nccu.edu/campus/echo/archive4-0405/c-vote.html (accessed March 24, 2005).

27. Matthew Jackson, "Students Rock the Polls on Super Tuesday," *Panther Online*, November 3, 2004, http://pvpanther.com/news/2004/11/03/ Campus/Student.Rock.The.Polls.On.Super.Tuesday-790713.shtml (accessed

March 24, 2005).

28. Mark Hugo Lopez, Emily Kirby, and Jared Sagoff, "The Youth Vote 2004," *Center for Information and Research on Civic Learning & Engagement,* July 2005, http://www.civicyouth.org/research/areas/pol_partic.htm (accessed January 6, 2007); "For Twenty-One Million Young Voters: What Next?" *MTV.com,* November 11, 2004, http://www.mtv.com/chooseorlose/headlines/news.jhtml?id =1493471 (accessed March 23, 2005); Mark Hugo Lopez and Emily Kirby, "Electoral Engagement Among Minority Youth," *Center for Information and Research on Civic Learning & Engagement,* July 2005, http://www.civicyouth. org/research/areas/pol_partic.htm (accessed December 29, 2006).

29. Rachel Dissell, "Younger Voices Get First Taste of Victory," *Cleveland Plain Dealer,* November 12, 2006, 5(B); Emily Hoban Kirby and Karlo Barrios Marcelo, "Young Voters in the 2006 Elections," *Center for Information and Research on Civic Learning & Engagement,* December 12, 2006, http://www. civicyouth.org/research/areas/pol_partic.htm (accessed December 29, 2006).

30. Kirby & Marcelo, "Young Voters"; Corey Moss, "Young Voices Are Heard: Midterm-Election Turnout Highest in Twenty Years," *MTV.com,* November 10, 2006, http://www.mtv.com/#/news/articles/1545509/20061110/story.jhtml (accessed December 29, 2006).

31. Dissell, "Younger Voices"; Kirby & Marcelo, "Young Voters"; "Young Voter Turnout Surges in 2006," *Rock the Vote,* November 8, 2006, http://www.rockthevote.com/media/press.php?ID=3 (accessed December 29, 2006).

32. Ian Urbina, "Democrats Fear Disillusionment in Black Voters," *New York Times* (Late Edition), October 27, 2006, 1(A).

33. Kirby & Marcelo, "Young Voters."

34. "2006 Civic and Political Health of the Nation Survey," *Center for Information and Research on Civic Learning & Engagement,* http://www.civic youth.org/research/products/youth_index_2006.htm (accessed January 2, 2007).

35. "WWE's Smackdown Your Vote! Encourages Voter Registration Using Mobile Phones," *WWE.com,* September 25, 2006, http://vote.wwe.com/press/2006_09_25.jsp (accessed January 2, 2007).

36. "About Music for America," *Music for America,* http://www.musicfor america.org/about (accessed January 2, 2007).

37. "Our Story," *League of Young Voters,* http://indyvoter.org/article.php?id=691 (accessed January 2, 2007).

38. Eric Stirgus, "Georgia 2006; Teen's Lyrics Address Voting; Lovejoy Student's Rap on Radio," *Atlanta Journal-Constitution,* November 2, 2006, 1(JI).

39. "Rappin' the Vote New Prop 89 Radio Spot is a Rap Song: About Time for 89 Hits Airways Today," *PR Newswire U.S.,* October 25, 2006, http://www.prnewswire.com (accessed December 29, 2006).

40. Chris Lee, "Pop Music; Fast Tracks; The J5 Go Jogging with Bush," *Los Angeles Times*, August 13, 2006, 41(E).

41. Steve Jones, "Diddy Presses 'Play' and Gets Back to the Music; It's First Studio Album in Five Years for Rap Celeb," *USA Today*, October 13, 2006 (Final Edition), 1(E).

42. "ASU Student Groups Work to Register Young Adults to Vote," *Arizona Republic Online*, November 4, 2006, http://www.azcentral.com/arizonare public/local/articles/1004B1-talker1004.html (accessed December 29, 2006).

43. "Student PIRGs' New Voters Project Posts Huge Vote Increase," *New Voters Project*, November 8, 2006, http://www.newvotersproject.org/new-voters-project-posts (accessed December 29, 2006).

44. "Exit Poll Shows Young Voter Turnout Up by More than Two Million Voters Over 2002; Precinct Tallies Show the Number of Votes Cast in Targeted Areas Doubled," *Young Voter Strategies*, November 8, 2006, http://www.young voterstrategies.org/index.php?tg=articles&idx=More&topics=37&article=282 (accessed December 29, 2006).

45. Joe Garofoli, "Growing Youth Turnout is Good News for Dems; Phone Calls, Handshakes, Even Text Messages Encouraged Those Under Thirty to Go to Polls," *San Francisco Chronicle*, November 9, 2006, 1(A).

46. Elizabeth Redden, "Crafting a 'Youth Culture,'" *Inside Higher Ed*, November 8, 2006, http://www.insidehighered.com/news/2006/11/08/turnout (accessed December 29, 2006).

47. Cherryl Aldave, "2006 NHHPC in Chicago: National Plan to Take Down the Man?" *Hip Hop DX*, August 2, 2006, http://www.hiphopdx.com/index/lifestyle-features/id.607 (accessed December 29, 2006).

48. Malik Cooper, "Turning Outrage into Power," *Wiretap*, August 16, 2006, http://www.wiretapmag.org/stories/40441/ (accessed December 29, 2006).

49. Quoted in Bynoe, *Stand and Deliver*, 108.

50. Howard Kurtz, "A Candidate's Not-So-Candid Camera?" *Washington Post*, January 8, 2007, 1(C).

51. Glen Ford, "Bigger Than Hip-Hop," *Wiretap*, September 19, 2006, http//www.wiretapmag.org/stories/41361/ (accessed December 29, 2006).

52. Howard Zinn, *A People's History of the United States: 1492-Present* (New York: Perennial Classics, 2003).

Part III: Evaluating the Show

Chapter 8

Soft News and Young Voters:
Why They Tune into It and
What They Get Out of It

Xiaoxia Cao

Americans have witnessed an ever-expanding media marketplace in recent years, with the number of television channels that the average household received increasing 80 percent just between 1995 and 2000.[1] As a result, politically apathetic citizens now have even greater opportunities to tune out traditional news programs.[2] Indeed, public opinion surveys show that a growing number of Americans—particularly those under the age of thirty—report not only watching entertainment-oriented soft news programs but also relying on them for campaign information.[3]

According to some, the rise of soft news media has undermined the foundation of democracy by diminishing public interest in and knowledge about politics.[4] Baum, on the other hand, argues that soft news media may benefit democratic politics by encouraging the politically apathetic to pay attention to public affairs, by informing them about politics, and by helping them to choose the political candidates that best represent their preferences.[5] This study contributes to the debate on the political implications of soft news media by exploring the uses of such media among the citizens who consume more soft news than anyone else: young voters, defined as those under the age of thirty who are eligible to vote in presidential elections.[6] Specifically, this study uses in-depth interviews to examine why and to what extent young voters tune into soft news media as well as how and why such media may have affected their political knowledge and opinions in the context of the 2004 presidential campaign. By doing so, this study advances our understanding of how such media may engage young voters in the political process in the future and therefore benefit the health of democracy.

Soft News and Hard News

Soft news is defined by "a set of story characteristics, including the absence of public policy component, sensationalized presentation, human-interest themes, and emphasis on dramatic subject matter such as crime and disaster."[7] Media focus on stories with these features are soft news media which, as some researchers have suggested, include television news magazine shows (e.g., *60 Minutes* and *20/20*), morning shows (e.g., *Good Morning America* and *Today*), entertainment-oriented talk (or E-talk) shows (e.g., *Oprah*, *The Tonight Show with Jay Leno*, and *The Late Show with David Letterman*) and political comedy shows (e.g., *The Daily Show with Jon Stewart*, *Real Time with Bill Maher*, and *Saturday Night Live*).[8] This category can also include entertainment-oriented newspapers (e.g., *The Onion*), magazines (e.g., *Cosmopolitan, People*, and *Rolling Stone*), cable channels (e.g., Black Entertainment Television and MTV), and radio shows (e.g., *Bob and Brian*).[9]

The hard news media, on the other hand, devote at least part of their coverage to public policy themes.[10] Media that fit into this category include newspapers, news magazines, network news programs, television news talk shows (e.g., *Face the Nation* and *Meet the Press*), cable news channels (e.g., CNN and Fox News), radio news programs (e.g., *Morning Edition* and *All Things Considered*), political talk radio (e.g., *Rush Limbaugh* and *Mark Belling*), news pages of internet service providers (e.g., Yahoo News), websites of traditional news media (e.g., newspapers, news magazines, news networks, and cable news channels), and online news magazines and opinion sites (e.g., Slate.com, Nationalreview.com, and Drudgereport.com).

Consistent with these definitions, empirical research into the content of soft and hard news media has found that each covers politics in a distinctive way. For example, a series of content analyses of late-night comedy shows found that jokes on these programs mainly targeted personal failings of the president and presidential candidates rather than political issues.[11] Similarly, another analysis showed that interviews with candidates on soft news shows focused more on the candidates' personal qualities and biographies than on their issue stands.[12] Thus, soft news media tend to pay little heed to issues. In contrast, hard news media pay at least some attention to public issues in covering political campaigns. For example, during the 1996 presidential election season, 25 percent of hard news stories on PBS and 11 percent on ABC dealt with issues.[13] Thus, those who tune into hard news media for campaign information may have greater opportunities to learn about candidates' stands on issues, whereas those who rely heavily on soft news media may learn something about the personal characteristics and biographies of political candidates but little about their issue positions.

Some Like It Soft: Young Americans and Political News

Numerous studies have shown that young people are less interested in politics than older people.[14] For example, a recent survey found that 54 percent of people thirty-years-old or above showed at least some interest in the 2004 primary campaign, whereas the percentage for those under the age of thirty was 35.[15] Given that people with less interest in politics tend to expose themselves to soft news media rather than hard news media, it is not surprising that people under the age of thirty were less likely to consume hard news media regularly—for example, by reading newspapers (42 percent) and watching network (18 percent) or cable news (28 percent)—than were older people (58 percent for newspapers; 39 percent for network news; 41 percent for cable news).[16] At the same time, young respondents were more likely to tune into soft news media on a regular basis—for example, by reading *People* (12 percent) and watching late-night E-talk shows (17 percent) or *The Daily Show* (9 percent)—than were older people (6 percent for *People*; 10 percent for late-night shows; 2 percent for *The Daily Show*).[17]

Moreover, a growing proportion of young people have cited soft news media as their campaign information sources in recent presidential campaigns. For example, 21 percent reported learning about the 2004 primary campaign from political comedy shows (up from 6 percent in 2000); 26 percent mentioned television news magazines (up from 19 percent).[18] Meanwhile, the number of young people who claim to learn from hard news media has declined. For instance, 23 percent cited network news in 2004 (down from 42 percent); 29 percent mentioned local news (down from 42).[19] As a result, soft news media began to rival hard news media as key campaign information sources among young people in the 2004 campaign.[20]

Soft but Still Influential

Though people consume soft news media mainly for entertainment purposes, these media nevertheless present political information and, thus, may influence public knowledge about politics.[21] According to Downs, the small chance that an individual may influence a political outcome does not justify much time and effort spent on gathering large amounts of political information.[22] Thus, people should tend to rely on free information that they receive as a by-product of their nonpolitical activities—for example, watching soft news television programs for entertainment—to reduce the costs of becoming informed.[23] Building on this idea, Baum developed an "incidental by-product model" to explain how soft news media may foster public attentiveness to and even knowledge about politics.[24] In this model, soft news media lower the cognitive cost of paying attention by repackaging political information in an entertaining and accessible way; consequently, even people who consume such media for entertainment may receive the information.

In line with this reasoning, some studies have suggested that watching soft news television programs may increase the political knowledge of the audience. For example, research based on cross-sectional survey data has found that exposure to such programs is associated with greater political knowledge among viewers under certain circumstances.[25] Watching candidate interviews on these programs was also found to be positively related to audience members' campaign knowledge.[26] Similarly, a recent experimental study concluded that exposure to entertainment-oriented television programs could increase viewers' political knowledge.[27]

In addition, soft news media can shape political opinions. According to the reception-acceptance model of opinion formation, the likelihood of encountering and accepting political messages varies with political awareness.[28] Relative to their more knowledgeable counterparts, poorly informed people are less likely to receive political messages but more likely to be influenced by them. It follows that people with lower levels of political awareness should be more responsive to political information from soft news media than to information from hard news media given that these people tend to consume the former more than the latter.[29] Even when they encounter information from hard news media, they may fail to absorb it due to their lack of interest in it or ability to comprehend it.[30] By comparison, they should be more inclined to absorb information from soft news media because it is entertaining and easy to understand.[31] Thus, soft news media should have a greater impact on the opinions of the politically unaware than hard news media. Indeed, Baum found that daytime E-talk shows exerted more influence on low-awareness viewers' attitudes toward political candidates than hard news media.[32]

Highly aware individuals, on the other hand, tend to resist the influence of soft news media because they usually have well-formed belief systems supported by a large store of political knowledge, which enables them to counterargue or reject political messages that are inconsistent with their pre-existing attitudes.[33] As a result, exposure to political information from such media usually reinforces rather than changes their political attitudes.[34] Consistent with this, Young found that exposure to late-night E-talk shows may have influenced ratings of presidential candidates' traits among people with lower levels of political knowledge but not among those with high levels of knowledge.[35] In a similar vein, Baum found that watching day-time E-talk shows may have affected candidate preference and voting intentions among less informed viewers but not among their more knowledgeable counterparts.[36]

In sum, young people differ from their older peers in being less interested in politics, consuming less hard news media, and consuming more soft news media. They are also more likely to cite soft news media as campaign information sources. Those who consume soft news media may gain information from them through incident exposure. Still, voters who rely primarily on such media for campaign information may be less aware of candidates' stands on issues than are those who learn from hard news media. Moreover, soft news media should have a greater impact than hard news media on the political opinions of relatively uninformed young people. With all of this in mind, the present study used in-depth interviews to explore why and to what extent young voters tune into soft news media as well as how and why such media may affect their campaign knowledge and political opinions.

Research Method

In answering these research questions, the present study used the 2004 presidential campaign as a case study. This campaign is of particular interest given that it was the first one in which soft news media rivaled hard news media as campaign information sources among young people.[37] Unlike previous studies based on quantitative research methods, this study used individual in-depth interviews to examine the role of soft news media. Though this method has its weaknesses—for example, one cannot generalize from the results to the broader population—it allows for a rich understanding of the topic.[38] The method is well-suited to the purposes of this study because it offers a means to understand why young voters tune into soft news media and why they are influenced by such media.

This study recruited two types of young voters—those with low levels of political interest and those with higher levels of interest—for comparison purposes.[39] To identify these two types of voters, a screening questionnaire was administered to potential respondents. Individuals who scored two or below on the questionnaire were considered politically apathetic whereas those who scored three or above were deemed politically attentive. Individuals whose scores fell between two and three were screened out of the study (see Appendix for the questionnaire wording and scoring method).

All participants were recruited from a public university in the Midwestern United States through snowball sampling. Multiple start points were used to minimize the impact of the sampling technique on the results. The researcher first went to twelve classes to recruit potential participants from different majors (e.g., electrical engineering, business, geography, and communication) and then met with them individually at either an office or a small conference room to assess their political interest levels. Regardless of whether they were eligible to participate in the study, they were asked to refer their classmates rather than their roommates or close friends. This was done to reduce the likelihood that the first-recruited respondents and referrals would share media with each other. The referrals were then contacted through e-mail and recruited as potential respondents. If potential respondents passed the screening test, then the researcher explained to them the purpose and procedures of the study and invited them to participate as volunteers. Those who agreed were asked to sign a consent form. The resulting sample included twenty-seven politically apathetic and twenty-four politically attentive young voters.

Participants were interviewed twice: once before the 2004 general election (between October 2 and October 31) and once after the election (between November 10 and November 22). All interviews were recorded on a tape recorder. The first wave of interviews explored 1) what kind of media participants used, 2) why they used these media, 3) where they acquired information about the campaign, and 4) which candidates they preferred and why; the second interviews focused on whom they voted for in the election and why.

Due to the tight schedule, the second interviews were completed in less than two weeks—seventeen days less than the first interviews. As a result, nineteen respondents were unable to participate in the second interviews and were eliminated from the present study.[40] Two other cases were removed because of technical problems (broken tapes). Thus, the findings from this study came from interviews with thirty young voters—fifteen in each political interest category. Among the politically attentive participants, seven were men and eight were women; among the politically apathetic, five were men and ten were women. The age of the participants ranged from eighteen to twenty-five with a mean of twenty-one.

Findings

Who Consumes Soft News?

Most participants consumed at least some soft news media. E-talk radio programs, morning shows, television E-talk shows, political comedy shows, and entertainment newspapers and magazines were widely popular. There were no discernible differences between politically attentive and politically apathetic respondents in terms of the amount and types of soft news media consumed. Samantha$_{(H)}$, for example, spent most of the time on her way to school listening to *Bob and Brian*: "I would say the station that I listen to most in the morning is probably 102.9 because I like *Bob and Brian*."[41] She subscribed to *Cosmopolitan* and read *People* occasionally. Sarah$_{(H)}$, tuned into *Today* every weekday morning: "I watched the *Today* show on channel 4 . . . It's three hours in length, but I usually only watch the middle hour . . . That's convenient for me." She was also a regular reader of *Cosmopolitan*. Michael$_{(H)}$ watched *The Daily Show* sometimes, in addition to "the comedy special *MADtv*." Tim$_{(H)}$, was a fan of *The Late Show with David Letterman* and liked reading *The Onion*. Troy$_{(H)}$ also read *The Onion*, in addition to visiting the websites of BET and MTV "every once in a while."

Like their politically attentive counterparts, many inattentive respondents were also regular consumers of soft news media. Lauren$_{(L)}$, for instance, listened to *Bob and Brian* in the morning most the time and watched Jay Leno at night occasionally. When she didn't "have homework," she read "*The Onion* sometimes at home." Elaine$_{(L)}$ watched *Today* in the morning: "A lot of time in the morning before I go to school or work, if I have time, I will turn on the *Today* show and watch that." She also listened to KISS FM—a hip pop music station where DJs sometimes briefly mentioned current issues. She read *Cosmopolitan* "once in a while." Nicole$_{(L)}$ followed both *Oprah* and *Dr. Phil* and read *People*. Jim$_{(L)}$ said, "when I get home from school at night, I watch Conan O'Brien, a late-night comedy show . . . Instead of newspaper, I read *The Onion*." Joe$_{(L)}$ watched *Real Time with Bill Maher* on a regular basis: "I know that I watch it whenever it's on. The show is on HBO. It's really political . . . [The name of the show is] *Real Time*."

Why Young Voters Consume Soft News

All of the participants who consumed soft news media said that they tuned into such media to be entertained. Only some of them, however, used such media solely for entertainment. Others considered them both entertaining and informative. Again, politically attentive participants did not differ from their inattentive counterparts in why they tuned into such media.

To some participants, the appeal of soft news media lies only in their entertainment value. Tim$_{(H)}$, for example, watched *The Late Show with David Letterman* solely for entertainment: "I watch it for entertainment. Usually there's not a whole lot [of] news value or anything like that." When the researcher asked him why he read *The Onion*, he replied: "It's hilarious. That's about it." Similarly, Rebecca$_{(H)}$ told the researcher that she watched *The Daily Show* because "it's funny." Like some of their politically attentive counterparts, a number of inattentive respondents also tuned into soft news media solely to be entertained. Nicole$_{(L)}$, for instance, explained why she watched *Oprah* and *Dr. Phil*: "I guess mainly for entertainment. They don't make me knowledgeable. They are not very informational." Paul$_{(L)}$ listened to *Bob and Brian* because it was funny. He did not consider it as a "source of good solid information."

Yet for other participants, soft news media had both entertainment and informative value. Elaine$_{(L)}$, for instance, said that she got news from a morning music program on KISS FM while listening to it for music: "I don't sit down [to] watch the news, I don't have much time to do that and

I don't get the paper . . . The DJ doesn't cover a lot of stuff but he mentions some of the more important things, so I know them . . . Normally I listen to this station for music but get the news along with it." Lauren$_{(L)}$ also deemed *Bob and Brian* entertaining and informative: "It's a really good show . . . It's a combination of entertainment and news . . . It's funny and informative." Though politically attentive participants regularly tuned into hard news media for information, some of them also consumed soft news for the news of the day. Samantha$_{(H)}$, who often listened to *Mark Belling* and read news on the websites of *Milwaukee Journal Sentinel,* Fox News, CNN, and MSN, also listened to *Bob and Brian* for both entertainment and information:

> I like *Bob and Brian.* I think it's pretty funny . . . the way they interview people and their viewpoints, everything is funny I guess. It's entertaining . . . Also if I go to school, if the teacher talks about something happening in the news overnight, maybe because I listen to *Bob and Brian* in the morning and they mention something, I will have a little background.

Similarly, Sarah$_{(H)}$, who read *Milwaukee Journal Sentinel* and watched network evening news, watched *Today* in the morning because she liked "the news and the fun stuff" it covered.

Several respondents consumed soft news media not only for entertainment but also to specifically seek out perspectives on political issues. For instance, Troy$_{(H)}$ went to the MTV website for music and celebrities' opinions on the election: "MTV is more entertaining . . . I learn about music, learn about how artists view the election." Similarly, Amanda$_{(H)}$ reported that she watched *The Daily Show* for entertainment and for "the whole different take on everything that is going on," including "the upcoming presidential election." Some politically apathetic voters in this study also tuned into soft news media for entertainment and views on issues. For example, Joe$_{(L)}$ explained to the researcher that he liked to watch *Real Time* "because [Bill Maher] is a really funny guy. He will take the serious issues and make jokes of them . . . It keeps me informed about the stuff that's going on and brings in more humorous insights."

Soft News as a Campaign Information Source

Although both politically attentive and politically apathetic participants cited soft news media as campaign information sources, they differed in the extent to which they relied on such media for information. Among attentive participates, the soft news media were typically only one of multiple media venues for learning about the campaign. For example, Michael$_{(H)}$ cited CNN and Fox News along with *The Daily Show* as his campaign news sources when the researcher asked him where he learned about the campaign. Similarly, Samantha$_{(H)}$ cited the *Milwaukee Journal Sentinel, Mark Belling,* and several news websites along with *Bob and Brian.* Among apathetic respondents, however, the soft news media were sometimes the only media venue for obtaining campaign information. *Bob and Brian,* for example, was the only media source that Lauren$_{(L)}$ cited, though she also reported learning about the campaign from her fiancée, brother, and instructor at school. Similarly, Joe$_{(L)}$ reported that, besides his family and friends, *Real Time* was one of his main campaign news sources. As a result, political messages on soft news media may be more important for these less attentive respondents.

Moreover, those who rely heavily on such media for campaign news may tend to be relatively unaware of where candidates stand on political issues even though they may know some information about the personal characteristics and biographies of the candidates.[42] Joe$_{(L)}$, for instance, told the researcher that he was not quite familiar with where candidates stood on issues though he knew Democratic Presidential Candidate John Kerry was a Vietnam veteran. Similarly, Lauren$_{(L)}$ said that she did not know candidates' issue positions but was aware that John Kerry was "a flip-flopper," which bothered her. In contrast, participants who claimed to learn about the campaign from both soft and hard news media may learn more about candidates' issue stands, given that hard news media usually devote at least some of their coverage to such topics.[43] In line with this, Michel$_{(H)}$ was familiar with the issue stances of both the presidential and senatorial candidates, and Samantha $_{(H)}$ was aware of where some political candidates stood on issues.

The Impact of Soft News on Political Opinions

Though both attentive and inattentive respondents claimed to tune into and learn about the campaign from soft news media, only the latter said that soft news media affected their opinions about presidential candidates—a pattern that paralleled Baum's and Young's results.[44] Jim$_{(L)}$, for example, described how *The Onion* affected his opinions about John Kerry: "It had an article making fun of Kerry. It was before he chose

Edwards as his vice president. It said Kerry chose 97.2 percent of Kerry as running mate because he is relying on his Vietnam record . . . That's the impression I got on Kerry. He is relying on some of his history and anti-Bush stands." Similarly, *Real Time* swung Joe's$_{(L)}$ voting decision at the final stage of the campaign. He was undecided in the first interview, but after the election he told the researcher that he had voted for John Kerry. When the researcher asked him why, he said that *Real Time* helped to push him toward John Kerry because Bill Maher was "more for Kerry than for Bush." No politically inattentive participants reported being influenced by hard news media, though many of them cited their family and friends as sources of influence.

Whereas some of the inattentive respondents said that they were influenced by soft news media, none of the attentive respondents said so. Moreover, the attentive respondents tended to discount political messages from such media when those messages were inconsistent with their own pre-existing attitudes. For example, Michael$_{(H)}$, a strong Republican who made up his mind at the early stage of the campaign, told me that he watched *The Daily Show* and learned from it but considered Jon Stewart's opinions "with less respect" because "he is very liberal."

Why Politically Apathetic Young Voters Were Susceptible to Soft News

The evidence from this study suggests that soft news media had a greater impact on politically apathetic participants than hard news media because 1) these respondents chose to consume soft news media more than hard news media; 2) they paid more attention to political messages from soft news media than to messages from hard news media; and 3) they were more likely to comprehend political information in soft news media than information in hard news media.

Compared to their politically attentive counterparts who sought to learn about current issues and events from hard news media on a regular basis, those with less interest in politics were less likely to tune into such media. Most of them only consumed hard news media incidentally, though they did make efforts to consume soft news media. Paul$_{(L)}$, for instance, had little interest in hard news and consumed little of it: "I don't really watch the news, I don't read the paper . . . I'm just not interested in the news for [the] most part . . . Let's say if I stand here and there's a paper on the table, I might glance the headlines in the paper but

I won't sit down and read it." Nevertheless, he listened to *Bob and Brian* in the morning and read *The Onion* on a regular basis. Similarly, Joe(L) told the researcher that he would not "make any effort to" watch television news:

> It's something that doesn't come to my mind. I'm not going to walk down the street one day, thinking about what's going on in another part of the country . . . But if I'm flipping through [channels] and it's on I will watch it . . . If I get to my parents' house . . . if they are watching the news, depending on if I sit down, talking to them or anything, then I usually watch whatever they are watching on TV . . . I go there once a month maybe.

However, he "tried to watch" *Real Time* "whenever it's on."

Political messages from soft news media, in turn, were more likely to reach politically inattentive young voters than messages from hard news media. Suzanne(L) for example, said that she would like to watch candidate interviews on *Oprah* even though she normally tuned out politics:

> I like watching the *Oprah* . . . If she has politicians on, I'd like to watch some of it just [so] I can have an idea of what they are talking about, what they are running for and really supporting, things like that. But I do turn off politics usually. Especially now it's getting closer to the election, things are getting so [over]whelming . . . I don't want to hear it anymore.

Moreover, politically inattentive participants tended not to pay attention to political information in hard news media even when they were exposed to such media. Suzanne(L) described how she watched national and international news on television: "I listen to it, but I don't really pay close attention to it. I may be not really thinking about what's going on." When Nicole(L) watched evening news, she did not pay much attention to it either: "It might be on the whole time, but I might watch a little of it or talk on the phone, I won't give it my undivided attention." When these two participants watched daytime talk shows, however, they paid more attention.

Finally, political information in soft news media was more accessible to politically inattentive participants than information in hard news media. For example, Joe(L), thought that *Real Time* was easier to understand than hard news: "I find that it's a lot easier [to] watch [*Real Time with Bill Maher*] and take it in than the straight news" because sometimes traditional news media—the newspapers in particular—"give too much detail" that he did not quite understand. Elaine$_{(L)}$ also said that it was hard for her to comprehend political news, though she did pick up information about current events from the morning music programs on KISS FM:

> It would be beneficial for me to get news . . . but I haven't really done it yet . . . I like entertainment news more than political or election related whatsoever. It's easier and more fun to read . . . I don't have to know a lot to read entertainment news . . . I don't want to hear them talking about the war all the time or listen to the candidates bashing [each other] back forth and back forth. It's just so hard for me to determine anything. I'd rather just read something that I can completely understand.

All in all, the findings suggest that politically inattentive participants tended to expose themselves to and receive political messages from soft news media rather than hard news media. Given their lack of attentiveness—and, thus, their relatively low levels of resistance to political messages—these respondents were also more susceptible to the influence of the soft news media than their attentive counterparts.[45]

Discussion

Given the growing proportion of young voters who cite soft news media as significant campaign information sources, it is important for political communication scholars to understand why and to what extent such media attract young voters' attention as well as how and why they may affect political knowledge and opinions. To answer these questions, the present study drew on interviews with two types of young voters—those with high levels of political interest and those with lower levels of interest—before and after the 2004 presidential election.

The findings indicate that most participants, regardless of their levels of political interest, consumed at least some soft news media. There were no discernible differences between the two types of participants in terms of the amount and kinds of soft news media consumed or their reasons for using such media. All of the participants who exposed themselves to soft news media did so for entertainment, a finding consistent with Baum's and Prior's results.[46] This, however, was not the only reason why they tuned into such media. Some of them—surprisingly, including both politically attentive and politically apathetic participants—also considered soft news media informative and/or turned to them for perspectives on the election.

Moreover, both politically inattentive and attentive participants claimed to have learned about the campaign from soft news media, which implies that such media may have the potential to foster political knowledge among young voters. To be sure, my findings suggest that those who mainly relied on soft news media for campaign information knew little about candidates' stands on issues but gained some knowledge about what Popkin calls "information shortcuts"—that is, candidates' personal characteristics and biographies.[47] However, these shortcuts are, "by no means devoid of substantive content" and can tell voters more about candidates than they initially appear to do.[48] For example, based on personal characteristics, voters can draw inferences on whether or not a candidate would have the ability to handle the issues facing the country if he or she takes office. Given that not all citizens follow campaigns just to be informed, information shortcuts obtained from soft news media may provide voters with substantive information that they would otherwise fail to acquire, thereby helping them to choose among candidates. Indeed, Baum found that watching E-talk shows enabled low-awareness viewers to vote for the candidate that best represented their interests.[49]

The present study also found that soft news media affected opinions about political candidates among politically inattentive participants, whereas hard news media did not, another finding that parallels results from earlier studies.[50] Soft news media may have had such impact because, consistent with Baum's argument, politically inattentive participants typically chose not to consume hard news media. Instead, they chose to consume soft news media. Moreover, they tended to receive political messages from soft news media because such messages attracted their attention and were easy to absorb. As a result, politically apathetic young voters were more susceptible to the influence of soft news media than to that of hard news media,

In drawing conclusions from these findings, one should be appropriately cautious. Admittedly, a convenience sample of thirty young voters from a public university by no means represents young American voters as a whole. Moreover, the nature of the research method—in-depth interviewing—also raises inevitable concerns. For example, the findings of this study may be susceptible to the influence of subjective factors such as the communication skills of the researcher and the accuracy of the respondents' memories. Thus, the findings cannot be projected to the population in question. Yet they can serve as a basis for future research on the impact of soft news media on young voters. Future studies might examine the extent to which American young voters consume soft new media for information and for perspectives on current issues. They could also investigate whether soft news media affect young voters with different motives in different ways.

This study examined young voters' soft news consumption and its impact at a particular stage of a particular campaign—that is, the final stage of the 2004 presidential election. Future research might examine the impact of soft new media on young voters in other stages of the campaign. Such research could even go beyond the context of presidential campaigns.

A final caution is that young voters in this study were asked to self-report their media consumption, their campaign information sources, and the factors shaping their opinions. Thus, the present study did not assess how much participants truly learned from soft news media, nor did it ascertain whether their opinions were indeed affected by such media. Future research could yield stronger evidence of the effects of soft news media on political knowledge and candidate preferences among young voters.

Patterson, among others, has argued that the rise of soft new media helps to account for a downward trend in public interest in and knowledge about politics.[51] Contrary to such an argument, the findings of this study suggest that soft news media may benefit democratic politics by directing politically inattentive young voters' attention to politics, offering them accessible political messages, and even helping them to choose among political candidates. Such roles may be particularly important for the health of democracy, given both the low interest in politics and the relatively high levels of exposure to soft news media among young voters.

Having said this, the prominence of soft news media seems likely to grow rather than diminish in future elections. With the increasing popularity of soft news media has come greater opportunities for young voters to engage in the political process. The fact that the young crowd could be the force that shapes election outcomes in the years ahead points to the importance of understanding the impact of soft news on young voters.

Notes

1. P. J. Bednarski, "More Than I Can Watch," *Broadcasting and Cable*, July 9, 2001, 18.

2. Stephen Earl Bennett, *Apathy in America: 1960-1984 Causes & Consequences of Citizen Political Indifference* (Dobbs Ferry, NY: Transnational Publishers, 1986), 131-35.

3. Pew Research Center, "The Tough Job of Communicating with Voters," *Pew Research Center for the People & the Press* 2000, http:// people-press.org/reports/display.php3?ReportID=46 (accessed January 1, 2007); Pew Research Center, "Cable and Internet Loom Large in Fragmented Political News Universe: Perceptions of Partisan Bias Seen as Growing, Especially by Democrats, *Pew Research Center for the People & the Press* 2004, http://people-press.org/reports/display.php3?ReportID=200 (accessed January 1, 2007).

4. Thomas E. Patterson, "Doing Well and Doing Good" (Faculty Research Working Paper Series, #RWP01-001, Cambridge, MA: John F. Kennedy School of Government, Harvard University, 2000); Robert D. Putnam, *Bowling Alone* (New York: Simon & Schuster, 2000), 230-31.

5. Matthew A. Baum, *Soft News Goes to War: Public Opinion and American Foreign Policy in the New Media Age* (Princeton, NY: Princeton University Press, 2003), 132-33, 279-81; Matthew A. Baum and Angela S. Jamison, "The *Oprah* Effect: How Soft News Helps Inattentive Citizens Vote Consistently," *Journal of Politics* 68, no. 4 (November 2006): 946.

6. Pew Research Center, "Cable and Internet."

7. Matthew A. Baum, "Sex, Lies, and War: How Soft News Brings Foreign Policy to the Inattentive Public," *American Political Science Review* 96, no. 1 (March 2002): 92.

8. Baum, "Sex, Lies and Wars," 93; Baum, *Soft News*, 58-62; Markus Prior, "Any Good News in Soft News? The Impact of Soft News Preference on Political Knowledge," *Political Communication* 20, no. 2 (April 2003): 150-54.

9. *Bob and Brian* is a radio E-talk show on 102.9 FM—a rock music radio station in Milwaukee, Wisconsin. The show is very popular among young people.

10. Baum, "Sex, Lies and Wars," 92; Baum, *Soft News*, 6.

11. David S. Niven, Robert Lichter and Daniel Amundson, "The Political Content of Late Night Comedy," *Press/Politics* 8, no. 3 (July 2003): 125-27.

12. Matthew A. Baum, "Talking the Vote: Why Presidential Candidates Hit the Talk Show Circuit," *American Journal of Political Science* 49, no. 2 (April 2005): 215; "Primary Campaign TV Talk Shows," *PresidentialCampaign2004*, 2004, http://presidentialcampaign2004.coas.missouri.edu/primary/primarytalk shows html (accessed January 1, 2007).

13. Matthew R. Keerbel, Sumaiya Apee and Marc Howard Ross, "PBS Ain't So Different: Public Broadcasting, Election Frames, and Democratic Empowerment," *Press/Politics* 5, no. 4 (October 2000): 26.

14. Pew Research Center, "The Age of Indifference," *Pew Research Center for the People & the Press* 1990, http://people-press.org/reports/ display.php3? ReportID=19900628 (accessed January 1, 2007); Pew Research Center, "Cable and Internet"; Putnam, *Bowling Alone*, 36-37.

15. Pew Research Center, "Cable and Internet."

16. Baum, "Talking the Vote," 216; Bennett, *Apathy in America*, 131-35; Pew Research Center, "News Audiences Increasingly Politicized: Online News Audience Larger, More Diverse," *Pew Research Center for the People & the Press* 2004, http://people-press.org/reports/display.php3? ReportID=215 (accessed January 1, 2007).

17. Pew Research Center, "News Audiences."

18. Pew Research Center, "Cable and Internet."

19. Pew Research Center, "Cable and Internet."

20. Pew Research Center, "Cable and Internet."

21. Baum, "Sex, Lies and Wars," 94; Paul R. Brewer and Emily Marquardt, "Mock News and Democracy: Analyzing *The Daily Show*," *Atlantic Journal of Communication* (n.d.); Niven et al., "The Political Content," 118; Prior, "Any Good News," 149; Dannagal Goldthwaite Young, "Daily Show Viewers Knowledgeable about Presidential Campaign, National Annenberg Election Survey Shows," *Annenberg Public Policy Center* 2004, http://www. annenbergpublicpolicycenter.org/naes/2004_03_late-night-knowledge-2_9-21_ pr.pdf (accessed January 1, 2007).

22. Anthony Downs, *An Economic Theory of Democracy* (New York: Harper Collins, 1957), 244-45.

23. Downs, *An Economic Theory*, 221-23; Samuel Popkin, *The Reasoning Voter* (Chicago: University of Chicago Press, 1991), 212.

24. Baum, "Sex, Lies and War," 92.

25. Baum, *Soft News*, 279-81; Barry A. Hollander, "Late-Night Learning: Do Entertainment Programs Increase Political Campaign Knowledge for Young Viewers?" *Journal of Broadcasting & Electronic Media* 49, no. 4 (December 2005): 410-41; Young, "Daily Show Viewers."

26. Paul R. Brewer and Xiaoxia Cao, "Candidate Appearances on Soft News Shows and Public Awareness of Primary Campaigns," *Journal of Broadcasting & Electronic Media* 50, no. 1 (March 2006): 18.

27. Young Mie Kim and John V. Vishak, "Just Laugh! You Don't Need to Remember: The Effects of Entertainment Media on Political Information Acquisition and Information Processing in Political Judgment" (paper presented at the annual meeting of the International Communication Association, Dresden, Germany, June 2006), 23. But also see Prior, "Any Good News," 162, for a different opinion on whether soft news affects political knowledge.

28. John Zaller, *The Nature and Origins of Mass Opinion* (New York: Cambridge University Press, 1992), 42-48.

29. Baum, "Talking the Vote," 216.

30. Ruth Hamill and Milton Lodge, "Cognitive Consequences of Political

Sophistication," in *Political Cognition*, ed. Richard R. Lau and David O. Sears (Hillsdale, NJ: Lawrence Erlbaum, 1986), 71-73; James T. Hamilton, *All the News That's Fit to Sell: How the Market Transforms Information into News* (Princeton, NJ: Princeton University Press, 2003), 113.

31. Baum, "Sex, Lies and War," 94.
32. Baum, "Talking the Vote," 228.
33. Zaller, *Nature and Origins*, 52.
34. Baum, "Talking the Vote," 217.
35. Dannagal Goldthwaite Young, "Late-Night Comedy in Election 2000: Its Influence on Candidate Trait Ratings and the Moderating Effects of Political Knowledge and Partisanship," *Journal of Broadcasting & Electronic Media* 48, no. 1 (March 2004): 14-15.
36. Baum, "Talking the Vote," 228.
37. Pew Research Center, "Cable and Internet."
38. Earl Babbie, *The Practice of Social Research* (Belmont, CA: Wadsworth, 2004), 307-9.
39. Baum, "Talking the Vote," 228; Bennett, *Apathy in America*, 161.
40. In terms of political interest and media consumption, the participants who dropped out of the study did not differ substantively from those who remained. One might suspect that those who had little interest in politics tended to withdraw because they felt uncomfortable telling the researcher that they did not care about the election or that they did not vote. This was apparently not the case, however; among those who returned for the second interviews, some admitted that they did not vote because they had not followed the election closely enough to do so.
41. H refers to a high level of political interest; L, on the other hand, means a lower level of interest. Participants' real names are not used in this chapter.
42. Baum, "Sex, Lies and War," 92; Niven et al., "The Political Content," 125-27.
43. Baum, "Sex, Lies and War," 92; Keerbel et al., "PBS Ain't So Different," 26.
44. Baum, "Talking the Vote," 228; Young, "Late-Night Comedy," 14-15.
45. Zaller, *Nature and Origins*, 44.
46. Baum, "Sex, Lies and Wars," 94; Prior, "Any Good News," 149.
47. Popkin, *The Reasoning Voter*, 44.
48. Popkin, *The Reasoning Voter*, 44.
49. Baum and Jamison, "The *Oprah* Effect," 946.
50. Baum, "Talking the Vote," 228.
51. Patterson, "Doing Well," 2; Putnam, *Bowling Alone*, 230-31.

Appendix: Screening Questionnaire and Scoring Method

Please tell me whether you agree or disagree with the following statements.

1. You follow what's going on in government and public affairs most of the time.
   a. Completely agree
   b. Somewhat agree
   c. Somewhat disagree
   d. Completely disagree
   e. Don't know or Refuse to answer

2. You follow the news about this year's presidential election closely.
   a. Completely agree
   b. Somewhat agree
   c. Somewhat disagree
   d. Completely disagree
   e. Don't know or Refuse to answer

3. You enjoy keeping up with the news about this year's presidential election.
   a. Completely agree
   b. Somewhat agree
   c. Somewhat disagree
   d. Completely disagree
   e. Don't know or Refuse to answer

4. You have given much thought to the coming presidential election.
   a. Completely agree
   b. Somewhat agree
   c. Somewhat disagree
   d. Completely disagree
   e. Don't know or Refuse to answer

Coding method: For each statement, A was coded as 4, B as 3, C as 2, D as 1, and E as an invalid answer. The political interest score was calculated by dividing the total score for each respondent by the number of valid answer(s).

Chapter 9

Thin Democracy/Thick Citizenry: Interactive Media and Its Lessons for Young Citizen/Consumers

Shawn McIntosh

Democracy does not need to go on a diet. In fact, one could argue that democracy in the United States is already runway-model thin and that there is no place for heroin chic in a healthy, modern democracy. Social commentators have long lamented the decreasing levels of engagement in politics and civic institutions by the public, blaming the decline on everything from widespread cynicism about political leaders and the influence of television on political campaigns to socio-cultural shifts.[1] Other scholars, such as Benjamin Barber, claim that it is liberal democracy itself that has led to cynicism and lack of participation—what he calls "thin democracy."[2] He claims that the emphasis on liberal values actually works against inculcating an atmosphere of spirited, democratic civic engagement.

Lack of civic engagement and a decline in voting has been especially noted among young adults. Since 1972, when eighteen-year-olds were first given the right to vote, voting rates among eighteen- to twenty-four-year-olds has steadily declined, except for surges in 1992 and 2004.[3] The percentage of eighteen- to twenty-four-year-olds who voted in 2004 jumped to 47 percent, representing an 11 percent increase over the percentage who voted in 2000.[4] Many commentators attributed the rise in youth voter turnout in 2004 to an increased number of active voter registration drives, the closeness of the race, and the Internet's capacity to facilitate communication and mobilization.[5] Activists hope that the surge in 2004 is part of a long-term trend and not simply a temporary blip like the 1992 elections turned out to be.

To be sure, compared to older groups, young people are still less likely to vote and are more likely to lack political knowledge and have a range of attitudes and beliefs that contribute to their low civic engagement.[6] These attitudes did not develop overnight and are also not likely to drastically change after one close election. Rather, an array of strategies will likely be needed to encourage young voters to become more engaged in politics. Some commentators claim that getting youth more civically engaged has to start with restructuring schools so they operate on democratic principles and give young people first-hand experiences in participation, decision-making, and seeing that their actions can make a difference.[7]

The development of the Internet and especially the World Wide Web has led to predictions that people would be able to super-size a low-involvement political menu as more citizens go online, get informed, and become politically engaged. Despite great unevenness among age, income, and ethnic groups regarding Internet availability and usage,[8] the Internet penetration rate in the U.S. reached 73 percent in 2006, making the Internet an important site of cultural production, including popular culture.

Peer-to-peer networks have helped spur the easy distribution of popular songs, TV shows, and movies among consumers while also facilitating the production of culture in the form of mash-ups, or user-generated mixes of material, or entirely new creations that are freely shared in what is broadly termed "social authorship."[9] Volunteers working together in loose collaboration or ad hoc virtual organizations have created such cultural forces as Wikipedia, the collaborative online encyclopedia, and the open source movement of software developers has created free software to rival those of major corporations, all in an environment that eschews traditional market principles.[10]

But even these phenomena fail to capture the evolving cultural role the Internet plays in our lives and subsequently in business. Country code domain names such as .us (United States) or .in (India), originally created simply as a type of post office address for the Internet, have taken on a range of cultural meanings in countries throughout the world, as well as generated revenues for countries like Tuvalu (.tv) and Niue, whose .nu became popular as a domain name among Swedes partly because it means "now" in Swedish.[11] There are many other examples regarding the Internet in which ostensibly dry or technical matters have taken on cultural, legal, financial, and political meanings.

This essay uses the 2004 presidential campaign as a foundation from which to examine current and future dynamics between youth, politics, and democracy in relation to interactive, digital media. Practices developed in 2004 and in coming elections may well have an undue influence on what citizens expect from their interactive media regarding politics, which in turn could greatly affect the way tomorrow's voters use and perceive the Internet in political campaigns and in civic involvement.

Will it be a tool of engagement and empowerment, in which interactivity helps give rise to practices that enable people, especially young people, to see being involved in their communities as a normal part of their lives? Or will the Internet further entrench the current divide between producers and consumers, between politicians selling a product (in this case, themselves) and a disengaged, cynical electorate that knows it is being sold a bill of goods? Do the 2004 presidential campaigns presage the development of a new type of politics in which citizens have a voice and can effect important changes to the political system, or will consumers simply be better targeted with slicker campaign messages and cajoled into a form of limited or carefully directed participation that enhances the political power structures and today's thin democracy?

The likely answer is that the future will combine elements of both. In order to avoid a "thick citizenry" that passively accepts what it is told by political elites, a democratic civic culture must be formed that encourages people to educate themselves and recognize the communal nature of modern society even as they acknowledge their competing yet overlapping individual interests that in part make up this web of communality. Just as the Internet can give people a voice and a chance to build community, it can also be used as an extremely efficient marketing tool that is able to better track and target citizens as consumers. It pulls in two very different directions simultaneously, and this essay explores that tension through the lens of the 2004 presidential campaigns. So the question for people hungry for a different menu, for an active, engaged citizenry and participatory democratic culture becomes: Does the Internet deliver?

Creating a conceptual framework from which to examine how the Internet is fulfilling or not fulfilling its democratic potential is vital for better understanding some of the important dynamics taking place. A useful starting point is the concept of what Barber calls "strong democracy," a form of democracy that attempts to balance the contrasting views of human nature found in different theories of democracy while avoiding many of the pitfalls and weaknesses in those theories. He wants to avoid the totalism that republicanism can lead to, yet bolster a democratic spirit that he says liberalism sacrifices on the altar of individual rights and private interests. For Barber, strong democracy "envisions politics not as a way of life but as a way of living—as, namely, the way that human beings with variable but malleable natures and with competing but overlapping interests can contrive to live together communally not only to their mutual advantage but also to the advantage of their mutuality."[12]

The Internet would seem to be the perfect communicative space to practice the activities that could inculcate a strong democracy. The rhetoric of revolution has long been used in discussing the Internet and its potential for revitalizing democracy and a sense of community. Although it may be true, to borrow Gil Scott-Heron's enticing 1971 song title, that "the revolution will not be televised,"[13] it can also be argued that in regard to the Internet and democracy the revolution has not finished downloading.

Many scholars are critical of the revolutionary rhetoric and technological utopianism, choosing to focus on the question of whether a democratic, participatory spirit can truly be achieved online. Cass Sunstein asks in his book, *Republic.com*, if the time spent in virtual communities is at the expense of time interacting and being engaged in the real world. Others keep firmly in mind the influence that political, cultural, and corporate elites have in determining how various media technologies develop or are regulated.[14] Journalist Howard Rheingold recommends that citizens need to educate themselves in order to ensure that they can take full advantage of emerging technologies. He writes, "The odds are always good that big power and big money will find a way to control access to virtual communities; big power and big money always found ways to control new communications media when they emerged in the past."[15]

Peter Dahlgren says that in looking at the Internet and democratization it is important to distinguish the political system of democracy from civic culture, although the two are in principle mutually dependent.[16] He proposes that examining four dimensions of civic culture provides the best way to study salient media in terms of modern democracy. Dahlgren outlines four dimensions: relevant knowledge and competencies; loyalty to democratic values and procedures; practices, routines, traditions; and identities as citizens.[17]

Other scholars have used similar factors to examine the potential the

Internet has for democratizing U.S. politics and civic engagement. Jennifer Stromer-Galley, in an essay that uses Barber's notion of strong democracy as an overarching framework in examining the Internet and its potential for fostering democracy, focuses on six characteristics of the Internet that could have a democratizing effect: cost, volume, directionality, speed, targeting, and convergence.[18] Stromer-Galley claims that "directionality," which she clarifies as more akin to "interactivity," is the most important feature of the Internet to foster democracy.

For such a fundamental and unique characteristic of the Internet as a medium, defining what exactly "interactivity" is has proved remarkably difficult.[19] What differentiates, if anything, the type of interactivity found by clicking on an internal hyperlink to read a candidate's issue statement and that found when answering an online poll? Does one engage citizens better than the other? And if so, why?

While some scholars have focused on the process of interactivity, others have examined the features of interactivity, and still others have looked at user perceptions or mixed approaches in trying to define the term. Three general concepts emerge from the literature over the years: direction of communication (primarily two-way communication), user control, and time.[20]

The ability of a producer of media content and the consumer of that content to easily communicate with each other—and for the consumer's "voice" to have a greater chance to be read or heard than in traditional media such as letters to the editor or call-in radio shows—is one of the aspects at the heart of the democratic potential of the Internet. More importantly, the ability of people to communicate easily with each other and to distribute their messages to a wide audience highlights how one characteristic of interactivity differentiates it from other forms of media.

User control of content is also an important aspect of interactivity. Through hyperlinks, users have control over not only how they access the content, but in what order they access it and even, in some cases, the way they see, read, or hear it. Time also must be considered with interactivity; while a letter to the editor in response to an article may take a week or more to get published in the newspaper and thus deter some people who would otherwise write, conversely, the ability to get responses quickly may help encourage interaction.

Still, even with a clearer definition of interactivity and what it potentially enables, there has been little research on the effects of interactivity. John Tedesco conducted a study that attempted to look at young adult political efficacy, or how knowledgeable and empowered young people felt about politics and political issues, as well as whether they believed politicians actually listened to them; he found that websites with higher levels of interactivity scored higher in political efficacy.[21] Although his findings cannot be generalized, it does seem that the dialogic process found in online interactivity helps engage online users to some extent in comparison to websites that do not allow interactivity. Whether this is because of an interactivity effect or stems primarily from what online users have come to expect from their online media is an open question. What does seem clear, however, is that interactivity allows for communication dynamics that are largely impossible to find in other forms of media.

In defining characteristics of the Internet in relationship to democracy, Lloyd Morrisett outlines six important features that he says must be taken into account: access, information, discussion, deliberation, choice, and action.[22] Morrisett says that access is the most important issue, because without access to information technologies such as the Internet no other component really matters. Although true on a fundamental level, this chapter examines the lessons learned by audiences that are already online, so the question of access is less important for our purposes here. Likewise, the more people who have access the less of an issue it becomes. The second factor he mentions, information, is the most similar to how traditional media are supposed to function in terms of informing and educating citizens, and most closely follows a more or less unidirectional, transmission model of mass communication. The other factors he mentions—discussion, deliberation, choice, and action—all strike at the heart of what interactivity should allow: the formation of an engaged citizenry and an interactive information system that enables people to develop an active and democratic civic culture.

A useful framework from which to analyze online political information and engagement was used by Steven Schneider and Kirsten Foot in their analysis of presidential primary campaign websites from 2000 and 2004.[23] The 2004 presidential elections are widely considered as a turning point in the importance of the Internet in political campaigns.[24] Howard Dean's widely publicized Internet campaign and the money he raised from mostly small donations was emulated and improved upon by several other candidates, even as Dean's primary campaign eventually crumbled. The Pew Internet & American Life Project called 2004 "a breakout year for the role of the internet in politics," finding that "seventy-five million Americans—37 percent of the adult population and 61 percent of online Americans—used the internet to get political news and information, discuss candidates and debate issues in e-mails, or participate directly in the political process by volunteering or giving contributions to candidates."[25]

Schneider and Foot analyzed presidential primary campaign websites in both election years along four functional dimensions: informing, involving, connecting, and mobilizing. They state that each dimension involves a different type of relationship between the political campaigns and the audiences they are trying to reach. We will examine each of these briefly to see how each dimension may or may not help citizens become more engaged in politics, noting similarities to the components that both Stromer-Galley and Morrisett used in their analyses and how it maps to Dahlgren's four dimensions of civic culture and the notion of encouraging the development of strong democracy.

Informing

Informing the public through a politician's website involves making biographical information, issue statements, press releases, and other relevant information available.[26] Often called "brochure ware," it was the first use of the Web by political campaigns, dating from the mid-1990s.[27] By 2004, it became *de rigueur* for any serious presidential candidate to have a website that included informing functions, which Schneider and Foot characterize as "when online structures are created to support the campaign in presenting information to potential 'consumers' or 'users.'"[28]

Given that most young people cite lack of knowledge about politics or politicians as a reason for their lower rate of voting and political participation in general, it would seem that more information about candidates and their issues that is easily available would be a good thing for democracy.[29] Related to this, it could be argued that the low cost of creating a website and sending information to a mass audience helps democratize the political campaign process, giving candidates without large financial resources for television or other mass media advertising a forum with which to reach people on more or less equal footing as better-funded candidates.[30] However, this view also tends to ignore the important complementary role that various media channels play today. Candidates who are deemed to be unimportant or "fringe" to the mainstream media tend not to get covered in news stories or invited to debates, making it less likely that citizens will even hear about them through the mainstream media, much less find their websites and learn about the candidates.

Furthermore, the information that is being transmitted via a candidate's website is highly controlled by the campaign or politician, raising questions about how credible or useful the information is to the public that comes to learn about the candidate's positions on various issues. Although the information found on such websites is more expansive than what can typically be found in television news, it is, inevitably, considerably biased. At the same time, as of 2004, the primary source of political information for people online and offline remained television, with 79 percent of all Americans saying television was their main campaign news source.[31] The Internet lagged far behind, with 28 percent of Internet users saying it was their primary news source.

The Internet has caught up to radio and is closing in on newspapers as a primary news source, according to Pew. Yet only 5 million people went to candidate websites most often for political news (double the number of 2000); on the other hand, 31.5 million people online went to websites of major news organizations most often (up from 16.2 million in 2000).[32] In addition, the Pew report also noted that people seeking political information online could be divided into two distinct camps: those who find the Internet a convenient way to get information, and those who believe that mainstream media do not give them all the information they need and thus look at other online sources. Nevertheless, the primacy of the mainstream news media and to some extent its gatekeeping function still play a role in directing the kind of information most people will receive.

It could be argued, then, that simply informing citizens through a unidirectional transmission model of communication actually strengthens thin, or representative, democracy. Political elites, whether candidates or parties, transmit information either directly through their websites or through mainstream media outlets to an audience, usually conceptualized as passive and comprised of "consumers" of that information. They are not talking with their publics, but talking *to* them.

Barber's conception of strong democracy involves communication technologies that enable not only easy information access, but also promise more involvement and engagement by citizens with each other as amateurs and without the "intermediary of expertise."[33] Another function of campaign websites, involvement, would seem to lead in the right direction as far as encouraging the growth of strong democracy but, alas, it turns out to also fall short.

Involving

Involving the public with campaigns is the second-most common practice of the 2000 and 2004 primary campaign websites that Schneider and Foot looked at. The features they examined within the practice of "involving" include the ability to make online donations, volunteering, signing up to get e-mail news and alerts from the candidates, a campaign calendar of events, and online stores.[34] In the 2004 presidential campaign, fourteen million people signed up for e-mail newsletters or other online alerts to get the latest news about politics, and seven million signed up to receive e-mail from the presidential campaigns directly.[35]

Although such features do have the ability to get citizens more engaged in political campaigns, they still, to a very large extent, represent a unidirectional approach. Just as the Internet lowers the costs of production and distribution, thus making it easier for more people to mass distribute information, it also lowers the barrier for involvement in making it easier for people to contribute to the candidate of their choice, either with time or money. There may be more involvement on the part of citizens in some campaigns, but this type of involvement largely reinforces the status quo regarding the running of political campaigns, party platforms, and the choosing of candidates. The public is now seen as an active consumer that can contribute to a campaign rather than a passive consumer of information—but a consumer nonetheless.

Integrally tied to one aspect of involvement is the ability of campaigns to more thoroughly track and target potential voters through opt-in e-mail lists and site registrations. A database of information on even a portion of the fourteen million people who signed up for e-mail newsletters can be extremely valuable to marketers inside and outside the political arena. Campaign sites can collect a vast amount of information from site visitors through registration information, and send highly targeted messages to segmented audiences that could not have been easily segmented with traditional direct mailings or mass media advertising.

The ability to send highly targeted messages to selective groups actually works against instilling a democratic civic culture and, if anything, could lead to even stronger feelings of inefficacy among youth voters; moreover, the practice raises important questions regarding privacy. The fact that the advertising sent to them may resonate better with their views on the issues or put a candidate in the best possible light matters little in terms of truly engaging citizens, because the real dynamic taking place is still very much one directed from the campaign site to a consuming audience.

Connecting

Schneider and Foot define the function of "connecting" as follows: when a campaign site tries to connect the site user with "another political actor, such as a press organization, a political party, a government agency, or even an electoral opponent."[36] Some of the features include endorsements, links to government entities, links to civic and advocacy groups, links to press organizations, comparisons to opponents, and links to political parties.[37]

Connecting may at first seem simply like an online version of informing, but the concept is fundamentally different. Whereas informing and involving can be seen as "vertical" or unidirectional functions from the campaign site to the user or consumer, connecting and mobilizing both take a social network approach in providing links across and outside the site. In connecting, a campaign website tries to act like a hub in a network, becoming valuable not only in terms of the information contained within the site itself, but also through the site's ability to provide the user with useful links or connections to other sites of value or interest. A considerable part of the jump in use of the Internet for political news between 2002 and 2004 was due to people researching candidates' positions on issues, examining their voting records, and taking online polls, with thirty-one million visitors checking out how candidates were doing in opinion polls.[38] This trend would seem to indicate that the more a campaign site can become a hub that links a user to other sites to easily perform additional research, the more the site will be perceived as useful.

Encouraging users to visit other sites whose content a campaign has no control over raises a number of thorny issues for campaigns. It should be no surprise, then, that connecting and mobilizing features, although showing impressive growth on the presidential primary sites studied between 2000 and 2004 by Schneider and Foot, were still not nearly as common as informing and involving features.[39]

Part of the problem is that campaigns are primarily interested in keeping visitors on their sites, rather than encouraging them to go elsewhere and learn or discover on their own—a clear example of how links in an online network inherently conflict with established practices and goals of campaigns in a liberal democracy. To be sure, campaign sites do face other practical issues regarding linking to other sites, including dealing with legal issues such as copyright (which itself raises some interesting questions about the role of intellectual property rights in hampering a more open and communicative information space, a concern that is beyond the scope of this essay but that scholars like Yochai Benkler and Lawrence Lessig, among others, cover very well). Still, the disruptive potential of a less structured, more networked information environment in which a message cannot be easily controlled has undoubtedly been considered by political campaigns, even as they understand how it could benefit them as well.

Mobilizing

If connecting is a function that allows site users to connect to other "approved" sites from the perspective of the campaign website, then the mobilizing function flattens and distributes the network even further and allows users to connect directly with each other, albeit with campaign goals and objectives in mind. Specific features include links sent from sites, e-paraphernalia, offline distribution of campaign materials, letters to editors, and action management sections of sites.[40] In Pew's survey of online political activities, they included several new categories to account for mobilizing functions, even if they are limited in scope. For example, thirty-two million users traded e-mail jokes about candidates, and seventeen million people sent e-mails about the campaign to groups of family members or friends, sometimes within the context of listerv or discussion group activity.[41]

The mobilizing function has similarities to four of six of Morrisett's features, namely discussion, deliberation, choice, and action, which would seem to put it closest to being able to fulfill the democratic potential of the Internet along the lines of a strong democracy.

Two other mitigating factors must be considered when looking at mobilizing functions from the perspective of campaign websites. First, it should be no surprise that campaigns, as risk-averse organizations, are hesitant to use a new technology and, if they do use it, attempt to maintain some element of control. Second, the 2004 Howard Dean presidential primary campaign, which spectacularly rose because of its use of involving and mobilizing functions—and dramatically fell through some of those very same dynamics—provided several valuable lessons regarding the promotional potential (and potential destructiveness) of the Internet in political campaigns. The now-famous "I Have a Scream" speech by Howard Dean after his disappointing third place finish in the Iowa caucuses was circulating the Internet within two days as music and video remixes, or mash-ups, and making the rounds of the late-night talk show host routines.[42] This in turn generated mainstream media coverage, which kept the story going longer than it probably would have otherwise.

Several campaigns in 2004 emulated and refined elements of Dean's Internet campaign (sans scream), and it is expected that presidential campaigns in 2008 and beyond will use all four functions, with involving and mobilizing becoming more widespread practices on campaign websites.[43] Dean, now chairman of the Democratic National Committee, has promised to use many of the same mobilizing techniques for the Democratic Party in 2008. He claimed that the most important innovation his campaign organizers had was that they "learned to take ideas from the bottom," or the grassroots, and use those ideas during the campaign.[44]

If online communication practices will be used by campaign websites that favor a more distributed, interactive, and democratic communicative structure along the lines of what Barber envisions with strong democracy, that brings us back to the question raised earlier concerning what lessons we learned from the 2004 election in terms of the roles youth may play in the political process and what we understand as democracy or civic culture.

Citizens do not need to go to a campaign website to mobilize online. Through discussion groups, blogs, chat rooms, listservs, independent websites, and media content created by individuals, people have shown a willingness to engage and form interactive communities of interest without the filter of mainstream media or established political organizations guiding them. Granted, some of the communication has been limited in depth or range, such as simply sending e-mail jokes, but in the more robust and politically oriented discussion groups and listservs—and even the Meetups held by the Dean campaign—their interactions have been remarkably similar to Barber's notion of strong democracy:

> Community grows out of participation and at the same time makes participation possible; civic activity educates individuals how to think publicly as citizens even as citizenship informs civic activity with the required sense of publicness and justice. Politics becomes its own university, citizenship its own training ground, and participation its own tutor. Freedom is what comes out of this process, not what goes into it.[45]

However, as noted earlier, a large number of online users primarily got their information about political candidates and politics from online news websites or television, which means that mainstream political and news organizations still play an important role as filters or hubs within this network of information, even if their role as gatekeepers has diminished to some extent in comparison to the past. Mainstream news organizations are integrally tied to the political system and capital, which, some argue, is to the detriment of our democracy.[46]

The fact that a large number of people will always find it easier to passively receive and believe information from traditional news sources rather than question or critique the information they get cannot be downplayed, and it raises the question of whether a "new elite" may form under the guise of creating a participatory civic culture that may nevertheless undermine that very culture.

Indeed, not everyone sees a strong democracy and civic activism as worthy goals to strive for. Besides threatening many established corporate and political interests and the elites that have a vested interest in seeing the status quo continue, notions of civic activism, some argue, at best, may be utopian or Pollyannaish and, at worst, may actually do more harm than good as the losers in any civic strife are ignored. "Casualties litter civic battlefields and participants might have been better off watching TV soap operas," claims one world-weary civic activism scholar.[47]

The mid-term elections of 2006 seem to indicate the development of a "new class of online political activist," one that tends to be young, socially upscale, and well-educated, according to a Pew report.[48] The organization estimated the number of Americans taking part in online political activism, which, according to Pew, includes posting their own political commentaries, forwarding others' commentaries, and creating or sharing videos or media created by others, at fourteen million people. People eighteen to twenty-nine made up 29 percent of this number, while thirty- to forty-nine-year-olds made up 39 percent, with almost 80 percent of this population consisting of non-Hispanic whites.[49]

Leaving aside the potential issues of this "new class" of political activist looking white and well-to-do, or very much like the social or political elite in the offline world except for skewing younger, the numbers do seem encouraging in that more citizens are using the communicative capabilities of the Internet to become more active in civic culture. Furthermore, teens are far more likely to use social networking sites, create and share content online, and generally feel more at ease in the fluid, interactive media environment of today than older demographics. A little more than half of all U.S. teens, or twelve million people (57 percent of online teens), have created content online either in the form of a blog or a website, or mixed and shared material.[50] Though the blogs and mixing are primarily for personal views or entertainment purposes, they do indicate a familiarity among youth with a culture of participation and sharing that could hold promise for the development of a vibrant civic culture as these people reach voting age.

Today's online teens, immersed in a media world unlike that of any prior generation, exemplifies the complex dynamics between entertainment media, news, politics, and advertising—and the blurring of all of them in media convergence. It raises the question of how active someone is considered to be if his or her political engagement is the occasional posting of a blog entry, forwarding of a video sent to them, or answering of an online poll. Just under fourteen million people participated in online surveys about politics in 2004, a jump of 15 percent.[51] Most would likely claim that such practices do not reflect any meaningful participation in civic culture, since the practice lacks the dialogue and deliberation that comes from a more robust form of participation (even though it is technically interactive). However, the power of opinion polls and their ability to shape perceived reality should not be underestimated, nor should the tendency of some people to think of answering polls or checking alternative sources of news on a candidate as "being engaged."

The power of video must also be considered, which is related to the growing number of broadband connections that make watching video online much easier than with slower Internet connections. Some researchers have said that citizen-created or shared online videos played key roles in the defeats of three incumbents in the 2006 elections: Virginia Senator George Allen after he called a rival campaign worker of Indian descent "macaca" at a rally, Montana Senator Conrad Burns when he was seen dozing during Senate hearings, and New York Representative Sue Kelly when she was shown running away from reporters rather than answering questions about Mark Foley's resignation due to a sex scandal.[52] If these damaging videos played a role in these politicians' defeats it is not because video has some special power in comparison to other types of media to captivate us (although something can be said for the power of the moving visual image), but because the video clips were able to be easily distributed to online users and because the interactive tools of the Internet made it easy to discuss them with other users.

The viral nature of such videos or other media content, regardless of who creates them, should not be underestimated as an element in helping form active and participatory communities. Short video clips are not only much easier to watch but, given how quickly they can be diffused, can receive a longer "shelf life" than if they had appeared once or twice in evening news and morning shows and then vanished from the screen. This dynamic of diffusion, combined with the inevitable remixes and mash-ups, acts as a counter-point to the conventional wisdom of everything happening online at "Internet speed" and online users having short attention spans as they look for the next interesting thing.

Yet in a different vein, the voyeuristic element of watching videos of public figures making career-ruining gaffes blurs the line between entertainment and political information or activism. Politicians are unlikely to subject themselves to an interactive yet viral video along the lines of the famed Burger King Chicken video, in which Burger King created what looked like an amateur video of someone dressed in a chicken suit standing in a living room that reacts to user commands. However, opponents of the candidate could create such a video or produce some sort of interactive entertainment that makes the politician appear silly, such as the Flash-based interactive game, "Dancing Bush."[53]

Although the "Dancing Bush" game seems to be primarily created as a simple piece of interactive entertainment rather than political parody, would something similar to this but with a sharper political point be an example of mindless entertainment, biting satire, a political ad to gain attention, or an example of informing or involving potential voters as they forward the video link to friends? Or could it be considered all of these things?

The equation could easily change if, instead of viewing interactive dance moves such as those in the "Dancing Bush" game, the user was able to see and hear contradictory statements the candidate has made over time or promises a politician has failed to keep, and access easy links to his or her voting record or stance on various issues. Checking a candidate's position on various issues was one of the most common actions among campaign Internet users in 2006, with 52 percent (20 percent of all Americans) doing so and 41 percent (14 percent of all Americans) checking the accuracy of claims made by and about candidates.[54] What's more, in February 2007, the popular online video site YouTube announced that it would be providing channels for politicians to post their own videos as part of a voter education initiative. "This is such an important election coming up that we just wanted to make sure we did everything we could in terms of helping candidates get their messages out, but also helping voters start a dialogue with those candidates on issues that really hit home at them individually," said Jordan Hoffner, YouTube's director of content partnerships.[55]

Reflecting on the combination of user-generated content that has viral qualities and more traditional political information demonstrates that the categories of informing, involving, connecting, and mobilizing used by Schneider and Foot may not be so easy to separate in a digital, networked world of political activism. Perhaps interactive digital media is not only taking us beyond traditional campaign politics, but is also playing an important role in casting ourselves as citizen-consumers—a type of "life politics," to borrow Giddens's phrase, that blurs the line between civic duty and consumer self-interest.[56]

Fortunately for us, the Internet does give us the tools and ability to speak up and talk with one another—here, the Internet has the potential to deliver. Whether it does or not will depend on a number of complex and powerful social, political, cultural, and technological factors, most of which, from a political economy perspective, are working against the emerging communication characteristics of the Internet. Much of the battle over what Benkler calls the "institutional ecology" of the Internet is not taking place in political campaigns, but in lobbying efforts by media and technology companies to have laws and regulations revised in ways that can help them maintain their dominant business models and expand intellectual property rights.[57] This is the intersection where a large part of how the Internet will be used and perceived lies: whether it will be able to maintain the openness that it was founded on, or become a largely enclosed, commodified sphere that is used by the media as yet another profitable content distribution channel. It is also where a dynamic civic culture is most needed.

There are some encouraging signs that an active and networked public can mobilize to effect change. The discussions on net neutrality in Congress in 2006 were a hot topic among several different activist groups, such as MoveOn.org and the media reform group, Free Press. Their use of e-mail alerts, calls to action among members to contact their representatives, and online tools to encourage local meetings—sometimes with media entertainment (i.e., a film) providing further incentive to gather—helped bring one attempt by corporations to influence the future direction of the Internet into the public spotlight and played a role in these major companies backing down from their demands.

Change from a thin democracy to a strong democracy, if it comes at all, will most likely happen only gradually and will probably not have defining, dramatic moments like those that occurred with Dean's 2004 online campaign strategy and tactics. This is partly because as various practices online become integrated into our normal ways of communicating with each other, we will stop seeing them as something special, or something "extra" we must do as citizens. It becomes, as Barber points out, "a way of living" rather than a "way of life." There will be strong forces that will encourage us to be passive consumers, albeit highly entertained, passive consumers. Some of this entertainment may come in the form of making it look as if we are getting engaged in the political process; for many people, we can assume, that will seem like enough involvement.

But there is also the power of people re-establishing a sense of community with each other, discussing important issues even as they forward jokes about candidates to each other, sharing ideas online and in face-to-face gatherings, and trying to change things. An important question in future elections is whether these active communities will be minimized or mostly ignored in our fragmented, multi-channel universe of entertainment, or whether, through our daily practices, we are able to organize and work together to truly produce change. Today's youth have incorporated a range of interactive communication technologies and media content and creation into their lives far better than their elders have to date, and if political ignorance and apathy are replaced by knowledge and activism, then the nascent lessons we have been learning in the elections of the early twenty-first century could be precursors to fascinating changes to come in our democracy and civic culture.

Notes

1. One such example is Robert Putnam, *Bowling Alone: The Collapse and Revival of American Community* (New York: Simon & Schuster, 2000). Another book that addresses downward voting trends directly is Tom Patterson, *The Vanishing Voter: Public Information in an Age of Uncertainty* (New York: Knopf, 2002).

2. Benjamin R. Barber, *Strong Democracy* (Berkeley, CA: University of California Press, 1984), 4-6.

3. Mark Hugo Lopez, Emily Kirby, and Jared Sagoff, "The Youth Vote 2004," *Fact Sheet* (The Center for Information & Research on Civic Learning and Engagement, 2005), http://www.civicyouth.org/PopUps/FactSheets/FS_Youth_Voting_72-04.pdf (accessed January 25, 2007).

4. Lee Rainie, Michael Cornfield, and John Horrigan, "The Internet and

Campaign 2004," *Research Report* (Washington, DC: Pew Internet & American Life Project, 2005), http://www.pewinternet.org/pdfs/PIP_2004_Campaign.pdf (accessed January 22, 2007).

5. Zack Pelta-Heller, "Voters, Fighters, Citizens, Youth," in *Start Making Sense: Turning the Lessons of Election 2004 into Winning Progressive Politics*, ed. Don Hazen and Lakshmi Chaudhry (White River Junction, VT: Chelsea Green Publishing, 2005), 62-64.

6. Michael X. Delli Carpini, "Gen.com: Youth, Civic Engagement, and the New Information Environment," *Political Communication* 17, no. 4 (October 2000): 341-49.

7. Ralph Mosher, Robert A. Kenny, Jr., and Andrew Garrod, *Preparing for Citizenship: Teaching Youth to Live Democratically* (Westport, CT: Praeger, 1994).

8. Mary Madden, "Internet penetration and Impact April 2006," *Data Memo* (Pew Internet & American Life Project, 2006), http://www.pewinternet.org/pdfs/PIP_Internet_Impact.pdf (accessed February 25, 2007).

9. Chris Atton, *An Alternative Internet* (Edinburgh: Edinburgh University Press, 2004), 103-5.

10. Yochai Benkler, *The Wealth of Networks: How Social Production Transforms Markets and Freedom* (New Haven, CT: Yale University Press, 2006), 63-74.

11. Erica Schlesinger Wass, ed., *Addressing the World: National Identity and Internet Country Code Domains* (Lanham, MD: Rowman & Littlefield, 2003), xv-xvii.

12. Barber, *Strong Democracy*, 117-18.

13. Joe Trippi also borrowed this title for his book on his experiences with the 2004 Howard Dean campaign: *The Revolution Will Not be Televised: Democracy, the Internet, and the Overthrow of Everything* (New York: Regan Books, 2005).

14. Many examples can be found in the writings of political economists such as Herbert Schiller and Robert McChesney, although Schiller deals mostly with mainstream media. For instance, see Robert W. McChesney, *Rich Media, Poor Democracy: Communication Politics in Dubious Times* (New York: New Press, 1999).

15. Howard Rheingold, *The Virtual Community: Homesteading on the Electronic Frontier* (Cambridge, MA: MIT Press, 2000), 8.

16. Peter Dahlgren, "The Internet and the Democratization of Civic Culture," *Political Communication* 17, no. 4 (October 2000): 335-340.

17. Dahlgren, "The Internet," 337-38.

18. Jennifer Stromer-Galley, "Democratizing Democracy: Strong Democracy, U.S. Political Campaigns and the Internet," in *The Internet, Democracy and Democratization*, ed. Peter Ferdinand (London: Frank Cass Publishers, 2000), 36-58.

19. Tanjev Schultz, "Mass Media and the Concept of Interactivity: An Ex-

ploratory Study of Online Forums and Reader E-Mail," *Media, Culture & Society* 22, no. 2 (March 2000): 205-21.

20. Sally J. McMillan and Jang-Sun Hwang, "Measures of Perceived Interactivity: An Exploration of the Role of Direction of Communication, User Control, and Time in Shaping Perceptions of Interactivity," *Journal of Advertising* 31, no. 3 (Fall 2002): 29-42.

21. John C. Tedesco, "Web Interactivity and Young Adult Political Efficacy," in *The Internet Election: Perspectives on the Web in Campaign 2004*, ed. Andrew Paul Williams and John C. Tedesco (Lanham, MD: Rowman & Littlefield, 2006), 187-202.

22. Lloyd Morrisett, "Technologies of Freedom?" in *Democracy and New Media*, ed. Henry Jenkins and David Thorburn (Cambridge, MA: MIT Press, 2002), 27-31.

23. Steven M. Schneider and Kirsten A. Foot, "Web Campaigning by Presidential Primary Candidates," in *The Internet Election: Perspectives on the Web in Campaign 2004*, ed. Andrew Paul Williams and John C. Tedesco (Lanham, MD: Rowman & Littlefield, 2006), 21-33.

24. Rainie, Cornfield, and Horrigan, "The Internet," i.

25. Rainie, Cornfield, and Horrigan, "The Internet," i.

26. Schneider and Foot, "Web Campaigning," 24.

27. Elaine C. Kamarck, "Campaigning on the Internet in the Election of 1998," in *Governance.com: Democracy in the Information Age*, ed. Elaine C. Kamarck and Joseph S. Nye (Washington, DC: Brookings Institution, 2002), 99-123.

28. Schneider and Foot, "Web Campaigning," 24.

29. Lynda Lee Kaid, Mitchell McKinney, and John C. Tedesco, *Civic Dialogue in the 1996 Presidential Campaign: Candidate, Media and Public Voices* (Cresskill, NJ: Hampton, 2000).

30. Stromer-Galley, "Democratizing Democracy," 42-43.

31. Rainie, Cornfield, and Horrigan, "The Internet," 2.

32. Rainie, Cornfield, and Horrigan, "The Internet," 6.

33. Barber, *Strong Democracy*, 152.

34. Schneider and Foot, "Web Campaigning," 27.

35. Rainie, Cornfield, and Horrigan, "The Internet," 7.

36. Schneider and Foot, "Web Campaigning," 24-25.

37. Schneider and Foot, "Web Campaigning," 27.

38. Rainie, Cornfield, and Horrigan, "The Internet," 7.

39. Schneider and Foot, "Web Campaigning," 31.

40. Schneider and Foot, "Web Campaigning," 27.

41. Rainie, Cornfield, and Horrigan, "The Internet," 7.

42. Blake Morrison, "Dean Scream Gaining Cult-Like Status on the Web," *USA Today*, January 22, 2004, 4(A).

43. Schneider and Foot, "Web Campaigning," 31-32.

44. Don Hazen, "Interview with Howard Dean," in *Start Making Sense:*

Turning the Lessons of Election 2004 into Winning Progressive Politics, ed. Don Hazen and Lakshmi Chaudhry (White River Junction, VT: Chelsea Green Publishing, 2005), 17-23.

45. Barber, *Strong Democracy*, 152.

46. C. Edwin Baker, *Media, Markets, and Democracy* (Cambridge: Cambridge University Press, 2002).

47. Robert Weissberg, *The Limits of Civic Activism: Some Cautionary Tales on the Use of Politics* (New Brunswick, NJ: Transaction Publishers, 2005), x.

48. Lee Rainie and John Horrigan, "Election 2006 Online," *Research Report* (Washington, DC: Pew Internet & American Life Project, 2005), http://www.pewinternet.org/pdfs/PIP_Politics_2006.pdf (accessed February 25, 2007).

49. Rainie and Horrigan, "Election 2006."

50. Amanda Lenhart and Mary Madden, "Teen Content Creators and Consumers," *Research Report* (Washington, DC: Pew Internet & American Life Project, 2005), http://www.pewinternet.org/pdfs/PIP_Teens_Content _Creation. pdf (accessed February 26, 2007).

51. Rainie, Cornfield, and Horrigan, "The Internet," 7.

52. Rainie and Horrigan, "Election 2006."

53. Miniclip.com, "Dancing Bush Game," http://www.miniclip.com/ games/dancing-bush/en/ (accessed February 27, 2007).

54. Rainie and Horrigan, "Election 2006."

55. Jim Kuhnhenn, "YouTube to Give Politicians Video Boost," *Associated Press* March 1, 2007, http://news.yahoo.com/s/ap/20070301/ap_on_hi_ te/youtube_politics_1 (accessed March 1, 2007).

56. Margaret Scammell, "The Internet and Civic Engagement: The Age of the Citizen-Consumer," *Political Communication* 17, no. 4 (October 2000): 351-55.

57. Benkler, *Wealth of Networks*, 383-459.

Chapter 10

Just Don't Bother to Vote or Die, Bitch! A Giant Douche, a Turd Sandwich, Hardcore Puppet Sex, and the Reinvention of Political (Un)Involvement[1]

Marc Leverette

> *Turn, now, to politics. Consider . . . a campaign for the Presidency. Would it be possible to imagine anything more uproariously idiotic—a deafening, nerve-wracking battle to the death between Tweedledum and Tweedledee.*
> —H. L. Mencken, *The American Scene*

> *The fully developed ability to say No is also the only valid background for Yes, and only through both does real freedom . . . take form.*
> —Peter Sloterdijk, *Critique of Cynical Reason*

> *To see what is in front of one's nose needs a constant struggle.*
> —George Orwell, "In Front of Your Nose"

> *Withdrawing in disgust is not the same thing as apathy.*
> —An "Oblique Strategy"
> from Richard Linklater's film, *Slacker*

In the third episode of the first season of HBO's American version of *Da Ali G Show*, our eponymous host/hero, during his opening monologue, saunters in front of giant letters spelling the word "POLITICS." "Young people see the word politics and they immediately switch off," he states. "I wish I been told that before me got these fucking massive letters built." While the main aim here is its comedic punch, there is still a lot of truth we can glean from his plight, though not in the obvious ways media critics might think. The texts that litter our postmodern, media-saturated landscape are often said to be characterized by eclecticism, irony, self-reflexivity, intertextuality, and lack of depth.[2] This has prompted many critics to, well, *criticize* (and examine, to be fair) the conscious use of the elements, allusions, and gestures made by such texts. In the process, however, critics of postmodern media texts tend to ignore a centrality behind such texts: intention. Too often we find this oversight with respect to the especially problematic case of television, widely regarded as the "postmodern medium *par excellence*."[3] In treating the production of postmodern texts as a by-product of the postmodern condition, critics have misrepresented the ways in which texts can politically engage viewers (unlike the now standard ways of considering the ways in which audiences actually engage texts) and what this might mean for those who consider politics traditionally.

This essay will argue that apathy and un-involvement may be the most powerful political feats of the contemporary age.[4] For a media-laden landscape criticized for its superficiality, there is a seeming surfeit of political mouthpieces—by this I mean texts that not only engage a political message, but those that stress political involvement. How does one create a politics of apathy in an age when even our most vapid of media texts stress involvement? From the falsely democratic plurality of MTV's *TRL*, to CNN's instant "non-scientific" polling, to Ben Affleck telling me to "Rock the Vote," the detritus of popular culture begs us to engage in the democratic process, often outing those who turn a blind eye. In today's media environment, is there no greater sin than simply not giving a shit?

From the right to the left, all sides of the political spectrum demand not so much our loyalty as our participation. I believe a viable alternative for today's voting youth is to simply not: not vote, not blog, not opinionate in the verb sense, to simply not participate. And to take this action (and indeed it is an *action*) in today's world may be the most pressing stance within the American political landscape.

A simple problem may be that the popular misconception is that un-involvement is somehow equated with a kind of "American stupidity." For just a few examples: A 1996 poll showed that only 10 percent of Americans could identify William Rehnquist as Chief Justice (and in 1996, while still in high school, explaining even the function of the Supreme Court would have been baffling to yours truly). But let's go further back, using our politicians themselves: In 1981, Reagan's nominee for deputy secretary of state, William Clark, admitted at his confirmation hearings that he had no idea how America's allies in Western Europe felt about the U.S. having nuclear missiles located there.[5] Even "Dubya," who is probably our President most well known for his misinformed malapropisms, once referred to Kosovars as "Kosovians" and said the Slovenian foreign minister was from Slokavia.[6] This is, of course, the President that, in a statement during his 2000 campaign to *Glamour* magazine (of all places), confused the Taliban with "some band." Our celebrity culture certainly doesn't help at all. When young people hear more about politics from Brad Pitt and Susan Sarandon than they do on the news, something seems to be rotten in Denmark. While it's a given that more people vote for *American Idol* than the President, it's interesting to consider the place of something like the "Idol Gives Back" campaign which, along with The Red campaign, show how conspicuous politicking is becoming a commonplace tool for resituating American consumption and reifying the state of exception.[7] Bono's The One campaign is an example of this *par excellence*, with its onslaught of celebrity do-gooders, serving as a constant reminder of both American sovereignty and imperialist elitism, while at the same time perpetuating a hegemonic consumerism and American excellence as an ideal.[8]

With this as a base, how, then, can "young people" not become apathetic?

An extremely complex notion (and issue), apathy is commonly thought of as a polarization, an either/or: a social disease or a philosophical virtue.[9] In political terms, in today's context, it is often the former definition that reigns. Daniel Gross, in *The Secret History of Emotion*, characterizes it in almost epidemic, clinical language:

> apathy suggests a profound personal deficiency, a passionless condition fully detached from the cares and responsibilities of the world. Indeed, apathy . . . has been considered at least since the time of Augustine a condition of moral depravity, a defiant retreat from the world of God and humankind.[10]

This kind of language, of apathy as a disease, particularly among youth voters, is, of course, the standard lexicon of contemporary politics itself.[11] That contemporary society is apathetic, particularly to politics, is a commonplace belief, a message that is constantly broadcast from media sources themselves.[12] But, rather than simply label apathy a disease, I wish to consider apathy, after Joshua Riggs, specifically for how it functions "as a crucial tool for the postmodern citizen."[13]

Within the rhetorical tradition, "apathy is related to the Greek *apatheia* which means, literally, without passion-as-suffering."[14] This etymology and definition is important, because, as Page duBois notes, "Apathy is preferable even to pleasure because pleasure can become habitual and cause pain when it is absent."[15] As I will elaborate on below, one of the reasons for the turn from politics, I argue, is a lack of enjoyment. Thus when politics is good, it's good, when it's bad (as it more or less constantly is, as our media remind us, yet again), apathy's better. As Jim Collins argues, in *Architectures of Excess*, the current life-world is marked by "semiotic excess," a condition that accounts for the inestimable number of images and messages that litter our everyday lives, images filled with rhetorical appeals—emotional appeals—that, once overloaded, offer us only apathy as a tool for navigating the infinite glimmer.[16] As such, if apathy is to be treated as a reaction to the deficiencies in politics, the media system, and the vicissitudes of life in postmodernity, I argue that Trey Parker and Matt Stone thus consciously critique those characteristics that mark the current condition as one of apathy. Rather than simply contributing to the mélange of media texts that reinforce apathy as a disease, Parker and Stone, through their critique of these systems and the institutions themselves, offer apathy as a viable alternative for maneuvering through contemporary political culture.

To discuss this turn to political inaction I will examine two key texts in pop culture leading up to the 2004 election: the *South Park* episode "Douche and Turd," which aired on October 27, 2004, and the feature film *Team America: World Police*, released on October 15, 2004, both created by Parker and Stone.[17] Garnering a huge amount of flak from pundits on both the right and the left, Parker and Stone left no one safe in their attacks. These texts represent the simple statement that if one approves of neither candidate in a two-party system, then the most democratic option is to simply not participate, allowing one's voice to be heard loudly through its silence. *Team America* skewered the assault launched on America's youth from everyone, such as right-wing critics, to Hollywood's legions of self-appointed politburos, leaving no one with an opinion safe (though admittedly *Team America* is highly conservative in its ultimate conclusion). "Douche and Turd" explicitly took on P. Diddy's "Vote or Die" campaign as a reinterpretation of democracy through totalitarianism. These texts were some of the only sites of popular culture where voters were offered the idea that if you don't know who to vote for, then just don't vote. And while Parker and Stone have been highly criticized for sending out anti-democratic messages, they have actually offered what may be the most democratic message ever heard in popular media: anti-mobilization as a viable alternative.

South Park Libertarians

> *As actors, it is our responsibility to read the newspapers,*
> *and then say what we read on television like it's our own opinion.*
> —"Janeane Garafolo" in *Team America*

> *Let's get out and vote!*
> *Let's make our voices heard!*
> *We've been given the right to choose*
> *Between a douche and a turd*
> *It's democracy in action,*
> *Put your freedom to the test,*
> *A big fat turd or a stupid douche,*
> *Which do you like best?*
> —The Ending Song to the *South Park* episode, "Douche or Turd"

> *I thought I told you to vote or die, BITCH!!!*
> —"P. Diddy" in *South Park* episode, "Douche or Turd"

Are *South Park* Republicans/conservatives just a bunch of (oxy)morons? Let us return to this question in a moment. First, let us "head on down to *South Park* and have ourselves a time."

Since its humble beginnings as a video Christmas card and later premiere on Comedy Central, *South Park* has stood out as unique in the television landscape. The animated program, which utilizes its low-tech approach in favor of a more up-to-the-minute critique of society, has continually attempted to redefine television as we know it, gaining a reputation for offering high quality, original takes on stories that are at the forefront of global discourse, often masking it as foul-mouthed scatology.

Since 1997, *South Park* has consistently been regarded as the premier site for critical discourse on television, hailed by both critics and audiences (and a darling of the academic circuit as well—though scholarship almost exclusively places it within the context of other animated programs[18]). Along with other animated series such as *The Simpsons, Family Guy,* and *American Dad* (as well as Comedy Central's non-animated offerings of *The Daily Show with Jon Stewart, The Colbert Report, Chappelle's Show,* and *The Mind of Mencia*), *South Park* has taken the case for media literacy from the classroom and put it on television. With the show, and their feature films *South Park: Bigger, Longer, and Uncut*[19] and *Team America: World Police,* co-creators Trey Parker and Matt Stone have carved a uniquely transgressive[20] place in media culture: at once horrifying parents, offending sensibilities, engaging audiences across demographics, and presenting a site for discourse consistently absent in the rest of television's flow.

It is intensely ironic that South Park Elementary's mascot is the cow, for, as is shown time and again, none are sacred. The show knows no bounds when it comes to lampooning cultural discourse; environmentalism, religion, race, gender, sexual harassment, hot Catholic love, poverty in America, famine in Africa, SARS, WMDs, jingoism and xenophobia, murder, child molestation, child prostitution, celebrity (America's real version of the sacred cow), and, perhaps most importantly, political correctness are just some of the "issues" that *South Park* skewers on a weekly basis. If someone does or says something stupid, *South Park* will no doubt slap them with a cold reality check—and reality is always in need of checking. As Tim Jon Semmerling notes:

> While *South Park* may seem juvenile and cruel in dismantling serious and important cultural topics, the show in reality is brilliant when it forces us to see that the discourse about these highly sacred icons may be just paper tigers with as little dimension to them as the images of the characters in the series themselves.[21]

Likewise, the duo's 2004 feature film also presented a complex interplay between sophisticated commentary and lowbrow scatology. Known widely as the film with some of the dirtiest puppet sex around, *Team America,* Parker and Stone's most high-profile side-project, is ostensibly the story of Gary Johnston, a famous Broadway actor, who is recruited by Spottswoode, head of the elite counter-terrorist group of the film's title. His initial task, in this marionette tribute to the 60s television series *Thunderbirds* by way of a Jerry Bruckheimer spoof, is to work undercover in Cairo and infiltrate a terrorist cell to obtain information regarding their plans to destroy the world. In a series of unfortunate events (such as destroying the Eiffel Tower and most of Egypt's pharaohnic monuments), Johnston is central to the success of Team America in their stopping of North Korean dictator Kim Jong II. I say a "series of events," because it is in these sidebar moments where the movie truly takes place.[22] And did I mention it was a musical? I wish to take up these two texts in relation to the political climate of 2004 to better understand how a libertarian approach to apathy may be Parker and Stone's most democratic gesture.

If the 2000 election had been eerily similar to an episode of *Seinfeld* (i.e., it was about nothing, everyone more or less agreed on various issues, and the recount turned out like we were watching a formulaic sitcom),[23] then the 2004 version was much more like a hostile episode of *South Park* in that it was filled with reminders that we, as a nation, were in desperate need of skewering. With the left's main argument being vote to get rid of Bush and the right clearly in a position to not give up power, the nation more or less turned into the dim-witted citizenry of our favorite "quiet, little, redneck, Podunk, mountain town," with the country's greatest crime being simply to not give a shit.

The episode, "Douche and Turd," was a clear parody of the election process as the nation moved toward the eve of the 2004 presidential spectacle. When PETA protesters force the school to change its mascot, South Park Elementary has an election to find a replacement. Cartman and Kyle each come forth with a nominee and it's up to them to convince the body politic that theirs is the one to beat. Cartman, of course, tries to convince everyone that his turd sandwich is a far better candidate for a mascot than Kyle's giant douche. Stan quickly realizes that he likes neither candidate, cares little about the supposed "issues," and, rather publicly, decides to not vote. As such, Stan is then ostracized from the community and forced to live with the crazy, PETA hippies. Central to the episode are two things: 1) the critique of P. Diddy's "Vote or Die" campaign as hypocritical and anti-democratic and 2) the critique of the myth that every vote matters. The episode came at the perfect moment in American culture when youth voters were getting waylaid and carpet-bombed by voter initiative campaigns from both sides of the political spectrum, as it is largely celebrity politics at which Parker and Stone take their deadliest aim. Whereas Rock the Vote, MoveOn.org, and other celebrity driven campaigns seemed little interested in actually informing a body politic in their quest to register voters, "Douche and Turd" offered an extremely articulate and complicated assessment of the information onslaught faced by young, uninformed citizens, coupled with the crushing realizations that an Electoral College may not effectively "represent" them even if their vote counts at all.

Ultimately Stan does cast a vote—a careless picking of the turd sandwich—for a candidate whose loss could not have been a more crushing landslide. So we, as is Stan, are left with the question: did his vote matter? The episode leaves us on a highly ambiguous note. While Stan ultimately did not affect the outcome of the election one iota, it would seem that through his empty gesture democracy was reified. I do not wish to attempt to answer the question of whether or not one vote actually counts; rather, I want to briefly explore the commentary and implications of the episode.

The most obvious straw man here is P. Diddy, and with good reason. Once it becomes apparent that Stan wants little to do with a faux democracy, in which he feels his voice doesn't matter and the outcome affects him little, the town quickly turns on him and it's not long before the former Sean Combs comes knocking. Stan opens the door to Diddy and his entourage. "Puff Daddy?" "Your friend Kyle told me you don't understand the importance of voting." He continues, holding up his official T-shirt, "Apparently you haven't heard of my 'Vote or Die!' campaign." "'Vote or Die?' What the hell does that even mean?" Diddy then calmly pulls out a handgun, cocks it, and proceeds to point it at Stan. "What you think it means, bitch?" This sends us into what is arguably one of the most interesting moments in the episode, where we find a merging of Diddy's campaign rhetoric and his flashy, "baller" video aesthetics, as the episode becomes a P. Diddy video *par excellence*, with the imagery echoing the words in the song:

Posse: Vote or die, motherfucker, motherfucker, vote or die.
Diddy: Rock the vote or else I'm gonna stick a knife through your eye.
Posse: Democracy is founded on one simple rule.
Diddy: Get out there and vote or I will motherfucking kill you. *Yeah.*
    I like it when you vote, bitch. *Bitch.*
    Shake them titties when you vote, bitch. *Bitch.*
    I slam my jimmy through your mouth roof. *Mouth roof.*
    Now get your big ass in the polling booth.
    I said, vote, bitch. Or I'll fucking kill you.
Posse: Vote or die, motherfucker, motherfucker, vote or die.
Diddy: You can't run from a .38. Go ahead an' try.
Posse: Let your opinion be heard. You gotta make a choice.
Diddy: Cuz after I slit your throat, you won't have a fucking voice.
    Vote or die. VOTE OR DIE!!!

In the end, with Diddy and his posse's guns all in his face, Stan, with his arms planted firmly in the air, finally gives in: "Okay. I'll vote." The lesson learned by Stan (and, as we know, Stan and company always learn lessons on *South Park*) is not one of appreciating democracy, nor did he "learn the importance of voting." Rather, "I learned that I better get used to having to pick between a douche and a turd sandwich, because it's usually the choice I'll have." This, however, is interpreted by his parents and the townspeople as, "Yeah! He's going to vote!!!"

Similarly, *Team America*'s main target is not the terrorist organizations, but Michael Moore, as a crazed suicide bomber, and a cadre of celebrities that Parker and Stone clearly see as colonizing the left coast's lunatic fringe. The celebrities mocked in the film include: Alec Baldwin, Sean Penn, Janeane Garofalo, Susan Sarandon, Tim Robbins, Helen Hunt, Danny Glover, Ethan Hawke, Samuel L. Jackson, George Clooney, and Matt Damon, among others, all of whom get torn to shreds (metaphorically and quite literally in that they are decapitated, eaten by cats, and set on fire).[24] They are all a part of the "Film Actor's Guild," or F.A.G. Yet beyond simply pointing fingers and naming names, *Team America* presents a complicated treatment of political discourse in an age in which sending Alec Baldwin to talk peace with Kim Jogn Il doesn't seem that loopy. And there are, of course, jokes a-plenty about F.A.G. and its seriocomic political stylings—one of my favorites may be the moment I realized the leaves of Hollywood's palm trees behind Baldwin in the film were made of money. Another great example of the film's treatment of Hollywood's often nonsensical and insular world is the moment when F.A.G. decides to go to North Korea for itself and all its members (at their United Nations-meets-Justice League-esque headquarters) shout "Qapla'!"—which any geek worth his or her salt knows is the Klingon word for "success." In that brilliant moment we encounter an incredibly obscure intertextual referent coupled with a critique of celebrity megalomania; could we expect anything less from "the guys who brought you *South Park*?" The movie, at least on the surface, remains non-partisan: the duo decided quite wisely that the puppets they made resembling George W. Bush, Dick Cheney John Kerry, and Ted Kennedy would date the film too specifically. Additionally, the word "Iraq" is spoken only by Sean Penn, who brags he's been there.

The film ultimately offers a narrative wherein Team America prevails as being on the side of right, Kim Jong Il turns out to be a cockroach from another planet, and F.A.G. is exposed as ill-informed ideologues (hinted at in the quote that prefaced this section). The culminating moment comes when Gary delivers the climatic monologue (which he got from a drunken barfly).

> We're dicks! We're reckless, arrogant, stupid dicks! And the Film Actors' Guild are pussies. And Kim Jong Il is an asshole. Pussies don't like dicks because pussies get fucked by dicks. But dicks also fuck assholes. Assholes who just want to shit on everything. Pussies may think they can deal with assholes their way, but the only thing that can fuck an asshole . . . is a dick . . . with some balls. The problem with dicks is that sometimes they fuck too much, or fuck when it isn't appropriate, and it takes a pussy to show 'em that. But sometimes pussies get so full of shit that they become assholes themselves. Because pussies are only an inch and a half away from assholes. I don't know much in this . . . crazy, crazy world, but I do know that if you don't let us fuck this asshole, we are gonna have our dicks and our pussies all covered in shit.

It's this kind of collapsing of political distinctions into vulgarity that most on the right have a problem with, yet it's this kind of vulgarity masking a celebration of America's position as "world police" that irks critics on the left. A. O. Scott, in his *New York Times* review, seems to be straddling this very dialectic.

> Considering that it's all done with puppets, "Team America" is sometimes more satisfying as a straight-ahead blow 'em up than as a satire. Goofy as they are, the members of "Team America" are treated, in the end, with affection, even respect, which is part of the film's political gist. When Team America blows things up in other countries, they do it by accident, in the course of their sloppy but zealous fight against the people who want to do it on purpose. This is not a trivial moral distinction, and it is one the film hangs onto in impressive earnest.[25]

Likewise, the main theme song, "America, Fuck Yeah!" is so intensely hyperbolic it's laughable, but I doubt anyone could call it truly sarcastic (and it's infectious if nothing else). Like Gary's speech, the song is seemingly a response to both the "Hollywood peaceniks and to the wishy-washy world community," all of whom perhaps expected something different.[26] *Team America* is at once a clear parody of the War on Terror by way of Bruckheimer-esque puppets, yet also one of the most cogent, and arguably nuanced, defenses of the complexities of American military power on the world stage. As such, and as Scott himself notes, *Team America*, like *South Park*, is invariably critic-proof. Regardless of politics, their creators can always say they're just "two guys fucking around with construction paper and puppets," with the joke seemingly on anyone who attempts any sort of serious analysis or discussion (myself included). Which is not to say that everyone is impressed by their guerilla-style media literacy.

One of the largest, and strangest, controversies (if one can even call it that) surrounding the film was the very public criticisms launched at Parker and Stone by actor Sean Penn. Supposedly, Penn was so insulted by his portrayal in the film that he wrote the following letter that was published widely across news outlets. In the letter he asked Parker and Stone to join him in Iraq and was critical of the pair's stance on not voting. This letter was posted on the Drudge Report a mere nine days before the release of *Team America*:[27]

October 6, 2004

To Trey Parker and Matt Stone,

I remember a cordial hello when you guys were beginning to be famous guys around Hollywood at some party. I remember several times getting a few giggles out of your humor. I remember not being bothered as you traded on my name among others to appear witty, above it all, and likeable to your crowd. I never mind being of service, in satire and silliness.

I do mind when anybody who doesn't have a child, doesn't have a child at war, or isn't or won't be in harm's way themselves, is encouraging that there's "no shame in not voting" "if you don't know what you're talking about" (Mr. Stone) without mentioning the shame of not knowing what you're talking about, and encouraging people to know. You guys are talented young guys but alas, primarily young guys. It's all well to joke about me or whomever you choose. Not so well, to encourage irresponsibility that will ultimately lead to the disembowelment, mutilation, exploitation, and death of innocent people throughout the world. The vote matters to them. No one's ignorance, including a couple of hip cross-dressers, is an excuse.

All best, and a sincere fuck you,

Sean Penn

P.S. Take this as a personal invitation from me to you (you can ask Dennis Miller along for the ride as well) to escort you on a trip, which I took last Christmas. We'll fly to Amman, Jordan and I'll ride with you

in a (?) twelve hours through the Sunni Triangle into Fallujah and
Baghdad and I'll show you around. When we return, make all the fun
you want.

The impetus for the letter was a comment Stone had made in a *Rolling*
Stone interview wherein, along with Parker while promoting *Team Amer-*
ica, he was highly critical of the "voting without understanding" policy
of many celebrity campaigns—specifically the P. Diddy campaign. "I
think just saying 'Vote or Die' is a serious danger to democracy," Stone
argued, as Parker broke into a Cartman-esque voice for a mocking pub-
lic-service message: "Hey, nineteen-year-old who doesn't know anything—you choose." Stone continued: "If you don't know what you're
talking about, there's no shame in not voting . . . They say if you don't
vote, you can't bitch. But you can bitch all you want. This is America."[28]
And only in Hollyweird would an interview in response to the discourse
the letter generated have gone something like this:

> Trey: It was funny because all he did was take something that Matt said
> in *Rolling Stone* and take it out of context and then claim, "this is what
> I'm mad about" when in fact, we had heard from people who know him
> that he was pissed off as soon as he saw that he was in the movie.
>
> Matt: Because he was in the teaser.
>
> Trey: He was honestly like "How dare someone make fun of me?" And
> what was so funny is that in the movie what we have them do is be "I
> went to Iraq! I went to Iraq!" when all of us are like we don't give a
> rat's ass if you went to Iraq. Dude, I went to the Grand Canyon once,
> but that doesn't make me an expert, you know. It's funny that we then
> get this letter and it's like "PS: And I went to Iraq! I went to Iraq!"
>
> Matt: If you saw the movie, it's almost exactly what he said in the
> movie.
>
> Q: People probably think it was a joke.
>
> Trey: People thought we wrote it!
>
> Matt: Our lawyer and people from Paramount called us and said "Did
> you guys plant that letter? Because if you did, you just can't do that"
> and we were like "No, we didn't. He really wrote that."[29]

In other venues, Penn also claimed that Parker and Stone shouldn't have released the film as it may have affected the 2004 presidential election. In follow-up interviews, Parker and Stone, interestingly, were quick to point out that the furious Penn was ironically attacking their free speech, ostensibly stating that because their opinion differed from his it should have been kept to themselves. At the heart of Stone's comments that brought on Penn's critique is essentially a push toward a politics of (un)involvement, which is to say Stone made the mistake of publicly telling people that not voting might actually be a viable option.

There are many reasons to not vote, even if one is eligible, even if one is registered: not being able to leave work, simply being too busy, not having a candidate to support, not believing one's vote matters, or not voting as a protest of what can be seen as a failed system—that "turning away in disgust" so different from apathy. All of these are good reasons and should not be discounted. The problem with treating non-voters as politically apathetic is at the heart of a neoliberal turn toward promulgating a false sense of democracy within the post-millennial republic.

Comparatively, the turnout for 2004 wasn't actually that bad, around 55 percent, up 4 percent from the previous election, which itself was up 2 percent from 1996.[30] Even in light of the hardships we put other countries through to try and bring them democracy, American style, it would appear that a good portion of the country simply feels like Stan a good portion of the time. And while the trend has shown that voter turnout has been dropping steadily since the 1960s, popular media would have made it seem imperative that the 2004 election be somehow different. Potential voters were so drowned in initiative campaigns that any dissent toward voting was seen as anti-democratic—with much of this kind of rhetoric coming at us from the likes of Sean Penn and P. Diddy. One problem may be that while they were arguing for folks to get out and vote, it really seemed like much of the point was to ultimately take the White House out of the Bush administration's hands. Thus, if one didn't know how to vote based on issues alone, it became pretty apparent pretty quickly that the election was really about supporting your favorite cause célèbre. Another problem might be the Electoral College, particularly after the fiasco in Florida following the 2000 election.[31] While the popular vote is not something that is completely ignored, in reality for many, it often stands in the way of individual votes actually being counted. As such, presidential elections often boil down to battleground states such as Florida playing the biggest part, with average citizens being reminded of how quiet their voices actually are.[32] So, while Diddy's threatening of Stan's life (no doubt with a platinum .38, or something equally baller) is clearly an exaggeration of Diddy's ridiculous ultimatum, it would appear that this clearly represents the many social pressures felt by people who choose not to vote (or are voting simply out of duty as opposed to personal interest).[33]

It's not too imaginative a reading, then, to glean that this episode smacks of a distinctively bad-taste regarding left-leaning celebrity politics, particularly when coupled with *Team America*'s potentially rather conservative treatment of the war on terror, ostensibly attacking critics while attempting to defend, if not, celebrate the cause. However, if we treat Parker and Stone's *modus operandi* as playing the cultural "devil's advocate," then what we are offered is not so much a glorification of unilateral violence, as a scathing critique that seeks to tear down the paper tigers of celebrity politicking. Parker, during an interview on *The Charlie Rose Show*, discussed it as such: "Where we live is, like, the most liberalist liberal part of the world. There's a groupthink, and you only get to some truth by argument and dissent, and so we just play devil's advocate all of the time."[34]

As one can see, it's no wonder that the show is often "claimed" by both the left and the right, conservative and liberal, alike as "representing" their views.

One of the most widely-known misinterpretations of *South Park* is probably Brian Anderson's book, *South Park Conservatives*, which hijacks the show's representation of conservatism in the name of anti-liberal propaganda.[35] The problem is that it places the show squarely into the polarized political context it is actually seeking to critique. The phrase "*South Park* Republican" actually began circulating in articles and blogs around 2001 and 2002 to describe the young adults (and here I would include teenagers not yet of voting age) whose political beliefs often align with those espoused on the show. The term was actually coined by gay conservative commentator Andrew Sullivan, who identified himself as a "*South Park* Republican" upon hearing that Parker and Stone had "outed" themselves as Republicans at a 2001 award ceremony. The phrase has been used in the popular press to identify beliefs, rather than partisan identity. I would argue that *South Park* Republicanism is actually a thinly veiled form of Libertarianism sans label (which would make perfect sense if we consider both the show and the notion that libertarianism is a philosophy of freedom). Stone sums up his political stance as such: "I hate conservatives, but I really fucking hate liberals."[36] And while the poststructuralist in me would argue that the political identities of the show's creators should be irrelevant to any textual reading, it may be worth noting here that, while Stone is a registered Republican, Parker is, in fact, a registered member of the Libertarian Party.

When asked about their knowledge of the term "*South Park* Republican," Parker responded with the following:

> Yeah, we have seen that. What we're sick of—and it's getting even worse—is: you either like Michael Moore or you wanna fuckin' go overseas and shoot Iraqis. There can't be a middle ground. Basically, if you think Michael Moore's full of shit, then you are a super-Christian right-wing whatever. And we're both just pretty middle-ground guys. We find just as many things to rip on on the left as we do on the right. People on the far left and the far right are the same exact person to us.[37]

Also complicating this marking of political identity in the show is the fact that Parker and Stone have on numerous occasions proclaimed *All in the Family* creator Norman Lear, who helped write several episodes of *South Park* (most notably the 2003 episode "I'm a Little Bit Country"— which happened to be the series' one hundreth) and founded the liberal/progessive advocacy group People for the American Way, to be one of their heroes, both personally and in the industry.[38]

But how does libertarianism explain away *South Park*'s often ambivalent political stances? According to Tibor Machan, one of the major questions of political principles faced since the penning of the American Declaration of Independence is, "How ought we to organize our political societies?"[39] Since we are dealing with an announcement, a *declaration*, not a thorough and detailed treatise, this concise question is always and already in constant need of fleshing out. For Machan, the answer best lies not only in the Founders' original ideals, but also in libertarianism—the notion that "individual members of human communities are sovereign, self-ruling, or self-governing, agents whose sovereignty any just system of laws must accommodate."[40] But this emphasis on the individual and free will must exist within a world where juridical systems, fire and police departments, hospitals, schools, etc., all must operate fluidly for society to function. This is to say that the complex view of libertarianism is one in which a society of individuals must agree on particular points of governmentality to continue being free.[41] Libertarianism has been around as a political movement in the United States since the 1960s in various forms, but its roots can be found in the writings of John Locke, among others, who believed that political authority must come through the consent of the individual.[42] But it's only really since the Reagan/Thatcher era that libertarian ideas have increasingly come to matter in public discourse.

One of the complexities at work is that any argument that says a meaningful human life requires both individual freedom and the state to provide services and uphold promises is seemingly at odds with itself. To many, libertarians seem like a bunch of confused ideologues who want to have their cake and eat it too. What's really at stake though, is not a confusion of political identity; rather, it is the democratic consideration that to make one's argument articulate, one must understand the politics of the other. And while this completely goes against a bifurcated political system, libertarianism may be the most democratic "choice" out there, as one of its tenets is to not merely listen to, but understand the arguments of others. As such, *South Park*, I argue, espouses a libertarian political philosophy in that, if anything, the show is about the cubist presentation of an argument. If viewers see something from all sides, logically, then it is up to them to make an informed decision about the issue. As Parker went on to explain during his interview with Charlie Rose, "What we say with the show is not anything new, but I think it is something that is great to put out there. It is that the people screaming on this side and the people screaming on that side are the same people, and it's okay to be someone in the middle, laughing at both of them."[43] This is to say that the libertarian perspective of *South Park* and *Team America* is one that actually celebrates all sides, allowing for extremists on all sides to have their voices loudly heard; the consequence is that everyone will get made fun of. Is this not free expression at its finest?

Postmodern Lafargues and the "Certain Economy of Enjoyment": Toward a Politics of (Un)Involvement

In an interview with Glyn Daly, Slavoj Žižek blithely remarked that "all politics relies upon, and even manipulates, a certain economy of enjoyment."[44] For Žižek, Lacanian *jouissance* is the centerpiece for all criticisms of ideological fantasies and subjectivity under late capitalism. As he notes in *The Parallax View*, "our politics is more and more directly the politics of *jouissance*, concerned with ways of soliciting, or controlling and regulating, *jouissance*."[45] Rather than enter into an elongated discussion or interpretation of the Žižekian notion of enjoyment as a pure political theory, running inroads and outroads through his pomposities (and I mean that in a good way) and his often elusive rhetoric, I wish to, instead, simply meditate on the simplest of interpretations of this pronouncement. How can one be involved in politics if one does not enjoy it? I realize that this is actually an *incorrect* interpretation of Žižek insofar as politics is concerned with *jouissance* as a category of subjectivity upon which it can impose some kind of governmentality.

No, here I wish to ask and state the obvious. If one does not enjoy politics, how then can one be political? And I ask this without offering an answer or a political "side." For Žižek it seems to be a given that conservatives on the right don't want us to have any fun. What's interesting in his critique is his challenge to leftist, liberal politics as well in that, while on the surface we tend to see uncritical celebrations rise from the left—such as multiculturalism or political correctness—liberal tolerance is nothing more than a form of "zero tolerance" of the other's *jouissance*.[46] In this way, liberalism is as guilty of the ideology of "you're with us or you're against us" as the next guy.

In the original draft of this essay, the subtitle for this section was much shorter, something filled with both erudition and brevity, something like "Fuck Bono!" I ranted for what seemed like forever about everything I hate about celebrity politics. Rather than recapitulate that argument—which was suitable for no one upon reflection—I want to consider Parker and Stone's libertarian embracing of democratic individualism in light of our discussion of political apathy.

In 1883 a Cuban-born French revolutionary (who also happened to be Marx's son-in-law) wrote a small pamphlet from his prison cell. Paul Lafargue's *Le droit à la paresse* ("The Right to Idleness," but more well known as "The Right to Be Lazy") polemicized against the then common notion of work as it crossed conservative, liberal, and even socialist boundaries.[47] For Lafargue, arguing from both a Marxist and a utopian perspective, the idea of work is dogmatic and false in that it is a kind of enslavement. Once human existence becomes subsumed under the guise of a "right to work," passion, creativity, and spirit fall to the wayside. For Lafargue, laziness is central to recapturing these essences of all human progress. As such, I argue, as I believe Parker and Stone do as well, that if we are to truly believe in democracy then we have the right to be politically lazy. We have the right to not vote, and, perhaps more importantly, we have the right to not care. Given that Parker and Stone are the most obvious exponents of this opinion, it is clear that it has taken media a while to come to this point, as, for many, this is largely an undemocratic position.

At the dawn of television, political apathy was frequently considered a widespread phenomenon in American society; political scientists, even a decade before television's widespread adoption, were already articulating apathy as a serious problem.[48] Tom DeLuca, in one of the best overviews of American political apathy, discusses its "two faces": the first face represents the claim of the politicians who blame the individual and encourages the conceptualization of apathy as a social ill; the second face "is productive, and it is also produced, with great social effort."[49] In a traditional view, apathy is always and already something to be discouraged.[50] The main problem is that this view articulates a very specific vision of what it means to live in a democracy. Regarding our contemporary lack of historicity, the political theorist C. B. Macpherson wrote in 1966,

> Democracy used to be a bad word. Everybody who was anybody knew that democracy, in its original sense of rule by people or government in accordance with the will of the bulk of the people, would be a bad thing—fatal to individual freedom and to all the graces of civilized living. That was the position taken by pretty nearly all men of intelligence from the earliest historical times down to about a hundred years ago. Then, within fifty years, democracy became a good thing. Its full acceptance into the ranks of respectability was apparent by the time of the First World War; a way which the Western allied leaders could proclaim was fought to make the world safe for democracy. Since then . . . everybody claims to have it.[51]

It is not coincidental that the way in which Macpherson characterizes the post-war spread of democracy sounds eerily like the current war on terror's agenda. Thus, a sweeping move to spread this kind of democracy must open the gates of resistance, resistance such as the *South Park* libertarianism I have described. Contemporary media and politics have simply beaten "the plowshare of democracy into a sword of political apathy . . . severed the democratic wish from its root . . . sliced democratic aspirations in half . . . invented *demi-democracy*."[52] In other words, the spread of democracy perhaps caused the spread of apathy. As Americans, we are, thus, a democratic people living in undemocratic times.[53]

The unique problematizing of Parker and Stone is that, unlike the rest of media culture, they don't lay blame at any one perspective; rather, all sides of an issue are skewered. Alan McKee, in his book on the public sphere, notes that when it comes to the issue of apathy, "The voters blame the politicians. The politicians blame the voters. Nobody takes responsibility for the uninformed, uninterested population. And nobody blames what may be the largest source of [political apathy] yet: the media."[54] For McKee, the media are a kind of conductor of political apathy; yet at the same time, he points out that blaming the media is an oversimplified approach to understanding the larger issues. A kind of Burkean, comic framing is actually what seems to be happening on *South Park*, unlike the tragic frame which envelops the vast majority of media culture. This comic frame allows for a critique of the constant onslaught of America's misguided policies and politics, while avoiding the allure of a straightforward kind of cynical scapegoating and debunking, so evident in places such as late night talk shows, etc.[55] Also, this comic framing highlights human fallibility without a simple knee-jerk condemnation of human error. Kenneth Burke, in *Attitudes Toward History*, notes that

> The comic frame is charitable, but at the same time it is not gullible. It keeps us alive to the ways in which people "cash in on" their moral assets . . . By astutely gauging situations and personal resources, it promotes the realistic sense of one's limitations . . . yet the acceptance is not passive.[56]

Yet the device of the Burkean frame is but one way of understanding how we are presented with the notions of apathy and democracy. The question for DeLuca is: "What if apathy is not freely chosen, the problem is not all us? What if what appears as apathy is really a political attitude of another kind?"[57] What DeLuca seems to be getting at here, and what Parker and Stone so effectively articulate, is that apathy may in-and-of-itself be a political reaction. Apathy, as presented in texts such as *South Park*, can thus be used as a tool for negotiating all our "semiotic excesses."

But this certainly is not a new perspective. In a highly influential 1954 book entitled *Voting*, Bernard Berelson, Paul Lazarsfeld, and William McPhee made the claim that apathy is actually good for democracy.[58] Additionally, two decades later, Samuel Huntington, a former president of the American Political Science Association, made a startlingly similar claim, noting,

> The effective operation of a democratic political system usually requires some measure of apathy and noninvolvement on the part of some individuals and groups . . . in itself, this marginality on the part of some groups is inherently undemocratic, but it has also been one of the factors which have enabled democracy to function effectively.[59]

Here I both agree and disagree with Huntington. Apathy is needed to truly have a democratic society; however, I do not feel that those who choose freely to not participate are inherently undemocratic. Would it not be better if we could find some kind of . . .

A Middle Ground (or Whatever, You Know)

In an exchange from a 2004 interview promoting *Team America*, Parker and Stone were confronted with, "You seem to feel free to roast everybody equally." Their response:

> Parker: Everybody needs a good roasting.
>
> Stone: It's been pretty funny on both sides.
>
> Parker: And it comes from an honest belief we have, which is . . . George Bush doesn't know what's going on. Michael Moore does not know what's going on. And Alec Baldwin definitely does not know what's going on. Basically, this shit is gigantically complicated.[60]

And the fact that this shit is, indeed, gigantically complicated thus illustrates the necessity for complex, deconstructive texts such as *South Park* and *Team America*, narratives that do not scapegoat, do not pick sides, do not let celebrities off the hook, and do not ignore the most pressing issues of our times. Yet it also takes a special kind of courage to use these texts as a platform for anti-mobilization, to take a truly democratic stance, and to tell people to participate only if they truly desire to do so. For apathy, as I have argued, is not undemocratic; rather, it is a necessary component of a true libertarian democracy, whereby the state and the individual are both rendered central. As DeLuca notes in the closing of his book, *The Two Faces of Political Apathy*,

> Democracy is a process, a goal, a way of life. It is a challenge and a commitment. It is a challenge many Americans took up, believed in, an ideal they suffered in war to defend. Conservative scholars are right to remind us that the founders set up a republic, not a democracy. They are wrong to say, today, that alone is good enough. Democracy is a commitment we never fully made. It's time.[61]

At the beginning of this essay, I alluded to the connection between conspicuous consumption as a kind of false remedy to political apathy (i.e. "Idol Gives Back," etc.).[62] Kevin Mattson notes that this connection is what makes youth mobilization campaigns, such as Rock the Vote, interesting, arguing that there is a "slippery line between the noble act of increasing the vote and the corporate sponsors' self-interest."[63] He continues, "A spokesman for Coors, another funder of Rock the Vote, explained, I'm not going to sit here and tell you this about voting. We're talking about selling beer and decided to kill two birds with one stone."[64] Mattson's use of this example, considering that he uses it in a text designed to engage youth through public services, etc., raises a key assumption about the relationship between consumerism and political participation, and its consequences. If we treat democracy like a commodity, then it is simply another service industry (which, for many critics of apathy, is simply the wrong perception about the populace's relationship with its government). The standard fear here, as articulated by Mattson, is that more people will simply be convinced to buy consumer products and will see voting as simply another purchasing choice, noting:

> In this day and age, it is probably safe to assume that young people receive the message to buy things even when it is attached onto the message to vote; it is easy to imagine them failing to hear Madonna begging them to vote and rather thinking about buying her next CD.[65]

But what's evident from the above quote is not necessarily that it is really "safe to assume" anything about youth voters; rather, it is illustrative of Mattson being guilty of a language of othering that we find everywhere else in the very media he is criticizing. Mattson thus frames the media in a kind of Burkean "tragic" frame, thereby scapegoating both the media and the corporate sector, along with the youth population.

So is there even cause for alarm with regard to youth voting? It would seem not. Even with Stone telling people to not vote unless they truly feel compelled to do so with knowledge of what's at stake, the youth voter seems to care. Turnout was up 11 percent from the 2000 election, no doubt due to the efforts of P. Diddy and the like, with the largest turnout since the 1972 and 1992 elections for voters between the ages of eighteen and twenty-four (see Graph 1). But if youth voting seems to be on an upswing, why still focus media attention on apathy? One reason could be the rhetorical connection between apathy and cynicism. The detachment from politics described above correlates, for many, with a substantial increase in the political cynicism that has erupted over

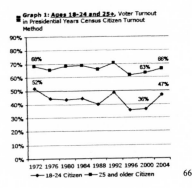

Graph 1: **Ages 18-24 and 25+**, Voter Turnout in Presidential Years Census Citizen Turnout Method

66

the past several decades—a cynicism stemming from scandals, an on-slaught of bad news, and a reaffirming of voter irrelevancy. For many critics, the danger lies in the potential moment when "citizens who are cynical . . . risk . . . getting trapped in a cycle" of apathetic behavior.[67] This kind of cynicism, whether real or projected, clearly relates to a lack of efficacy regarding politics itself. As Matthew Reed notes, if "politics is irrelevant and irretrievable, and there is no possibility of changing that (and therefore no reason to try). Better to conserve one's efforts, to apply them to something more productive."[68]

There's a wonderful moment in a *Lingua Franca* interview with Žižek when he argues that Yugoslavian socialism produced a thoroughly cynical citizenry and turned the country into a group of people who understood that the last thing the regime desired was for them to believe too ardently in the official principles of communism. This, for Žižek, is ideology at its most effective. "The paradox of the regime," he noted, "was that if people were to take their ideology seriously it would effectively destroy the system."[69] For Žižek, cynicism and apathy are explanations not for the failure of the communist regime, but, perversely, for its success.

> The conventional wisdom is that socialism was a failure because, instead of creating a "New Man," it produced a country of cynics who believed that the system is corrupt, politics is a horror, and that only private happiness is possible . . . But my point is this: Perhaps depoliticization was the true aim of socialist education? This was surely the daily experience of my youth.[70]

But is this what's happening in the American landscape? Is the political system in effect creating political apathy? Is the true aim of politics and the media to depoliticize us? And what is the place of public discourse?

As Nina Eliasoph observes, in *Avoiding Politics: How Americans Produce Apathy in Everyday Life,* "The act of carving out public space for open-ended, broad-minded political conversation could, potentially, implicitly call into question many unjust forms of power. When citizens assume that speaking in public is a source of power, public speech magically can *become* a source of power."[71] This is why celebrity politics are so dangerous. This is also why, perhaps, Parker and Stone have consistently avoided politicking over specific issues or lending their name to specific causes (other than, say, publicly protesting and criticizing the Motion Picture Association of America). And perhaps this is why, in April 2006, when the University of Georgia handed out its coveted Peabody Awards for "distinguished achievement and meritorious service" in electronic media, *South Park* was among the winners. In its award statement the committee cited the show with the following: "Primitive animation is part of the charm of TV's boldest, most politically incorrect satirical series. Its simple style also makes possible the show's unmatched topicality." And while the fact that they can make episodes in the days leading up to their Wednesday night timeslot does afford them a topicality unsurpassed in fictional media, it is the show's irreverence with regard to those current events that give it its strongest satirical—not cynical—edge.

What I mean by that last remark is quite simple, really. It is clear to see that, regardless of political identity (republican, libertarian, etc.), Parker and Stone are not cynical; rather, they are "kynics" of the purest sort. Peter Sloterdijk proposes the term "kynicism" as a subversive practice, whereby it becomes "the motif of self-preservation in crisis-ridden times . . . a critical, ironical philosophy of so-called needs."[72] For Sloterdijk, "kynicism" is "the antidote to modern cynicism"[73]—a kind of "shameless, 'dirty' realism that, without regard for conventional moral inhibitions, declares itself to be for how 'things really are.'"[74] What Sloterdijk is presenting here really is an explanation of *South Park*'s politics *avant la lettre*.

So, how are we to overcome the contemporary, "cynical" move toward a politics of (un)involvement—if this is what we desire? How are we to protect ourselves from the Bonos, the P. Diddys, and the Janeane Garofalos? How can we conflictingly embrace and mobilize into a more laissez-faire politics? There is an ambiguity that plagues political (un)involvement, perhaps explaining why public discourse about apathy is often so contradictory, with scapegoating on all sides. This is why *South Park*'s taking of the American pulse is all the more crucial. It would appear the youth of today are damned if they do and damned if they don't. For example, whereas a critic such as Mattson is quick to dismiss any kind of activism in contemporary society as "apolitical service," he is quick to provide a solution that would seemingly do more damage than good. He states, "Precisely because service offers an 'up-close and personal' feeling of commitment, it falls prey to the worst tendencies of a therapeutic culture—one that stresses *feeling good about oneself* rather than connecting to public life."[75] What is seemingly being claimed here is that volunteering in its variety of forms is somehow less valuable because it is superficially removed from direct political involvement. This is not to say that Mattson doesn't advocate curricular enterprises such as service learning (or "indentured servitude learning" as we called it when I was an undergraduate), which would seemingly be at odds with his overarching argument. How can one be less involved because of consumerism and volunteerism, yet more involved when one is forced to participate against one's will? This seeming contradiction is at the heart of many a debate surrounding service learning within higher education. And while critics of uninvolved youth, such as Mattson, are clearly not satisfied with leaving young people to their own devices, on the other hand, we find celebrants such as McKee, who witnesses "the ultimate face of political apathy [yet] at the same time, youth culture is shown to us in the media as the source of the most extreme forms of activism . . . organizing anti-global movements and protests."[76] What we have seen unfold in the space between recent elections is not simply an overarching move toward the politicizing of a generation, but the commodification of dissent on a large enough scale to confuse anyone. The Battle for Seattle seems to be just another way to sell Nike and Starbucks. The anti-consumerism of the film version of *Fight Club* not only serves as a steady money-maker for News Corp, but also provided the Gap with a "revolutionary" ad campaign. The lines are impossibly blurred; it's no wonder turning away becomes the best option we've got.

While I was writing this chapter I chatted with my grandfather, and as I told him about this book, he dispensed some of his typical wisdom: "Politics is the filthiest shit. And unless you devote all your time to understanding it, it's never going to make any fucking sense, 'cause that's how they want to play it."[77] But isn't this kind of obfuscation the only way American politics can function within its tiny swathe in the "information age?" Isn't confusion what American politics is seemingly all about?

In a 2002 Department of Defense briefing, Donald Rumsfeld offered what is perhaps the first, most important political philosophy of the twenty-first century.

Reports that say that something hasn't happened are always interesting to me, because as we know, there are known knowns; there are things we know we know. We also know there are known unknowns; that is to say we know there are some things we do not know. But there are also unknown unknowns—the ones we don't know we don't know.[78]

Even though the specter of Wittgenstein is standing behind me shouting in my ear, "Wovon man nicht sprechen kann, darüber muß man schweigen," there is a utopian beauty to Rumsfeld's admission of uncertainty.[79] For our purposes we can take this to mean that Rumsfeld is making an empirical claim about the limits of knowledge. While he is clearly lamenting the military's problem of verifiability, he is still making an argument regarding the difficulty in saying with certainty when, and if, anything actually happened. It's, sadly, this kind of rhetoric, which provides the true "equipment for living," that the media offer us.[80] Which is to say, if we want to retain a happy way of life, it's up to politics and the media to keep reminding us that's what we've got.

About one fifth of American children live in poverty and the paucity of national healthcare insures even more go without proper medical care. And although the United States is one of the four wealthiest nations in the world in terms of gross domestic product per capita, it fails on many other social levels.[81] For example, almost between thirty and forty-five nations are ahead of the U.S. in life expectancy, depending on whether we count various sovereign groups.[82] This is all to say that even though our chosen protected image is one of invincibility and global power, we might not be so tough after all. Where, other than *South Park*, are we reminded of this?

But it is not simply that *South Park* is a knee-jerk, anti-hegemonic critique; it exists as part of a complex interplay between creative artistry, the economic interests of corporate media, and the fickle (and often confused) intertexual knowledge of audiences and their discursive constructs. If the hegemonic perspective is one in which "apathy refers to citizens' unwillingness to exert some degree of effort to involve themselves in the political process in even the most basic forms of participation," then *South Park*'s politics is at once a challenge to the "apathy as social disease" label and a reification of the cultural complexities of democratic life.[83]

Throughout the history of any democratic enterprise (and it's worth noting the U.S. has *always* been a republic and not a democracy in its purest sense), there is always a large portion of the populace that votes and a large portion that does not—for a variety of reasons. Taken historically, apathy is not a contagious disease, spreading among youth like a political STD; rather, it functions, as has been shown, as a critical instrument with which citizens can navigate the symbolic environment—a tool with which they can voice their opinion through their deafening silence. And while some hold out an unrealistic, utopian vision that technology will save us,[84] a characteristic of democracy worth remembering is the simple fact that not everyone can participate in every public decision; for democracy to function it relies on the assumption that certain people will and will not take part. (Un)involvement is the moment of choice between the two. Readers will also notice that I have deliberately used a parenthetical break distinction to include both involvement and un-involvement in the same breath. For what many see as a blatant disregard for the political process, what we have seen is, in fact, a political action in itself.

One of the problems with political apathy from an academic perspective, the overarching problem perhaps, is the political unconscious, to use Jameson's phrase, that underscores much scholarly discourse. As Paddy Scannell notes:

> The only reality that media studies knows is a political reality, set in a field of discourse that . . . mobilizes concepts of power, struggle, conflict, ideology. It has great difficulty with any idea of ordinary *unpolitical* daily life, and its everyday concerns and enjoyments. Since for the politically minded all things are political—and what is not is either marginal or incorrectly understood—it follows that the only *interesting* questions about the media are political. I of course do not think so.[85]

I, of course, agree.

The argument here, then, is one of "negative utopianism," where the human field of struggle becomes one of *realizing the potential* for that struggle, for a becoming of the potentiality of differences, where guidance and direction by an (infra)structural system becomes phrased as a question, as opposed to an assumption. In other words, will we see anyone in 2008? 2010? 2012? 2014?

It will be up to them, now, won't it?

Notes

1. For Lehne Leverette and Frank Menczel, who remind me that not giving a fuck is my prerogative, my right, and nobody can take that away. I also what to thank Josh Riggs for sharing with me a wonderful literature review on political apathy, as well as Tony Kelso and Brian Cogan for their inestimable patience and all-around kick ass-ness and great ideas.

2. As literary critic Terry Eagleton defines the postmodern: "a depthless, decentered, ungrounded, self-reflexive, playful, derivative, eclectic, pluralistic art." Terry Eagleton, *The Illusions of Postmodernism* (Oxford: Blackwell, 1996), vii.

3. Marc O'Day, "Postmodernism and Television," in *The Routledge Critical Dictionary of Postmodern Thought*, ed. Stuart Sim (London: Routledge, 1999), 112.

4. The standard definition of apathy is as a particular state of mind—lacking passion, feeling, or interest in something others find moving. Political scientists, however, define it in behavioral rather than psychological terms (i.e., a lack of participation, a lack of direct action, etc.). I will be using the latter definition throughout, as some people clearly devote more time to politics than others and some clearly devote none. Involvement, as such, can be defined by things such as common activities, many of which are undemanding, specifically voting, but also seeking information, discussing politics, joining organizations, or even showing a general interest in politics on any level. For more, see Giuseppe Di Palma, *Apathy and Participation: Mass Politics in Western Societies* (New York: Free Press, 1970).

5. Michael Moore, *Stupid White Men: And Other Sorry Excuses for the State of the Nation!* (New York: Harper Collins, 2001), 88.

6. Mark Crispin Miller, *The Bush Dyslexicon: Observations on a National Disorder* (New York: Norton, 2000), 198.

7. On the state of exception, see Giorgio Agamben, *Homo Sacer: Sovereign Power and Bare Life*, trans. Daniel Heller-Roazen (Stanford: Stanford University Press, 1998); Giorgio Agamben, *State of Exception*, trans. Kevin Attell (Chicago: University of Chicago Press, 2005); and Andrew Norris, ed., *Politics, Metaphysics, and Death: Essays on Giorgio Agamben's* Homo Sacer (Durham: Duke University Press, 2005).

8. Bono, the part-time singer for U2 and full-time planetary guilt-trip, even fancies himself an "amateur economist." See, for example, Robert J. Barro, *Nothing Is Sacred: Economic Ideas for the New Millennium* (Cambridge, MA: MIT Press, 2002), 36-43. In all seriousness, as Barro observes, Bono's success in coalescing disparate groups, from the right and the left, and raising money for a wide-range of causes is nothing short of staggering. Barro, it should be noted, is also writing before the ubiquity of "The One" campaign, wherein celebrities of all shapes and colors implore their less wealthy sycophantic fans to end poverty by shopping at the Gap or buying Motorola phones and other such hypo-

critical acts of conspicuous consumption.

9. Joshua Riggs, "The Redemption of Apathy: Rhetorical Virtue or Social Disease?" Unpublished manuscript.

10. Daniel M. Gross, *The Secret History of Emotion: From Aristotle's Rhetoric to Modern Brain Science* (Chicago: University of Chicago Press, 2006), 51.

11. To wit: "Apathy and social disengagement seem[s] to be an epidemic among young people." Bruce E. Pinkleton and Erica Weintraub Austin, "Media Perceptions and Public Affairs: Apathy in the Politically Inexperienced," *Mass Perceptions & Society* 7, no. 3 (2004): 320.

12. See, for example, Russell Jacoby, *The End of Utopia: Politics and Culture in the Age of Apathy* (New York: Basic Books, 1999).

13. Riggs, "The Redemption."

14. Gross, *The Secret History*, 52.

15. Page duBois, "Violence, Apathy, and the Rhetoric of Philosophy," in *Rethinking the History of Rhetoric: Multidisciplinary Essays on the Rhetorical Tradition*, ed. Takis Poulakos (Boulder, CO: Westview, 1993), 127.

16. Jim Collins, *Architectures of Excess: Cultural Life in the Information Age* (New York: Routledge, 1995).

17. Even though he was writing pre-*South Park*, Doug Rushkoff, for example, reminds us that if we want to find social criticism, sometimes the best place to look is just under the surface of seemingly inane cartoons (as well as video games, comic books, etc.). See Douglas Rushkoff, *Media Virus! Hidden Agendas in Popular Culture* (New York: Ballantine, 1994), specifically chapters 4 and 6, "Kids TV" and "Alternative Media," 100-25, 179-209.

18. For one political read, see Robert Singh, "Subverting American Values? *The Simpsons, South Park*, and the Cartoon Culture War," in *American Politics and Society Today*, ed. Robert Singh (Cambridge: Polity, 2002), 206-29.

19. For more on the film version of the show, see Tim Jon Semmerling, "Conclusion: The *South Park* Lesson and Orientalist Fear," in *"Evil" Arabs in American Popular Film: Orientalist Fears* (Austin: University of Texas Press, 2006), 248-55; and James Hewiston, "The *South Park* Apocalyptic: Smaller, Shorter, & Undercut," in *Oh My God, They Deconstructed* South Park*! Those Bastards!*, ed. Marc Leverette and Brian Cogan (Lanham, MD: Lexington Press, forthcoming).

20. The argument for *South Park* being "transgressive" is nothing new. Nor is it very original at this point. Mary Dalton argues, for example, that in the episode "Proper Condom Use," the show renders condoms transgressive. I find this kind of logic regarding *South Park* to be superficial and somewhat ridiculous. All comedy, by definition, is transgressive, for all comedy needs to be offensive to derive energy from the transgressive prowess of its challenges to conventions, norms, and status quos. To say *South Park* is transgressive is like saying punk rock was transgressive. The real moment of transgression in *South Park* occurs when they are not being societally transgressive: episodes such as "Pip," which

was simply a retelling of Dickens's *Great Expectations*. Fans know these moments and tend to hate them; dilettante viewers simply don't understand them. If everyone thinks you are transgressive, are you? You can only be when you cease to be in these people's eyes. That's about as punk rock as it gets. For the standard view, see: Mary M. Dalton, "Making Condoms Transgressive: *South Park* and 'Proper Condom Use,'" in *Culture and the Condom*, ed. Karen Anijar and Thuy DaoJensen (New York: Peter Lang, 2005), 37-47. See also Michael V. Tueth, "Breaking and Entering: Transgressive Comedy on Television," in *The Sitcom Reader: America Viewed and Skewed*, ed. Mary M. Dalton and Laura R. Linder (Albany: State University of New York Press, 2005), 25-34; and Karen Anijar, Hsueh-hua Vivan Chen, and Thomas E. Walker, "Poofs—Cheesy and Other: Identity Politics as Commodity in *South Park*," in *The Sitcom Reader: America Viewed and Skewed*, ed. Mary M. Dalton and Laura R. Linder (Albany: State University of New York Press, 2005), 191-204.

21. Semmerling, "Conclusion," 248.

22. Before settling on the final plot for their script (ultimately penned by Parker, Stone, and *South Park* alum Pam Brady), Parker and Stone's original idea was to do an all-puppet remake of *Armageddon*.

23. Ryan Sager, *The Elephant in the Room: Evangelicals, Libertarians, and the Battle to Control the Republican Party* (Hoboken, NJ: John Wiley and Sons, 2006), 95.

24. It's worth mentioning here that Clooney was a driving force in getting *South Park* on the air. Additionally, as a close friend of Parker and Stone, he has lent his voice to the show and movie. Similarly, Matt Damon is also a friend of the pair and was originally going to be portrayed as intelligent and articulate. However, as rumor has it, when they saw his puppet, both noted that he "looked retarded" and decided to play it as such. Both Clooney and Damon have commented on their puppet caricatures in very positive terms and said they would have been offended if they hadn't been skewered in the film.

25. A.O. Scott, "Moral Guidance from Class Clowns," *New York Times*, October 15, 2004, http://www.nytimes.com/2004/10/15/movies/15TEAM.html?ei=5090&en=44a5437ea423a6ad&ex=1255579200&partner=rssuserland&pagewanted=all (accessed January 21, 2007).

26. Scott, "Moral Guidance."

27. As Stone notes, however, "that letter wasn't to us. It was an open letter. We got it a day before it was 'leaked' but he sent it to the *LA Times*." Quoted in Ethan Aames, "Interview: Trey Parker & Matt Stone on 'Team America: World Police,'" *Cinema Confidential*, October 15, 2004, http://www.cinecon.com/news.php?id=0410151 (accessed March 18, 2007).

28. Quoted in David Wild, "Puppetmasters: *South Park* 'Bad Boys' Take on Terror with Potty-Mouthed Puppets," *Rolling Stone*, October 5, 2004, http://www.rollingstone.com/politics/story/6539084/puppetmasters/ (accessed March 18, 2007).

29. Wild, "Puppetmasters."

30. http://www.presidency.ucsb.edu/data/turnout.php (accessed March 16, 2007).

31. Let us not forget the brilliant fourth-season episode, "Trapper Keeper," wherein Ike's ("Ike the Genius") kindergarten class has an election for class president. When it becomes clear that there is a tie between Ike and Fillmore all hell breaks loose, with undecided "Flora" clearly representing Florida and "the Absent Kid" clearly standing in for all the absentee ballots. Fillmore's aunt, Rosie O'Donnell, keeps insisting on a recount (which Mr. Garrison does well more than one hundred times). Jesse Jackson even gets involved. After countless lawyers take over the argument and fill the youngsters' lives with legal forms and endless meetings ad nauseum, Filmore ultimately concedes because "this game is stupid." With Ike as the new class president, the kids go and fingerpaint. The episode aired on November 15, 2000, a mere eight days after the election.

32. For more on the Electoral College, see, for example, André Blais, *To Vote or Not to Vote? The Merits and Limits of Rational Choice Theory* (Pittsburgh: University of Pittsburgh Press, 2000); Geoffrey Brennan and Loren Lomasky, *Democracy and Decision: The Pure Theory of Electoral Preference* (Cambridge: Cambridge University Press, 1993); Thomas E. Patterson, *The Vanishing Voter* (New York: Knopf, 2002); and Steven E. Schier, *You Call This an Election? America's Peculiar Democracy* (Washington, D.C.: Georgetown University Press, 2003).

33. For example, see Blais, *To Vote*, 8.

34. *The Charlie Rose Show*, September 26, 2005. In a recent interview with *Rolling Stone*, the duo talk at length about this aspect of their deconstruction of Hollywood (both artistically and politically). In the article they relate a story about how the quickest way to piss off Hollywood royalty is to tell them that George Bush is awesome. This is transgression at its finest. See Vanessa Grigoriadis, "Still Sick, Still Wrong," *Rolling Stone*, March 22, 2007, 58-62.

35. Brian C. Anderson, *South Park Conservatives: The Revolt against Liberal Media Bias* (New York: Regnery Press, 2005).

36. Quoted in Brian C. Anderson, "We're Not Losing the Culture Wars Anymore," *City Journal*, Autumn 2003, http://www.city-journal.org/html/13_4_were_not_losing.html (accessed November, 24, 2006).

37. "Interview: Trey Parker and Matt Stone Talk *Team America: World Police*," *USA Today*, October 4, 2004, http://www.movieweb.com/news/06/5406.php (accessed November 18, 2006).

38. Bill Keveney, "TV Icon Norman Lear is Goin' Down to 'South Park,'" March 17, 2003, http://www.usatoday.com/life/television/news/2003-03-17-south-park_x.htm (accessed November 24, 2006).

39. Tibor R. Machan, "The Case for Libertarianism: Sovereign Individuals," in *Libertarianism: For and Against*, by Craig Duncan and Tibor R. Machan (Lanham, MD: Rowman and Littlefield, 2005), 3.

40. Machan, "The Case." See, also, Tibor R. Machan, *The Passion for Liberty* (Lanham, MD: Rowman and Littlefield, 2003).

41. One major source of consternation among many political philosophers and theorists—for example, Karl Marx, C.B. Macpherson, Charles Taylor, Amitai Etzioni, and John N. Gray—is the individualist element in classical liberalism and, especially, libertarianism. Machan, "The Case," 14.

42. See, for example, John Locke, *Two Treatises of Government* (New York: Cambridge University Press, 1988).

43. *The Charlie Rose Show*, September 26, 2005.

44. Slavoj Žižek and Glyn Daly, *Conversations with Žižek* (Cambridge: Polity, 2004), 114.

45. Slavoj Žižek, *The Parallax View* (Cambridge, MA: MIT Press, 2006), 309.

46. Žižek takes on this very notion in his afterward to the reprinting of Lenin's 1917 writings. See Slavoj Žižek, "Lenin's Choice," in *Revolution at the Gates: A Selection of Writings from February to October 1917*, by V. I. Lenin (London: Verso, 2002), 174.

47. Paul Lafargue, *The Right to Be Lazy and Other Studies*, trans. Charles H. Kerr. (Chicago: C.H. Kerr & Company, 1907).

48. Morris Rosenberg, "Some Determinates of Political Apathy," *Public Opinion Quarterly* 15 (1954/1955): 5. Gordon Connelly and Harry Field, "The Non-Voter—Who He Is, What He Thinks," *Public Opinion Quarterly* 8 (1944): 175-87.

49. Gross, *The Secret History*, 52. Tom DeLuca, *The Two Faces of Political Apathy* (Philadelphia: Temple University Press, 1995).

50. DeLuca, *The Two Faces*, 10.

51. C.B. Macpherson, *The Real World of Democracy* (Oxford: Oxford University Press, 1972), 1-2.

52. DeLuca, *The Two Faces*, 246, emphasis original.

53. Seymour Martin Lipset, *Political Man* (Baltimore: Johns Hopkins University Press, 1981), 310.

54. Alan McKee, *The Public Sphere: An Introduction* (Cambridge: Cambridge University Press, 2005).

55. Kenneth Burke, *Attitudes toward History* (Berkeley: University of California Press, 1937), 167.

56. Burke, *Attitudes*, 107. For a meta-reading of *South Park* as ultimately a kind of Burkean comic framing, see Marc Leverette and George F. McHendry, Jr., "Appendix: How to Teach *South Park* (or Maybe Not)," in *Oh My God, They Deconstructed* South Park! *Those Bastards!*, ed. Marc Leverette and Brian Cogan (Lanham, MD: Lexington Press, forthcoming).

57. DeLuca, *The Two Faces*, viii.

58. How could a "mass democracy work," they asked, "if all the people were deeply involved in politics? Lack of interest by some is not without its benefits." Bernard R. Berelson, Paul F. Lazarsfeld, and William N. McPhee, *Voting: A Study of Opinion Formation in a Presidential Campaign* (Chicago: University of Chicago Press, 1954), 314.

59. Samuel P. Huntington, "The United States," in *The Crisis of Democracy*, ed. Michael J. Crozier, Samuel P. Huntington, and Joji Watanuki (New York: New York University Press, 1975), 114.

60. "Interview: Trey Parker and Matt Stone Talk *Team America: World Police*," October 4, 2004, http://www.movieweb.com/news/06/5406.php (accessed November 18, 2006).

61. DeLuca, *The Two Faces*, 251.

62. A very good study that takes this up as its central question, and is recent enough to discuss the Idol Gives Back campaign as well as The Red and One campaigns, is Kellie C. Keelan, *Conflicting Messages: The Logics of Consumption and Conservation in MTV's* Cribs & Think MTV (unpublished M.A. thesis, Colorado State University, 2007).

63. Kevin Mattson, *Engaging Youth: Combating the Apathy of Young Americans* (New York: Century Foundation Press), 40.

64. Mattson, *Engaging Youth*.

65. Mattson, *Engaging Youth*.

66. Mark Hugo Lopez, Emily Kirby, and Jared Sagoff, "The Youth Vote 2004," *CIRCLE: The Center for Information & Research on Civic Learning & Engagement*, http://www.civicyouth.org/PopUps/FactSheets/FS_Youth_Voting_72-04.pdf (accessed February 18, 2007).

67. Pinkleton and Austin, "Media Perceptions," 322.

68. Matthew Reed, "Apathy and Its Discontents: Social Capital and Social Awkwardness in American Life," *New Political Science* 23, no. 3 (2001): 443.

69. Robert S. Boynton, "Enjoy Your Žižek! An Excitable Slovenian Philosopher Examines The Obscene Practices Of Everyday Life—Including His Own," *Lingua Franca* 8, no. 7 (1998), http://linguafranca.mirror.theinfo.org/9810/zizek.html (accessed January 24, 2007).

70. Boynton, "Enjoy Your Žižek!"

71. Nina Eliasoph, *Avoiding Politics: How Americans Produce Apathy in Everyday Life* (Cambridge: Cambridge University Press, 1998), 263, emphasis original.

72. Peter Sloterdijk, *Critique of Cynical Reason*, trans. Michael Elrod (Minneapolis: University of Minnesota Press, 1987), 193.

73. William Chaloupka, *Everybody Knows: Cynicism in America* (Minneapolis: University of Minnesota Press, 1999), 171.

74. Sloterdijk, *Critique*, 193.

75. Mattson, *Engaging Youth*, 30.

76. McKee, *The Public Sphere*, 184.

77. It's not really hard to see where I pick up my linguistic patois.

78. Donald Rumsfeld and Gen. Richard Myers, "Department of Defense News Briefing, Tuesday, Feb. 12, 2002—11:31 a.m. EST," http://www.defenselink.mil/transcripts/2002/t02122002_t212sdv2.html (accessed May 15, 2005). Alex Galloway has incorporated this now infamous sound bite into a staggering critique of utopia within the gamespace of *Warcraft*. See Alexander

R. Galloway, "*Warcraft* and Utopia," *CTheory*, http://ctheory.net/articles. aspx?id=507 (accessed January 11, 2007).

79. Ludwig Wittgenstein, *Tractatus Logico-Philosophicus*, trans. C. K. Ogden (New York: Harcourt Brace, 1933), 189. "What we cannot speak of we must pass over in silence" or, alternatively, "Whereof one cannot speak, thereof one must be silent."

80. See Brian L. Ott, *The Small Screen: How Television Equips Us to Live in the Information Age* (Malden, MA: Blackwell, 2007). Consider what A. O. Scott says: "Without 'South Park,' I would scarcely know what to think about issues like stem cell research, 'The Passion of the Christ' or the Pokémon craze."

81. At the time of this writing, the only nations ranked ahead of the U.S. were Norway, Ireland, and Luxembourg. See Martha Nussbaum, "Foreword," in *Libertarianism: For and Against*, by Craig Duncan and Tibor R. Machan (Lanham, MD: Rowman and Littlefield, 2005), ix-xiii.

82. Additionally, the U.S. figure regarding probability at birth of not surviving to age sixty is around 12.6 percent, whereas most European nations are around only 8 percent.

83. Pinkleton and Austin, "Media Perceptions," 322.

84. Outside of the scapegoating of Al Gore on this topic, see, for example, Stuart Davis, Larry Elin, and Grant Reeher, *Click on Democracy: The Internet's Power to Change Political Apathy into Civic Action* (Boulder, CO: Westview, 2002).

85. Paddy Scannell, *Radio, Television, and Modern Life: A Phenomenological Approach* (Oxford: Blackwell, 1996), 4, emphasis original.

Index

About the Contributors

Marco Calavita is an Associate Professor of Communication Studies at Sonoma State University. He is the author of *Apprehending Politics: News Media and Individual Political Development*, and has published work in a variety of publications, including *Popular Communication, The Communication Review, Atlantic Journal of Communication*, and the *Journal of Film and Video*.

Xiaoxia Cao is a doctoral candidate at the Annenberg School for Communication at the University of Pennsylvania. Her research interests include the effects of entertainment media on political knowledge, public opinion, and political engagement. Her authored or co-authored scholarship has appeared in *Mass Communication and Society*, the *Journal of Broadcasting & Electronic Media*, and the *International Journal of Public Opinion Research*.

Brandy Chappell served as a program assistant at Rock the Vote, and was the organization's National Field Coordinator during the 2004 Presidential election. Currently, she is a Master of Public Policy candidate at the University of Southern California, and serves the City of Los Angeles as an Urban Planning and Council staff member for the Ninth Council District.

Brian Cogan is an Associate Professor of Communication Arts and Sciences at Molloy College. He is the author of *The Encyclopedia of Punk Music and Culture, The Punk Rock Encyclopedia* (forthcoming), and articles in numerous scholarly journals. He is also co-author of *The Encyclopedia of Heavy Metal* and, with Tony Kelso, the co-author of *The Encyclopedia of Politics, the Media, and Popular Culture* (both forthcoming). In addition, he has lectured and published on Irish immigrant assimilation in New York City in the nineteenth century, and received awards from the New York Irish History Roundtable and the Media Ecology Association.

Michael Grabowski is a filmmaker and teacher/scholar, who won two Emmy Awards while working on documentaries for Jonathan Demme, PBS, Lifetime, Court TV, commercials, and news. His films have played in numerous film festivals as well as at the Smithsonian and Guggenheim museums, on PBS, and in Cuba. Currently, he is writing the book, *Unreal: The Merging of Fact and Fiction in American Culture*. Michael teaches filmmaking at New York University and is an Associate Professor of Communication Arts at The College of New Rochelle.

Tony Kelso is an Associate Professor in the Department of Mass Communication at Iona College. He is co-author (with Brian Cogan) of *The Encyclopedia of Politics, the Media, and Popular Culture* (forthcoming). His research on advertising and religion has been published in the journal, *Implicit Religion*, as well as in the *Encyclopedia of Religion, Communication, and Media*. Other recent work includes the chapter, "And Now No Word from our Sponsor: How HBO Puts the Risk Back into Television," in the book, *It's Not TV: Watching HBO in the Post-Television Era*.

Robert J. Klotz is an Associate Professor of Political Science at the University of Southern Maine. His book, *The Politics of Internet Communication*, has earned *Choice* "Recommended" and *The Review of Communication* "Editor's Top Ten" designations. His research has been profiled in *The Chronicle of Higher Education* and has appeared in *Political Communication* and other peer-reviewed journals.

Marc Leverette is an Assistant Professor of Media Studies in the Department of Speech Communication at Colorado State University. He is author of *Professional Wrestling, the Myth, the Mat*; *American Popular Culture*; and *The Highway is Alive Tonight*. He is also co-editor of *Zombie Culture: Autopsies of the Living Dead*, *It's Not TV: Watching HBO in the Post-Television Era*, and *Oh My God, They Deconstructed South Park! Those Bastards!* His articles have appeared in numerous journals, including *Communication and Critical/Cultural Studies*, the *Journal of Communication Inquiry*, and *Studies in Popular Culture*.

Shawn McIntosh is a lecturer in the Strategic Communications Program at Columbia University's School of Continuing Education. Formerly, he was an editor and freelance writer for ten years in London and Tokyo. He is co-author (with John Pavlik) of *Converging Media: Introduction to Mass Communication*, and co-editor (with Marc Leverette) of *Zombie Culture: Autopsies of the Living Dead*.

Arthur Sanders is Professor of Political Science, Chair of the Department of Politics and International Relations, and Director of the Honors Program at Drake University, where he has been a member of the faculty since 1990. He received his BA from Franklin and Marshall College in 1978 and his PhD from Harvard University in 1982. His research has focused on citizen politics in the United States, including examinations of public opinion, the impact of mass media, and campaign finance. His most recent book, *Losing Control: Presidential Elections and the Decline of Democracy*, was published in 2007 by Peter Lange.

Aaron Teeter is a training specialist in the Office of the Coordinator for Reconstruction and Stabilization with the United States Department of State. Formerly, he was a program assistant with the United States Institute of Peace's Education and Training Center's Domestic Programs. Before that, he was a program and events management assistant with Rock the Vote and field coordinator for the DNC. In 2005, he was LA field office director of operations for the International Organization for Migration's Iraq Out of Country Vote program. He holds an MS degree in peace and stability operations policy from George Mason University.

Laura Tropp is an Associate Professor in the Communication Arts Department at Marymount Manhattan College. She received her Ph.D. at New York University. She teaches courses in communication theory, media history, youth and popular culture, campaigns and elections, and new communication technologies. Her areas of publication include interactive television, representations of pregnancy and motherhood in media, and the use of television in voter mobilization drives.